Christian Education Handbook

Christian Education Handbook

Bruce P. Powers

Editor/Compiler

BROADMAN PRESS
Nashville, Tennessee

Dewey Decimal Classification: 268.1

Subject Heading: RELIGIOUS EDUCATION

Library of Congress Catalog Card Number: 80-69522

Printed in the United States of America

Preface

Time management is one of my biggest problems. As a church minister, as an educational administrator, and now as a teacher, I have found that keeping up with developments related to my work is a major drain on my time and energy.

The key problem as I have come to see it has always been *administrative overload,* related primarily to information, organizations, and administrative procedures.

As an educational leader, I always sought resources that would enable me to be more effective in my work by providing basic information and administrative guidelines. As one responsible for the total educational ministry of a church, however, I soon experienced *resource* overload. It wasn't that this information was not helpful, but that each guidebook gave detailed instructions for administering a particular program or organization. This was excellent for directors of these activities, but was an overload for me.

What about pastors, ministers of education, and other key church leaders who have major responsibility for administering the *entire* educational program? What is there to help leaders at this level of responsibility?

As I discussed this need with church leaders, I found that many of us shared similar concerns. One answer that emerged was the idea of a handbook that would bring together essential information and guidelines for administering the overall educational ministry in a local church: one resource piece combining the why and the how-to, with information and procedures appropriate for the key leader.

The outcome is this volume, written by a cross section of persons who have served in churches and now are teaching in theological education.

In using this book, you will find that it can be read sequentially or that it can be consulted topically by referring to the expanded list of contents. Each chapter stands alone and references other portions as appropriate. Consequently, there is some overlap, but this is inherent in the design.

The topics move from general theological considerations and administrative processes to specific areas of leadership responsibility. In addition, each chapter focuses on practical ways to use the information presented.

Regarding the use of pronouns, we recognize the role of women as well as men in educational leadership. In some cases we reference both genders; at other times we use the generic, *he* or *him*.

Appreciation is due our publisher, Broadman Press, for encouragement and insightful participation in the planning process; The Sunday School Board of the Southern Baptist Convention, through its Church Programs and Services, for supporting the project and providing access to pertinent resources; to the many denominational and church leaders who reacted to our outlines, previewed materials in conferences, and otherwise helped in developing the product; and to our students who in their process of learning helped us to refine the concepts, values, and skills which we hope to impart.

I would like to express personal gratitude to the writers of this volume and to Carolyn Bailey, my very helpful secretary.

Bruce P. Powers
Wake Forest, North Carolina

The Authors

Daniel Aleshire, Assistant Professor of Church and Denominational Ministry, The Southern Baptist Theological Seminary, Louisville, Kentucky

Bob I. Johnson, Assistant Professor of Religious Education and Church Administration, Midwestern Baptist Theological Seminary, Kansas City, Missouri

Bruce P. Powers, Professor of Christian Education, The Southeastern Baptist Theological Seminary, Wake Forest, North Carolina

Jerry M. Stubblefield, Associate Professor of Religious Education, Golden Gate Baptist Theological Seminary, Mill Valley, California

Charles A. Tidwell, Professor of Church Administration, Southwestern Baptist Theological Seminary, Fort Worth, Texas

Contents

Introduction
Daniel Aleshire

I had arrived at my first church after graduation from the seminary. My world, for so many years, had consisted of going to school. It had been a world of growing ideas, growing convictions, growing faith, and growing commitments. Now, as I anticipated the task of the pastor, new questions were forming. How does one take the profound truth of faith and, guided by the ever-present Spirit of God, make that truth alive and available to others?

The first several days I moved into my new office and met the people of the congregation. I spent some time going through the church files. In those files, which had been patiently and appropriately gleaned by my predecessor, I happened upon a letter to the congregation which that pastor had sent years earlier. It made an impact on me that stayed through the duration of that pastorate and continues with me in my ministry. "The church is a school," he said. That pastor, R. Quinn Pugh, had an important idea which I had not really considered before. He expressed it in more detail several years later, and it is appropriate for his expression to become the basis for an introduction to Christian education.

THE CHURCH IS A SCHOOL. When that reality dawned upon me, it was like a rare morning in my Christian experience. I had been struggling with the mechanics of religious education and the competing loyalities of church organizations, when out of some unexpected quarter—which now I scarce remember—came the expression, "the church is a school." All of the structural fragments and the infinite number of organizational nuts and bolts appeared in one beautiful whole: the Church. It was suddenly alive for me—and is until this day. The Church does not simply have a school; it is a school.

For too long I had been fretting with getting people to join something which was adjunctive, a terribly exhausting experience. I instantly saw my task in a new light: that of declaring, informing, pointing persons within the Church to the truth that they are already in the School.

It simply can't be any other way, I began to feel. For the truth is that to be a disciple is to be a learner. And to be a disciple of the Christ is to be one absorbed in knowing Him. And to be joined with each other in the discipleship of Christ is to be joined in a fellowship of learning. With crystal clarity the picture leaped from my memory of Jesus, surrounded by the twelve, issuing the invitation, "Take my yoke upon you and learn of me." Did they not always call Him, "Teacher?"[1]

Of course, the statement that the church is a school might be considered an overstatement. But the church, in many significant ways, really is a school.

For example, the church is a school inasmuch as it completes through its life the commandment in Matthew to "Go therefore and make disciples of all nations, baptizing them in the name of the Father and of the Son and of the Holy Spirit, *teaching* them to observe all that I have commanded you. . ." (28:19-20, RSV, author's italics). Schools are those environments where teaching is a natural and valued activity. The church is a school inasmuch as the commission is to teach "them to observe all." The task that the resurrected Christ bequeaths to his church is not unlike the task of a good school: seeing that students have exposure to the kinds of teachers and opportunities that will lead to learning and change in their lives.

The church is a school in the sense that the teaching of faith is not an adjunct to the tasks of the church. It is inherently a part of being a church. It is appropriate to think of the church as a school inasmuch as its task is helping persons learn to love God and each other. It is a school in that it trains persons to serve and give their lives away for the cause of the saving Christ.

The church is a school inasmuch as every gathering—whether for worship, Sunday School committee meetings, training of leadership, or learning of mission—provides the forum for learning and redefining one's commitment to Christ.

Of course, the church is not just a school. It is far more. The outcomes of its efforts to educate should be persons whose lives have been transformed, who have found vision and meaning. Those are the gifts of conversion, to be sure. But they are also the gifts that are nurtured through education. They are the true fruit for which education hopes. In some ways, it might be true to say that not only is the church a school, it may be more a school than most of the institutions that go by the name. Through the grace and powerful presence of God, the church can do in its education what most schools could only wishfully dream of doing.

To be a school means that education is a central reality in the life of the church. To be valid, the education must be of a certain type and have a certain content. While many claims can be made regarding what is most central in the life of the church, no claim is any more valid than the claim that the tasks of teaching and learning, when properly understood, are central features.

Education is how the people of God gain insight into their mission and purpose. It is the means by which believing people gain vision of the magnitude of their belief. It is the vehicle by which the wise God of the Bible helps his children grow in grace.

Education is how the people of God become skilled in the tasks of doing the mission for which the church has been created. It is where they gain the sensitivities to identify those issues which require attention and the skills to render the needed attention. Education is a means by which people can be motivated to do the tasks of the gospel.

The church is a school for disciples who are learning to serve, to long for God, to live together, and to witness to the world. This volume deals with the education that occurs in the church—or at least should occur. It seeks to define the nature and goals of such an education, and to provide practical instruction in structure, organization, and leadership. It seeks a holistic description of the gift and ministry of education in the church.

Note

1. R. Quinn Pugh, quoted in *The Crescent Hill Beams* (Louisville, Kentucky: Crescent Hill Baptist Church, January, 1973).

1
Educational Ministry of the Church

Bruce P. Powers

Although the church has always been a teaching institution, only since the early 1900s have churches identified their formal teaching activities as an educational ministry or program.

The Sunday School, largely an extrachurch, lay-directed organization during the nineteenth century, was later adopted by denominations as a means for teaching the Bible to the masses. This influence, along with increased public concern for education and moral development during the early twentieth century, exerted strong pressure on churches to devise educational organizations and programs to help congregations convey to the young the content and values of their faith.[1]

The first educational administrators came primarily out of the public school tradition. In larger churches, volunteers could no longer handle the time-consuming tasks of selecting and training teachers, setting up and administering the Sunday School and other educational organizations, planning curriculum, staff planning, and facility management. Thus, larger churches began to turn to their best qualified volunteers and extended an invitation to broaden their responsibilities and opportunities in educational ministry.

From this modest beginning, a distinct area of church ministry has developed along with a corresponding administrative function—that of educational administration.

Education, along with worship, proclamation, and ministry, is now recognized as one of the four major functions of a church. Whereas the other functions have traditionally been administered by the pastor, educational responsibilities have been delegated in larger churches to a specialist, and in smaller churches to a number of volunteer leaders. Although at first educational specialists were not part of a church's ministerial staff, such leaders today usually are prepared theologically and educationally and serve on a ministerial team as minister of education.[2]

In smaller churches, the pastor is usually the key educational admin-

14

istrator, assuming this responsibility along with other duties.

To some degree, however well or poorly done, educational ministry is provided in a church. The beginning point is found in the statement of purpose or objectives of a congregation, or if not formally recorded, in the people's hopes and dreams.

The purpose of a church has been encoded in certain formal and informal activities designed to perpetuate the institution. Formal activities such as Bible study classes and training groups make up a large part of the educational ministry or program, and informal teaching through congregational life and family nurture comprise a significant complementing influence.

It is the formal activities under the direction and control of a church for which the educational administrator has primary responsibility. And it is these activities which comprise the intentional, structured, educational curriculum that will enable a church to achieve its purpose.

What Are We Trying to Do to People?

The answer to the question "What are we trying to do to people?" suggests a congregation's expectations about its educational ministry and the leader. If these expectations are clearly defined, appropriate structures and experiences can be provided. The alternative is to have unclear (or unsure) expectations, matched with structures and experiences which produce ambiguous results.

Teaching in the early church focused primarily on catechetical instruction, or indoctrination, which remained the major expression of Christian education until the development of the Sunday School in the eighteenth century.

Along with the idea of church school for laypersons came a renewed concern for education, somewhat dormant since the Reformation. An educated person could use the Bible and interpret God's message without depending on another. Commitments, freely chosen through personal study, could be the basis for one's Christian beliefs rather than adopting a set of beliefs passed down from others. Thus education took its place alongside indoctrination as a means for passing on the faith.

Revivalism, particularly in the United States during the eighteenth and nineteenth centuries, was a major influence in relating Sunday School and evangelism. The rapid growth of the Sunday School movement, the need for a way to teach converts, and the recognition of the Sunday School as an *outreach* organization to convert the young contributed to an identity that has become an inseparable part of educational ministry in strongly evangelical churches. In Southern Baptist churches, this influence has continued. Today there is general affirmation that the Sunday School is the outreach and witnessing arm of the church, and the educational minister has a major responsibility for church growth.[3]

Today the general view of a church educational ministry encompasses these three traditions: indoctrination, education, and outreach. Each denomination, indeed every church, incorporates elements of each in an effort to answer, "What are we trying to do to people?" And, not surprisingly, each tradition provides a unique and necessary ingredient in effective Christian education.

A Teaching Church

Whereas *teaching* encompasses any manner of imparting information, skills, and values so that others may learn, each of the above traditions embodies only a partial expression of a teaching church.

Indoctrination.—Devoted to instruction in fundamental beliefs and practices, indoctrination is used to infuse learners with a partisan and distinctly sectarian point of view. This is necessary to maintain the integrity of the beliefs passed from generation to generation, and to provide a foundation for the young and for new Christians so that they can effectively move into the mainstream of congregational life.

Education.—When this term became popular in churches during the early 1900s, the emphasis was on bringing out the latent, God-given capabilities of the young. As persons developed, they would be exposed to the history, beliefs, and practices of their faith appropriate for their level of readiness. This form of teaching would equip learners to pursue knowledge of their faith for themselves rather than relying only on instructors or tradition. Consequently, persons would become aware of and develop the capacity to interpret not only their own, but other faith traditions as well. Resulting religious convictions would be more personal than sectarian, and overall development would be in accord with each individual's ability.

Outreach.—Testifying or giving witness to what one has experienced is the basis for outreach being a third element of a teaching church. A desire to tell about and involve others in one's beliefs and practices gives clear indication that commitment is strong. Two aspects of outreach contribute to effective ministry: giving testimony to one's beliefs and experiences; and enlisting persons in the life and organizations of a church. Both are initiated by a believer in the hope that a convert and/or a new participant will result, thereby gaining the same benefits witnessed to by the believer. Outreach is necessary to spread the gospel message as well as to secure participation in the overt teaching activities of a church.

Educational Ministry Today

Most evangelical churches now use the term *educational ministry* to identify the functions of a teaching church described above. It is important to recognize that all three traditions have a place and, in fact, contribute to the effectiveness of each other. Where one is weak or ignored, the others will suffer; and where one is emphasized to the neglect of others, there will be eventual decline in overall effectiveness.

What are we trying to do to people? Consider this as a possible answer. The purpose of educational ministry is to develop within persons an understanding of, commitment to, and ability to practice Christian teachings. Another way to view this is to describe Christian education as the ongoing efforts of believers seeking to understand, practice, and propagate God's revelation.

Christianity may be viewed as the life of a community, and educational ministry as the *work* of that community. The aim is not so much to promote the community as it is to contribute to the reconciling mission to which the community is called. Thus, from an overall perspective, educational ministry may be viewed as the effort "to introduce persons into the life and mission of the community of Christian faith."[4]

Roger Shinn, who popularized this description, uses a family analogy to illustrate the process.

> The New Testament uses the figure of adoption to describe what happens to persons in Christian faith (Rom. 8:23; Gal. 4:5). In adoption a child enters a family; the family becomes *his* family, and he becomes its child. He adopts the style of life of the family, its practices and ideas, its precious symbols, and its family jokes. The family, adopting him, receives him in warmth, makes its resources his, transmits to him its habits and values. In this educational process deliberate instruction plays an important part, but it is less significant than the teaching and learning that inevitably go with life. Thus adoption is a suggestive metaphor for the educational ministry of the church.[5]

The response to the question "What are we trying to do to people?"

is really a hope, an objective. It is central to our role as leaders, and in today's ministry incorporates the best of the three traditions which make up our history.

Understanding Your Church and Its Educational Ministry

Whatever form your educational ministry has assumed, it exists as it does because someone believed that the programs, facilities, curriculum, organizational arrangements, and other components were the best way to do Christian education. It is these structures which enable a church to do its work.

Teachers in the social sciences often refer to a life cycle through which organizations develop. By applying this theory to a church, we can gain an understanding of how these structures develop, of potential problems, and of how to provide leadership.

As illustrated in Figure 1, a church moves through a life cycle involving several phases.

Birth

In the birth phase, the organization develops out of the hopes and dreams of a person or group. The initiators call others to join them in creating a church that will fulfill the expectations of the founders.

Development

The second phase focuses on development of the institution. Considering the expectations of the charter members and available resources, structures are developed to help the church fulfill the dreams of its founders. A helpful term for this process is *encoding*. Whereas ideas and dreams birth an organization, how it fulfills its purpose is determined by the structures that are created to perpetuate the institution. This is the encoding process—development of the means such as programs, facilities, and curriculum that enable a church to do its work.

Peak Ministry

In the peak ministry phase, the organization operates effectively, serving both congregational needs as well as accomplishing its task in the community. This is a time characterized by cohesiveness and good feelings as a church experiences growth in membership, strong support and commitment among members, community appreciation, and relative ease in decision making.

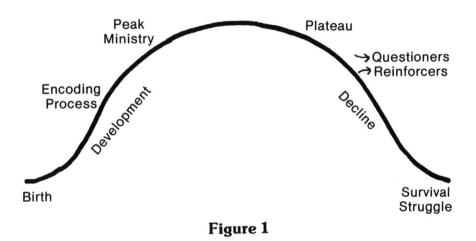

Figure 1

Plateau

Inevitably, however, whatever has been encoded begins to erode in effectiveness. In time, the situation and conditions change which brought forth certain programs, organization, facilities, staff, and procedures. There is a turnover in membership, resulting in many new persons who have no understanding of or appreciation for traditional forms or structures which have been encoded. Eventually, if adjustments and changes are not made, whatever was encoded to help the church achieve its purpose begins to lose effectiveness.

Evidences of the plateau phase are subtle. Interest and motivation for keeping things going as they are gradually replace efforts previously focused on innovation and adaptation to internal as well as external needs. The human urge to find security through familiar structure and organization results in a church that resists change. The result is declining effectiveness.

Attendance and participation begin to level off, evangelistic concerns moderate, and the fervor associated with peak ministry declines.

There is a distinct emphasis on making the existing organization work, with any changes being minor.

Decline

If the life cycle continues, decline sets in. This phase results when efforts to make the system work are not adequate to maintain the plateau level. Congregational resources shift from focus on mission and ministry to a maintenance orientation. Time and money formerly used in reaching others are channeled into ministry to church needs.

The teaching ministry, formerly devoted to a balanced emphasis on instruction, nurture, and outreach, usually now emphasizes nurture and neglects the other areas. Whereas participation in Bible study activities probably predominated during the church's development, involvement in worship services is more likely during decline.

Survival Struggle

The last phase, survival struggle, is faced by churches unable or unwilling to adapt to changing needs. For some congregations, existence will be an ongoing effort by persons committed to the organization's survival. For others with inadequate resources or endurance, the life cycle ends.

Questioners and Reinforcers

An interesting development begins during the plateau phase and intensifies as a church begins to decline. One by one, members begin to polarize into *questioners* and *reinforcers* as they sense that all is not well.

The initial response, usually among persons not involved in the encoding phase, is an expression of doubt about the effectiveness of some aspect of church life. Questions and comments emerge such as: "What's the matter with our church?" "Why do we have such difficulty enlisting workers?" "How can we improve the mission interest in our church?" "Why do we have to keep doing it this way?" "I think we need new leadership." "What should we be doing?"

In response to the unrest, persons strongly identified with the status quo begin to doubt that the congregation is putting forth sufficient effort to get the job done. Questioners are viewed more as troublemakers, persons who don't understand that the organization has worked well in the past.

Reinforcers tend to defend the existing structures and feel that renewal comes as members recommit and give of themselves unselfishly. There is a conscious effort to conserve resources and to preserve the institution. Staff, facilities, programs, and such must effectively serve membership needs. Other concerns are secondary.

If the reinforcers are strong enough to resist necessary change, questioners often will leave or will develop a subgroup within the congregation. This can be observed when like-minded persons begin to form "renegade" Sunday School classes, training groups, and mission activities. Occasionally questioners simply accept the situation and become chronic complainers or passive participants. Without significant adjustments to meet the changed situation, decline will continue.

On the other hand, if questioners predominate, there is potential for radical and unfocused change that disrupts continuity in and operation of the organization. There is a loss of commitment to the institution and of problem-solving capacity normally gained from history and experience. Concern for studied, well-defined, calculated responses by the congregation gives way to expediency and immediate action.

Clearly, both questioners and reinforcers are needed in a congregation for stability and for initiative in problem solving. And either group can create problems that will foster further decline. Without significant adjustments to meet changing circumstances, the church will continue its downward path.

Fortunately, however, most churches do not reach the final phase. There is an intriguing happening as a church begins its downward journey and the questioners and reinforcers begin to appear. The tension level builds as dissatisfaction surfaces, and leaders are faced with taking action. Some leaders choose this time to move to another church. Others become more assertive in seeking to resolve problems. Either way, leaders and congregation begin to address key issues such as:

- What are our problems?
- Why are we feeling as we do?
- What should we be doing as a church, as an organization, as a staff, as leaders?
- What are the best options for who we are and what we are trying to do or be?

It is this response by leaders and congregation that often creates opportunity for organizational renewal, for persons find themselves involved in the same type of creative, problem-solving environment which birthed the original structure. A congregation has an oppor-

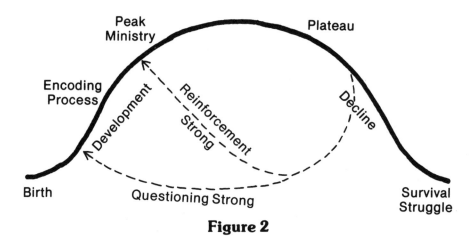

Figure 2

tunity to reencode what it is and how it does its work in light of present needs and resources.

As shown in Figure 2, this renewal might be extensive if questioning is strong, or might be minor if reinforcement concerns are dominant. In either case, there is a recycling of the stages through which the organization moves, with many of the same opportunities and problems to be encountered again.

Leadership Strategy

Your church is in one of these phases. Consequently, the way in which your church is doing educational ministry must be viewed not only from the present perspective, but also in relation to the previous and the anticipated phases. Ideally, educational leaders will continually evaluate and initiate adjustments so that decline never sets in. The questions such as "What should we be doing in light of our purpose?" and "What are the best options?" portray a leadership commitment that will encourage and assist a church in maintaining a viable organization and relevant ministries for the congregation as well as the world.[6]

In addition to understanding the developmental pattern of your church and being committed to maintaining an effective organization, certain leader actions are necessary to be successful. As you administer the educational ministry of your church, seek to:

- Involve in decision making persons who will be affected.
- Be flexible in meeting changing needs.
- Distribute leadership responsibilities widely among responsible people rather than centralizing responsibilities among a few.
- Support group values when appropriate and question them when necessary.
- Learn from and not be inhibited by the possibility of failure.
- Make decisions based on information and evidence rather than on emotion.
- Maintain a balanced concern for the individual and for the group.
- Encourage the development and use of individual gifts.
- Lead persons to establish, and assist them in achieving, common goals.
- Maintain a healthy relationship between task and maintenance activities in your own life as well as in organizational life.

A Leader's Commitment

As James Smart reminds us in *The Teaching Ministry of the Church,* Christians must live in obedience and response to the Word of God.

> Our goal must be no lesser goal than that which Jesus and the apostles had before them. We teach so that through our teaching God may work in the hearts of those whom we teach to make of them disciples wholly committed to his gospel, with an understanding of it, and with a personal faith that will enable them to bear convincing witness to it in word and action in the midst of an unbelieving world. We teach so that through our teaching God may bring into being a Church ... whose all-engrossing aim will be to serve Jesus Christ as an earthly body through which he may continue his redemption of the world.[7]

In essence, quality educational ministry demands commitment to reaching, teaching, developing, and involving persons in Christian service.

There is no greater need or opportunity facing educational leaders than to make disciples and bring them into the full life and faith of the Church. Helping persons find their life's fulfillment in being part of the body of Christ and sharers in his mission is a ministry that clearly embodies Jesus' teaching that effective leaders must be able servants (Matt. 20:26).

Notes

1. Dorothy Jean Furnish, *DRE/DCE—The History of a Profession* (Nashville: Christian Educators Fellowship, 1976), pp. 18-19.

2. Other titles include associate pastor for education, director of religious education, director of Christian education, and educational director.

3. Mavis Allen and Max Caldwell, "Growing Through Bible Teaching," *The Minister of Education as a Growth Agent,* ed. Will Beal (Nashville: Convention Press, 1978), p. 65.

4. Roger Shinn, "The Educational Ministry of the Church," *An Introduction to Christian Education,* ed. Marvin J. Taylor (Nashville: Abingdon Press, 1966), p. 12.

5. Ibid.

6. For assistance in implementing change, see Bruce P. Powers, *Christian Leadership* (Nashville: Broadman Press, 1979), pp. 34-60.

7. James D. Smart, *The Teaching Ministry of the Church* (Philadelphia: The Westminster Press, 1954), p. 107.

2

Christian Education and Theology

Daniel Aleshire

"Get on board little children, get on board!" That was the call that came ringing through the countryside. "Get on board, little children, get on Board!" It was a call to faith; a call to a new quality of life; a call to board the gospel train. It was a call to board the good news and set out on the journey of faith. That train, as it was sung about, was always a joyful vehicle rumbling through the countryside, picking up any passenger who flagged it down. There was joy because persons were discovering faith and joining the faithful on the train. There was joy because the train was heading on its way to the glory of God's presence.

But I wonder if the people on the train may not have experienced some problems—especially those who ended up spending a lifetime on the train. Could some have become concerned that the train made little headway toward its goal because it was forever stopping for new passengers? Would some have been frustrated because they had been thinking about faith for a long time, only to have their car filled with new passengers who were asking the beginning questions all over again? Could others have begun thinking that riding the train was the total task of Christian faith? I even wonder if a few passengers might have begun questioning whether the train's purpose was only to pass through the countryside, or should it be causing something to happen in the land where it was traveling?

The gospel train is a nineteenth-century vision of the life of faith. It clearly shouts the joy of the Christian's discovery of faith and eternal destination. But the image identifies a problem. It was this same problem which the early church was forced to confront.

The first years of the church's life were clearly distinguished by the *kerygma*—the proclamation of the saving grace of God, made available through Jesus Christ. The arguments and concerns in the early church dealt with such issues as: who was entitled to hear the good news (Acts 15:1-29) and how the missionary task should be staffed and undertaken (Acts 15:36-41). But many of the later records of the early church show an increasing concern with the refinement of the teachings of the faith and the need to explore fully their implications for living the faith. The task of the *kerygma,* the proclamation of the gospel to the lost, never ended. But as believers began to live through whole lifetimes, there was the increasing need for the *didache*—the teaching about the life of faith and its implications in the world.

"Get on board little children, get on board." That is the call of the *kerygma*—to hear the call to faith and to respond. But that call is not the totality of the journey.

Life on a train where there is no instruction in the faith does not live up to the whole gospel. The command to the early church was to teach, baptize, and make disciples (Matt. 28:19-20). It is never enough just to get the little children on board the train—though that is the undeniable beginning. They must also learn the profound truths of the Christian faith. They must come to understand the truths that breed excitement for the kingdom coming and patience in the days of the journey.

Education that leads to discipleship has several requirements. This chapter is about four of them.

First, education that is true to the grace of the gospel requires a vision of the church, its purpose and mission. Christian education cannot be relegated to the world of method and procedures. Rather it must emerge out of the mission of the church, move people toward authentic discipleship, and reflect the emphases of Scripture.

Second, Christian education requires theologically-informed objectives.

Third, the learning that results from Christian education requires some serious consideration. The learning must be of a special kind—the kind that provides knowledge, instills feeling, and leads to right living.

Fourth, there is also a need to evaluate the organizations, teachers, and leaders which this kind of learning requires.

The first task is to examine the purpose and mission of the church. It is from this vantage point that thinking about objectives, learning, and organizations rightly ensues.

The Nature and Mission of the Church

The gospel train is one image of the church. It is picturesque, and it surfaces part of the nature and mission of the church. But, like most images of the church, it does not do the job with precision. W. O. Carver has noted, "Since the New Testament nowhere has an explicit definition of the church, basic and determinitive criteria must be reached by an inductive study of the New Testament books."[1] The New Testament nowhere provides a single brief description of the nature and mission of the church. So, while images that reflect inductive study may be imprecise, they are the best available tool.

Why, on such an important issue as the mission and nature of the church, does Scripture not provide a clear statement? As in many other issues of profound significance (i.e., the nature of redemption, the quality of the disciples' life), no one image is adequate to capture the scope and meaning of all the concept implies. Frequently, we discover that the Scripture provides multiple images of some reality; and, like the blending of sounds in a symphony, the true vision emerges from the strength of the several parts. The Bible speaks profusely on the nature of the church—but always in models, portraits, and not in brief definitive statements.

Our attention will be centered on three of the several models which Scripture provides.

The Church as the People of God

In some places, the church is pictured as the people of God. This concept of the church shows its roots in the Old Testament. God made a covenant with the people of Israel, and they became God's own people. It would be through the people of God that the relationship between humankind and God—long ago broken by sin—could be restored. The idea of the "people of God" is that some people on this earth are given the responsibility to share the hopes and dreams that God had for his creation with the other people of the world. It does not mean that some people are chosen as God's favorites. Rather, it means that some people are given a special responsibility to share God's word with the world.

Through the covenant with Abraham, the nation of Israel became the people of God (Gen. 12:1-3; Gen. 17:1-8). They were God's people and were to be a blessing. But Israel failed at being the people of God. Though God continued to love and respect the covenant, the descendants of Abraham continued to disincline themselves from the covenant and its commands. The martyr Stephen declared that the sons of Jacob had "received the law as delivered by angels and did not keep it" (Acts 7:53, RSV). The New Testament teaches, though, that there was one faithful to the law—faithful unto death: Jesus Christ. It was through his faithfulness that the law was fulfilled. E. Glenn Hinson summarizes the New Testament teaching well:

> Upon the faithfulness of Jesus of Nazareth, then, the first Christians declared, God made a new covenant in fulfillment of that foretold by Jeremiah (Rom. 11:27) and Joel (Acts 2:16-21). He was not calling a new people, but transacting a new covenant with his people. They were to be no longer Israel "after the flesh" but Israel "after the spirit" (Rom. 9:6ff).[2]

Thus the followers of Jesus Christ become the people of God: the people charged with the responsibility of sharing the word of the Lord that can restore the broken relationship between sinful humanity and a just, loving God.

The Church as the Body of Christ

Another model of the church is frequently employed in the Pauline letters. In fact, one of Paul's most frequent descriptions of the church is the "body of Christ." Christ is always portrayed as the head, with the believers comprising the other parts. The members are grafted into the body through the redemptive love of Christ. As members of the body, their purpose is to do the divine will. As members of the body, different persons are gifted with different abilities and have different contributions to make to the body. As members, people work together to accomplish the bidding of the Christ. Though the body is characterized by diversity, it is unified in purpose and mission. The church as the body of Christ is God incarnating himself anew and extending himself into the midst of human life. When the church functions as the body of Christ, it is effectively delivering the love and word of God to the world.

The Church as the New Humanity

Some commentators combine the image of the church as the body of Christ with the image of the church as the new humanity. Both are images that are frequently found in the writings of Paul. The concept of the new humanity is most evident in Ephesians and Galatians. The new humanity is a new creation which God has brought into being through the redemptive mission of Jesus Christ. The old humanity was one of persons who were dead in their trespasses and sins (Eph. 2:1). But Christ has raised them up, and made them alive. "For we are his workmanship, created in Christ Jesus for good works, which God prepared beforehand, that we should walk in them" (Eph. 2:10, RSV).

The church as the new humanity is the result of God's continuing creative activity. It is people who are made to be a new people, and gifted with the ability to do what the old humanity could not accomplish. The new humanity is perhaps best described in relation to the old humanity.

Hinson, for example, distinguishes the new humanity from the old humanity in several ways. While the old humanity is self-centered, the new humanity is God-centered. The old humanity expressed hatred toward both God and humankind, while the new humanity expresses itself in love to God and humans. Factionalism and strife are characteristics of the old humanity, while the new humanity is characterized by unity and reconciliation. A high ethical sensitivity in the new humanity replaces the immorality or amorality of the old humanity.[3] The new humanity is God's new creation—made capable of righteousness and love.

The images of the people of God, the body of Christ, and the new humanity clearly emerge from the New Testament. But there are other helpful ways to characterize the nature of the church. Some of these bring sharp theological issues into focus. The need for this focusing can be seen in the possible overinterpretation of the images we have already discussed.

For example, while the church clearly is the body of Christ, it is not the incarnation in the same way that Christ was the incarnation of the *Logos* (John 1:1-18). The body does not always do the will of the divine head, and it would be very inaccurate for some to think that whatever the church did was clearly the same action that Christ himself would undertake if he were present in person.

Likewise, the church as the new humanity is an image that must be held with caution. While God has begun a new creative act in the new humanity and equipped them for love and righteousness, persons do not always live up to the endowment God has given them. It would be disastrous to think of some of the acts of church people as God's gift. Sometimes, the actions of the "new humanity" are nothing more than sin expressed in its most sinister form—the garb of piety.

Church as the "Subjective Pole"

As a way of affirming these cautions, some theologians talk about the church in ways that separate the church from God. For example, one such theological definition states that the church is the "subjective pole of the objective rule of God."[4] At first, that sounds very obtuse. But its power and meaning are not too difficult to clarify. It suggests that whatever else the church is, it is always the subject whose purpose is to point to the object: God. The clear, objective rule of God exists— but the church always reflects a subjective, editorialized version of God's rule.

For example, people gather together to decide what a particular congregation should do with its money, or what kind of programs it should design to minister to the community. The faithful pray that God will lead them in their decisions; and the people will do what they think God is leading them to do. However, they must always realize that they are doing what *they think* God is leading them to do. There may be times when they have misunderstood the nature of the gospel, or the rule of God in their lives. When this happens, the objective rule of God is not done through the church.

The church is the body of Christ; the church is the people of God; the church is the new humanity. Yet it never completely functions as the body—members sometimes go against the command of the head. It is never wholly all the new humanity was created to be—because there are constant regressions back to the region and behavior of the old humanity. The people of God continue to break and misrepresent the gospel—because they do not yield to the will of God.

But by God's grace the church is the new humanity, the people of God, the body of Christ. Each model reflects a portion of all that God intended when he planned the church.

What Is the Purpose of the Church?

These images and models help to identify the purpose of the church. It is to be the expression of God's will on this earth. It is to be a community of persons who are wholeheartedly and overwhelmingly committed to doing what God wants done on this earth. It is all that. But what is it that God wants done through his people?

Some theologians conclude that what God most wants to happen is "the increase of the love of God and the love of neighbor."[5] That is a good summary of the many commands which emerge from the teaching of Jesus and filter through the epistles. If the church fulfills its purpose, by this definition there will be more love—both for God and for humankind—in the world than would otherwise exist. Love of neighbor leads to reaching out, caring, giving, confronting, admonishing,

NO SALE

NO SALE

Baptist Book Store #86
5001 North Oak Street Tfwv
Kansas City, MO 64118
(816)455-3925

---- CUSTOMER NAME & ADDRESS ----

KELLY   DUNN
ROUTE 1 BOX 184H
LAWSON   . MO 64062

CLERK   : 10
REGISTER : 4
RECEIPT # : 8600019722
DATE   : 04/18/96
TIME   : 2:20 PM

ISBN/SPCN	PRICE	QUANTITY	AMOUNT
0805432299	1.97	1	1.97

TP CHRISTIAN EDUCATION HANDBOOK

SUB TOTAL	1.97
SALES TAX ON 1.97 @ 6.475	.13
GRAND TOTAL	2.10
PAID WITH CASH	2.10

Thanks For Shopping With Us.
Please come again.

5001 North Oak Street Trwy

----- CUSTOMER NAME & ADDRESS -----

RECEIPT # : 8600019722
79 CHRISTIAN EDUCATION HANDBOOK			

SUB TOTAL	1.97
SALES TAX ON 1.97 @ 6.475	.13
GRAND TOTAL	2.10
PAID WITH CASH	2.10

Thanks For Shopping With Us.

seeking justice and the common good. Love of God means prayer, devotion, commitment, a sense of piety, and growth in spiritual life. Both mean worship and fellowship. While this definition certainly provides a comprehensive scope, it is in many ways still abstract. We can conclude that God wants love done, but how does the church do this loving of God and neighbor?

Five Purposes of the Church

More detailed perspectives on the purpose of the church tend to summarize the church's primary purpose in several areas. They also provide clues as to how the church realizes its overarching goal to increase love of God and neighbor.

First, the church is to be the gathering together of people for the worship of God. Thus church is the people of God giving themselves to the God of their salvation. It is the body of Christ that gathers to reflect on the divine head, to seek to hear his voice, and to respond to his bidding. It is the people, called to be the new humanity, who gather to confess the sins that have kept them from fulfilling God's call and seeking to be made more into God's workmanship. Worship is vital. It is one of the purposes of the church.

Second, the church has the task of proclaiming the word to people who do not know the Christ of the gospel. Evangelism is the way in which the church becomes a caring distributor of good news of Jesus Christ. It is the people of God giving love, hope, and glad tidings to people who do not know God.

The church also exists for the purpose of doing missions. *Missions* has been characterized as "what the church does to achieve her mission in areas of human need which are on the growing edge of the church's confrontation with the non-Christian world."[6] The task of missions is taking the whole gospel of Jesus Christ to the world—including the gospel's call to salvation, social justice, physical healing, and wholeness. The task of missions is to see that the gospel's response to every human condition is implemented at the intersection where the Christian community meets the rest of the human family.

A fourth purpose of the church is the fellowship of believers. Christianity stands uniquely among the world's religions as a faith that calls its believers to community. While many religious traditions are content with the solitary worship of a deity, the Christian faith calls people into relationship with each other. The church is not comprised of isolated persons who just happen to worship the same God. Rather, it is a deliberate calling of people together to share the burdens and joys of life together.

Part of the purpose of the church is that individuals come into community, contribute their gifts to the common good, and give encouragement, support, and discipline to one another. Christians cannot serve God and remain separated from each other. Jesus emphatically endorses the idea that we give service to God as we care for one another (i.e., Matt. 25:31-46). The church serves the purpose of providing a community in which persons find each other, discover the meaning of love and care, and find fellowship.

There is another purpose for the church, and it is tied up with the others that have already been mentioned. The church must educate its members. The education must be wide-ranging. Persons must be educated in the content of the faith: the teaching of Scripture; the doctrines that interpret these teachings; and the ways in which believers should live. There must also be education concerning the nature of the church, its functions, and the ways by which it becomes the authentic vehicle of God's word and will into the world. There must also be education in the ethics that emerge out of biblical principles. Christians must be taught about right and wrong, both for individuals and for the social order.

The content of faith is important. But it is never enough for Christian education just to communicate the content of the faith. Believers must also be educated to the ways in which they live out their faith in meaningful discipleship. Knowing what is right is very useless unless one has also been taught how to do the right. Scripture is full of stories of people who knew the right thing to do, but who failed to do it.

Christians must also be educated to the emotions which are part of faith. The God who has loved us and given his Son for us calls us to love him with all of our personhood. To love well is to learn not only how to think about faith and to respond in action, but also how to feel devotion, commitment, and surrender to the Source of life and hope.

Each of the purposes or tasks of the church is crucial. It is not correct to see one as superior to the others. A church that only does evangelism is no more what God intended than the church that only does education. The church that only engages in worship is only doing part of what God intended. Each task is necessary to the church fulfilling its purpose and claiming its identity as the people of God, the new humanity, and the body of Christ.

The Undergirding Role of Christian Education

While no task is paramount, each task brings its distinctive contribution. The distinctive task of education is its undergirding of all the other tasks. Before people can worship in mature ways, they must understand what worship is and how believers engage in it. Before persons engage in mission, they must understand the task of mission and the methodology of mission, as well as the motivation to launch out on mission. People are more likely to engage in the efforts of evangelism as their own faith is growing. People grow through exposure to Christian education. Education also helps the fellowship life of the church. As people learn together, as they share ideas and burdens, and discover new understandings, they grow together.

Thus while education should not be seen as the premier task of the church, it does provide a positive influence on the entire catalog of the church's tasks. It informs and undergirds all the purposes of the church.

The church is the new humanity, the body of Christ, the people of God who gather together for worship, fellowship, mission, evangelism, and education. It is through these tasks that the body of Christ is animated, the will of the divine head is done in the world, the influence of the new humanity spreads, and the responsibility of the people of God is rightly discharged.

The Objectives of Christian Education

Christian education has the task of providing the support necessary for the church effectively to accomplish its other tasks. But the task must be more precisely stated for the purposes of this book. We must ask the question: What is it that Christian education should do? How does it support the other tasks of the church? In short, what should be the objectives of Christian education?

The Concept of an Objective

In order to answer this question, it is necessary to have a clear idea about the nature of objectives. An objective provides a focus and serves as a magnet within an ongoing enterprise. For example, the objective of a construction project is, ultimately, to complete a building. That's the focus. That ultimate objective has many other objectives subsumed under it. For example, the foundation must be completed—though completing the foundation can never be substituted as the final objective. The objective acts as a magnet pulling the organization toward its ultimate purpose.

The Objectives in the Teaching Ministry of Jesus

The task of forming the objectives of Christian education can well begin with identifying the objectives which appear to be expressed in the teaching ministry of Jesus. James Smart in *The Teaching Ministry of the Church* has attempted such an analysis and concludes that Jesus reflected three objectives in his teaching.

First, Jesus used his teaching ministry to proclaim the gospel of the coming of the kingdom in relatively small group settings. To Jesus, the gospel was not just for the multitude on the mountainside. It was also for the few around the table who would hear and seek to understand. In fact, there is a dimension of the gospel that requires the interaction of persons that is possible only in the small group settings.

Second, Jesus used his teaching—particularly the teaching of the disciples—as a means of instructing them fully in the nature of the gospel "so that they might leave behind their old inadequate understanding of God, of themselves, and of all the things in their world."[7]

Third, the teaching of Jesus reflected the objective that the disciples would be able, both in mind and in heart, to carry on the ministry which Christ had done in their midst. These three objectives provide an excellent foundation for structuring objectives for the contemporary practice of Christian education.

The Objectives of Contemporary Christian Education

What is the objective of Christian education? One that seems to be faithful both to the mission of the church and the objectives expressed in Jesus' teaching has been stated by Randolph Crump Miller. He writes: "The main task [of Christian education] is to teach the truth about God, with all the implications arising from God's nature and activity, in such a way that the learner will accept Jesus Christ as Lord and Savior, will become a member of the Body of Christ, and will live in the Christian way."[8] This statement identifies three objectives in Christian education which reflect Smart's summary of objectives in Jesus' teaching.

The first is that persons will seek to come into right relationship with Jesus Christ. There is disagreement among Christian educators as to how this objective is accomplished. For example, some have argued that the role of Christian education is to help nurture children who are born to believing parents into the faith of their families. In this view, there is no need for conversion. Children are taught the gospel and grow up never knowing a time when they did not believe and accept the good news of Jesus Christ.

Others, however, argue that persons can never be nurtured into Christian faith. Ultimately, faith is something which each individual must claim personally. John Westerhoff takes this side when he argues that "The Christian faith by its very nature demands conversion. We cannot gradually educate persons through instruction in schools to be Christian. Of course, persons need to be and can be nurtured into a community's faith and life."[9]

At some point the individual must come to own the faith that has been taught. The language of the Baptist tradition is likely correct in saying that the individual accepts Christ and "professes his or her faith" in him. That profession is a time when the individual claims that the truth that has been taught and preached about the gospel is now a part of his or her own experience and affirmation. Westerhoff goes on to say that "Conversion, I believe, is best understood as this radical turning from 'faith given' (through nurture) to 'faith owned.' "[10] This objective of Christian education focuses on teaching people that they are in need of a Savior and sharing the faith of the community of believers with them in hope that they will adopt it as their own.

The second objective of Christian education is to help the convert become a mature disciple. Miller reminds us in the imagery of the Scripture that the goal is a "maturity which feeds on the 'solid food' of the gospel, which is for the full-grown (Heb. 5:14). Strong meat is our goal, and we are to leave the milk which is for the babies behind."[11] The biblical image of "milk to solid food" suggests that faith matures and develops. True believers are forever relearning their faith. Concepts that were useful at one time (milk) must be supplemented by new vision (solid food). While the adult may still enjoy the milk of childhood, it can no longer be the only food that is consumed. The believer does not necessarily abandon his or her first understandings of the gospel. Rather, those first understandings are supplemented by more mature appreciation for the magnitude of the God of the universe and the salvation he offers through Jesus Christ. The movement in faith requires the continuing influence of education.

A third objective for Christian education is that contemporary disciples be equipped to carry out the work of ministry. Competent ministry requires that persons be sensitized to the right issues, trained in appropriate skills, and motivated by both understanding and commitment to the Christ.

These various objectives point to a consistent view of the role of Christian education: that persons become believers, mature as believers, and function as believers. It is as people learn these lessons that they enable the community—the church—to become the effective body of Christ, the faithful new humanity, and the redemptive people of God. Education, of course, in no way replaces the necessary presence of the Holy Spirit. Education alone cannot convict people of sin, preserve them in the hour of temptation, or comfort them at times of loss and grief. The ministry of the Spirit—power, boldness, comfort, presence—can never be replaced by an educational experience. But with the enabling presence of the Spirit, the word and work of faith come alive through the ministry of education.

I have summarized the objective of Christian education as facilitating persons in becoming believers. This objective is expanded in a set of objectives that have been associated with Christian education since the 1930s. Paul Vieth introduced them to the discipline, and they have become an enduring statement. According to Vieth, Christian education seeks:

1. To foster in growing persons a consciousness of God as a reality in human experience, and a sense of personal relationship to him.
2. To develop in growing persons such an understanding and appreciation of the personality, life, and teachings of Jesus as will lead to experience of him as Savior and Lord, loyalty to him and his cause, and manifest itself in daily life and conduct.
3. To foster in growing persons a progressive and continuous development of Christlike character.
4. To develop in growing persons the ability and disposition to participate in and contribute constructively to the building of a social order throughout the world, embodying the ideal of the Fatherhood of God and the brotherhood of man.
5. To develop in growing persons the ability and disposition to participate in the organized society of Christians—the Church.
6. To develop in growing persons an appreciation of the meaning and importance of the Christian family, and the ability and disposition to participate in and contribute constructively to the life of this primary social group.
7. To lead growing persons into a Christian interpretation of life and the universe; the ability to see in it God's purpose and plan; a life philosophy built on this interpretation.

8. To effect in growing persons the assimilation of the best religious experience of the race, preeminently that recorded in the Bible, as effective guidance to present experience.[12]

Baptists would revise the language in some of these statements, but the central truth they pronounce reflects a noble focus for efforts in Christian education, and provides a strong magnet drawing those efforts toward gospel purposes.

The Kind of Learning Christian Education Requires

The objectives make it clear that holding classes and conducting programs are not the primary issue in Christian education. Ultimately, the only issue that really counts is that somebody has learned something, and that faith has somehow become alive. So, the question emerges, what kind of learning does Christian education require?

Learning comes in many forms. Some learning, for example, deals with the acquisition of facts. Much of the learning of geography, elementary math, or spelling is the acquisition of facts. Another kind of learning deals with physical skills—like driving a car or learning to figure skate. Still another kind of learning deals with understanding, which is different than the acquisition of facts. What kind of learning is the desired outcome of Christian education?

The objective of Christian education—that persons become believers, mature as believers, and function as believers—dictates the kind of learning that must be part of Christian education. A central theme expressed by the objective is the issue of belief. The learning that is appropriate for belief is the learning most appropriate for Christian education. But before we can determine the most appropriate form of learning, we must identify the nature of religious belief.

Religious Belief and Learning

Belief, as the term is used in religious language, frequently reflects two traditions. The distinction between these two uses of the concept of belief is important to understand. The *Oxford English Dictionary* identifies these two traditions in its definitions for *belief.* The first defines *belief* as "The mental action, condition, or habit, of trusting or confiding in a person or thing; trust, dependence, reliance, confidence, faith." The second definition reads: "Mental acceptance of a proposition, statement, or fact, as true, on the ground of authority or evidence;

assent of the mind to a statement, or to the truth of a fact beyond observation, on the testimony of another. . . ."[13]

Many persons appear to view the task of Christian education as imparting the propositions that can be discerned from the teaching of Scripture. This kind of learning is *fact* learning and clearly relates to the second definition of belief. However, it is not the kind of learning that the objectives of Christian education, as we have stated them, require. The learning that aids persons in becoming believers, maturing as believers, and functioning as believers cannot be based on one's ability to remember or agree with a catalog of propositions. It must be more. When John says: "He who believes in the Son has eternal life" (John 3:36a, RSV), it does not mean that people who can affirm a variety of true facts about Jesus will be saved. That is the kind of believing that even the devils do (Jas. 2:19)!

The belief of which John speaks is the belief that follows the first definition. It is the individual putting trust and confidence in Jesus Christ. It is more than answering "true" to a statement about Jesus. It is a profound confidence in the saving grace of Jesus; it is a trust in him as Savior; it is a commitment—both a rational and emotional commitment—to Jesus as Lord of life. Education must be toward the "belief in"—the state of confidence that breeds hope and commitment, the sense of truth that breeds surrender to the lordship of Christ.

But education that seeks this kind of belief is a very difficult process. Learning to say what is true or false about a proposition of faith requires nothing more than memorization and recall. But learning how to place an increasing degree of confidence in Jesus Christ, or learning to deepen the commitment one makes to Christ, or learning a willingness to follow—even when the way is unmarked and unknown—that is indeed a difficult kind of learning. No educational tools can effect it. It is a learning that is possible only through God's grace.

Of course, it is at this point we are reminded that even faith is the gift of God. It is not something that we can acquire through the right kind of education, effort, or religion. Although it entails careful educational efforts, an individual can never come to this kind of belief solely by education. It comes as a gift that must be tutored, nurtured, and matured.

The Kinds of Learning Christian Education Requires

The kind of learning that facilitates believing involves at least three aspects. First, the learning should include cognitive content—things that people think about their faith. There are a number of biblical guides concerning what content must be a part of vital faith (for example, 1 John 4; 1 Corinthians 15:1-18). While belief must be more than assent to propositions, it must include content.

The learning must also deal with the feelings of love and trust. Pascal is right, I think, when he notes that "The mind has its order by premise and proof; the heart has another. We do not prove that we should be loved, by setting forth in order the causes of love; that would be too foolish."[14]He concludes, "the last step that Reason takes is to recognize that there is an infinity of things that lie beyond it, Reason is a poor thing, indeed, if it does not succeed in knowing that."[15]The education that facilitates believing must touch the heart, as well as the head.

There is yet another characteristic of learning that belief requires. It is the learning to do one's faith in ways consistent with the content and feeling of that faith. The importance of this characteristic is illustrated in the parable of the Good Samaritan (Luke 10:29-37). The problem in the story, as Jesus tells it, is that the first two passersby should have stopped to help, but didn't. The reason they should have stopped was that helping was a part of their belief system. It is likely that the priest and the Levite knew what they should do to help a wounded person, but they did not act according to the content of their belief.

The epistle of James admonishes us not to be hearers only, "But be doers of the Word" (James 1:22, RSV). It is not enough for the Christian to think the precepts of faith; it is not enough just to feel one's faith; and it is not enough for the individual only to do the actions of faith. Belief that is mature reflects the learning of thoughts, feelings, and behavior. This is the kind of learning that the objectives of Christian education require.

Teachers, Leaders, and Structures for Christian Education

The kind of learning that we have been proposing as the heart of Christian education has several implications for the teachers and leaders who staff the programs and the kind of structure that the program employs.

People are the key resource for Christian education. The learning of faith that is the belief in Jesus Christ is a person-to-person kind of learning. It would be all but impossible for persons to learn about being

Christian from any context that does not put them into close and constant contact with other people.

Propositions and facts can be learned from teaching machines or
correspondence courses. But learning to love and care and learning to
be faithful and obedient to the tasks of discipleship are possible only as
people share the experience of faith together. John Westerhoff affirms
this idea when he recalls Baptist layman Benjamin Jacob's saying that
"teaching is leading others by example on the road to spiritual maturity."[16]

People are so profoundly important because the learning that leads
to faith is more than the accumulation of facts and ideas. It is skills and
attitudes, feelings and ways of acting on one's faith. People learn these
best from other people, as their lives touch under the leadership of
God's Spirit. People learn a great deal about Christianity as they
encounter others dealing with the joys, frustrations, anxieties, and
burdens of day-to-day life. While "celebrity religion" seems to be very
highly valued by some, it is all but impossible to learn about lives that
are full of faith when people never come closer to their teachers than
the television set. Christian education—at least the kind that readily
facilitates the maturing of disciples—requires persons sharing faith
with persons.

The Real Teachers

The real teachers are not just the persons who fill the formal role of
Sunday or church school teacher. They are all the persons who are
struggling to find and live their faith in the local church. Westerhoff
summarizes well the central value of persons when he notes that the
historical function of the Sunday School "was to give persons an
opportunity to share life with other faithful selves, to experience the
faith in community, to learn the Christian story, and to engage in
Christian actions. Sunday school was not curriculum, teaching-learning strategies, or organization; it was people in community."[17]

Everyone who participates in the life of the local church becomes a
teacher of the other persons who are part of that congregation. The
church officers are teachers; the deacons are teachers; the people who
speak for or against issues in business meetings are teachers; the people who always come, and those who never come, are teachers. The
people who are critical and the ones who are supportive are teachers.
The people who pour out their lives in love and service are teachers,
as are the persons who always voice their opinion that the church

should be doing more and more for members. It is from the sinners that many people learn about sin, and from the faithful believers that many people really learn what the Christian faith is.

The persons who serve as the formal teachers in the church's program of Christian education are a part of this total teaching environment. There are certain educational agendas for which they must accept responsibility, but they must never view themselves as the only teachers in the church.

With the total community as teachers, the total life of the church becomes the teaching environment. Thus two kinds of events can be viewed as teaching events: those that are structured and intentional, and those that are quite unstructured and unintended. Both contribute to the education of persons in the process of believing. But each is very different in the kind of learning it produces.

Much of this book is about the structured, intentional kind of educational experience. Structure, in a program of Christian education, should include comprehensiveness in presenting the content of Christian faith, as well as balance in the sequence and emphasis with which that content is presented. The structures should be designed to serve the purpose of education for faith. They need to be sensitive to the local church environment and should reflect the needs of the people the program is seeking to serve.

In most administrative structures, there are basic principles that should be carefully considered, while there are few models that should be exactly copied. Structures will vary with size as well as with a church's overall style of doing ministry. Congregations are populated with variously gifted persons and variously experienced needs. The structure of Christian education must be subservient to these gifts and to these needs.

Learning also emerges from the unstructured events of community life. For example, some have learned from a church leader who failed in his own moral life and hurt the people who had placed their trust in him. Others learned from business meetings where people differed in their opinions and resorted to power plays, deception, and public displays of anger and disgust to make their points. It is some of the hard education that makes some people want to give up and walk out. But it is education.

There is also education provided by the people who are willing to forgive and to stick with their commitments to serve Christ through a particular congregation. Roger Shinn talks about the teaching value of unplanned events in his own life when he writes about being a soldier. "What I learned was not primarily what the military teachers taught me. Neither they nor I planned that education. But it took hold."[18]

The people of God acting as if they are the people of a rampaging devil is a perverse distortion of the gospel. But it happens, and when it does, it becomes a much-remembered teaching event. A program of Christian education must be sensitive to these unplanned teaching events. It must learn to seize them and incorporate them into the total ministry of education.

Qualifications for Teachers-Leaders

We have asserted that persons are the most important educational force in the church. All people teach, whether their influence is positive or negative. Some people teach in the structured environment, while others teach in the unstructured emotions and inspirations of life in the community. Whereas it would be difficult to choose those who would influence others in the total context of the church, choice is possible for those who teach in the programmed and intentional forms of education. Assuming there are more persons who can teach than there are teaching positions (an assumption that is not always valid), there need to be some criteria for the selection of the intentional teachers. I would emphasize two qualifications without which individuals should not be entrusted with the faith-lives of growing disciples.

The first of these is that the teacher must be a person of real faith. So many of the unstructured teaching events will be dominated by those who have halted in their life of faith. The structured teaching events must not be surrendered to those who are not working at their own faith. If teachers are to lead others in growth in discipleship, then they must be persons who are seeking to mature in their own expressions of belief.

The qualification is not that all teachers must be fully mature in their faith; it is that they have a measure of maturity and the commitment to grow toward more wholeness. Arthur Adams, in discussing the qualifications for church leaders, argues for the necessity of faith. "The important requirement is that conviction be powerful enough to give life its main thrust."[19]

The teacher must not, however, teach with the desire to influence everyone to believe exactly as he or she does. Such a position is contrary both to the teaching of Scripture (we are each priests unto God) and to the affirmation that the Holy Spirit may work uniquely among different persons. But the teacher must be a person of conviction and willing to express those convictions and make them available to the students.

A second qualification for those who teach in the intentional program of instruction is that they be persons who love and who are willing to develop skill in sharing that love. Much of the educating that is part of faith is helping persons understand how persons should love the Lord with all their minds, hearts and souls, and to love their neighbor as themselves (Matt. 22:34-40). Those who are afraid of love being overemphasized in the teaching ministry of the church would probably be offended by the ministry of Jesus. When Jesus was asked to reduce the law to its most important dimensions, he affirmed the need to love God and other human beings.

One simply cannot teach the faith of the gospel of Jesus Christ apart from some firsthand experience with loving and caring. Long after students will have forgotten the point of the Sunday School lesson, they will clearly remember the teachers who cared for them, who rejoiced and cried with them, and who encouraged and chided them.

As persons are taught by individuals who are on the growing side of faith and love, the gospel becomes, in its own miracle-ful way, incarnate once again. Only to talk about such things as faith and love is like trying to learn about a symphony by only studying the musical score. One may be able to understand what the music would sound like, but the lesson becomes real when the symphony is heard. Education with a teacher who has neither faith nor love may provide opportunity to see the possibilities of faith, but it can never provide the experience of it.

These criteria are so important that if there is only one person in the church who possesses these qualities, then the only class structure that church should have is one class with that person as teacher. Education for faith is too important to be left to those persons who are loveless and faithless.

Of course, there are other qualifications which would be pursued in the choice of persons to be the formal faculty. But there is a great gap in importance between these two qualifications and any others that could be listed.

Scripture speaks of those whose gift is teaching, and those persons so gifted should be secured for the teaching program of the church. Teaching is a skill, and skills require training and development. Teachers who are willing to develop skills should be selected.

Teaching is hard work—especially if it is done as an expression of one's faith and love. Those who are willing to work should be recruited for the task. Any invitation to persons to teach that is prefaced by the explanation "this job won't take much time" is an invitation to fill a vacancy more than it is an invitation to teach the Christian gospel.

These are only a few of the additional qualifications which could rightly be placed on those who should serve as teachers in the formal educational program. But the theological affirmation is that the qualifications of faith and love must be the two seen as preeminent. The skills which constitute other qualifications help the message of faith to be delivered with more precision and clarity. They make it more accessible to the persons seeking to learn. However, skills without faith and love are of little value.

Conclusion

Education for faith requires qualified teachers though it recognizes that everyone in the congregation is a teacher. Education for faith requires a special kind of learning—the kind of learning that leads to behavior and feeling as well as ideas. Education for faith requires a clear sense of purpose and objectives. Education for faith is a function of the church that helps the church be the church. It makes the gospel train a very special vehicle.

Notes

1. W. O. Carver, "Introduction," *What is the Church?* ed. Duke K. McCall (Nashville: Broadman Press, 1958), p. 3.

2. E. Glenn Hinson, *The Integrity of the Church* (Nashville: Broadman Press, 1978), p. 47.

3. Ibid., p. 44.

4. H. Richard Niebuhr, *The Purpose of the Church and its Ministry* (New York: Harper and Row, 1956), p. 19.

5. Ibid., p. 31.

6. Albert McClellan, comp., *A Basic Understanding of Southern Baptist Missions Coordination* (Nashville: Inter-Agency Council, SBC, 1972), p. 10.

7. James Smart, *The Teaching Ministry of the Church* (Philadelphia: Westminster Press, 1954), p. 85.

8. Randolph Crump Miller, *The Clue to Christian Education* (New York: Charles Scribner's, 1950), p. 37.

9. John Westerhoff, *Will Our Children Have Faith?* (New York: Seabury Press, 1976), p. 38.

10. Ibid., p. 39.

11. Miller, p. 37.

12. Paul Vieth in Randolph Crump Miller, *Education for Christian Living* (Englewood Cliffs, New Jersey: Prentice Hall, 1956), p. 57.

13. *The Oxford English Dictionary,* I (Oxford: The Oxford University Press, 1933).

14. Blaise Pascal, *Pensées,* trans. H. F. Stewart (New York: The Modern Library), p. 13.

15. Ibid., p. 31.

16. Benjamin Jacob in Westerhoff, p. 83.

17. Westerhoff, p. 83.

18. Roger Shinn, "Education is a Mystery," *A Colloquy on Christian Education,* ed. John Westerhoff (Philadelphia: Pilgrim Press, 1972), p. 19.

19. Arthur Adams, *Effective Leadership for Today's Church* (Philadelphia: Westminster Press, 1978), p. 5.

3
How to Plan and Evaluate
Bob I. Johnson

Planning is both old and new. It is both spiritual and technical. Planning is as old as God's intentionality for creating the universe and as new as the latest theory and principles for effecting planning in today's concern. Planning is spiritual, for from all accounts God in Christ made and is following a plan to provide redemption for the responsive ones. It is technical in that theorists and practitioners apply the various sciences and disciplines to develop finely-tuned approaches to planning.

Evaluation evokes a variety of responses, much of which depends on the respondent, the evaluator, or the one being evaluated. To say that a church does not have evaluation parallels saying that a church doesn't have teaching or preaching. In reality, the church lives with evaluation; and, like its preaching and teaching, some is good, some is bad, and some is dressed with an overabundance of mediocrity.

Planning and evaluation form an inseparable partnership with potentiality for overcoming significant amounts of the inertia embedded in the institutional church. They stand neither in isolation from nor out of harmony with an authentic understanding of the nature and function of the church. Is it really fair for the people of God in the churches to set aside planning and evaluation and approach the greatest work in the world from a *laissez faire* stance? The "if God wants something done he will see to it that it is done" syndrome seems greatly off-key from the melody produced when God's best and man's best merge to produce a masterpiece of purposeful forward movement in the church's life and mission. The intent of this chapter, then, is to provide a foundation, both philosophically and practically, for planning and evaluating in a church's educational program.

Developmental Planning

Much of what the local church does relative to planning can be characterized as troubleshooting. Often there exists only time for reaction to a nagging problem or an unexpected crisis. Planning should enable the church to act in positive ways at being the servant of God in the world, not merely fighting brushfires. The term *developmental planning* is used here, not for its novelty but for its implications. This use of the term *developmental* highlights and focuses on aiding maturity in the church, both collectively and individually. This presupposes that the educational ministry as well as the entire church should and can improve in important areas. The church educational leadership may profit from considering planning which seeks to lead toward maturity by:

1. *Developing decision making and decision makers.* One crucial question in any church is, how do you make decisions? God doesn't treat us as many television audiences are treated—as if they had no brains! We have decision-making responsibilities.

2. *Developing the consistently best use of nonhuman resources.* Each church has its limits on such resources as money, space, and time; therefore, serious attention should be given to their use.

3. *Developing the proper use of human resources.* Each church likely has the persons it needs to staff its educational programs. Planning helps determine how to relate persons to positions.

4. *Developing an interrelational understanding with other areas of the church's life.* The church is made up of parts, the whole of which is greater than the total of the parts. This demands that collegiality and interrelatedness be respected as basic.

5. *Developing a rationale for being and ministering.* The educational ministry as a means for the church's winning and maturing its constituents can find reason for its existence and purpose for its ministry.

6. *Developing quality individuals.* The educational ministry leadership shows astuteness by remembering that they are in the people-growing business. While leadership persons may have their goals, individuals also have directions for themselves set by what they believe to be God's guidance. The two sets of goals don't have to be antagonistic to each other. Developmental planning emphasizes individual maturity while at the same time reaching for church organizational goals without either running disrespectfully over the other.

Purpose and Description

As with most any enterprise imaginable, planning, especially longer-term planning, suffers from some misunderstanding. To clarify thinking about planning, Peter Drucker's thoughts are helpful in saying what long-range planning is not:

1. *It is not "forecasting."* It is not masterminding the future. The only thing Christian workers can predict with accuracy is the ultimate victory of God and his people. Could any one have predicted yesterday's headlines ten years ago?

2. *It does not deal with future decisions.* It relates to the futurity of present decisions. Decisions exist only in the present. The task of the planner is to determine what we have to do today to be ready for the opportunities of tomorrow. "How well will today's decisions stand up for how long and to what degree of effectiveness?" is a valid question for church educational planners.

3. *Long-range planning is not an attempt to eliminate risk.* Unable to avoid risk, the planner wants to take the right risks. Actually, planning should provide the capacity to take a greater risk—a fact not out of keeping with the Christian faith. Drucker, as a part of his definition, states that long-range planning is risk-taking decision making.[1]

Definition—It is important to consider some definitions applicable to educational planning which enhance the developmental idea. Robert K. Bower says, "Planning is the process of examining the past and present in order to construct the best program for achieving the church's objectives."[2]

Reginald McDonough states that the planning process is primarily a decision-making one. He believes that the process of planning is asking and answering these questions: 1. Why are we here? 2. Where are we going? 3. How are we going to get there? 4. Who is responsible?[3]

Arthur Adams in *Effective Leadership for Today's Church* states the steps involved rather than a formal definition. "The steps in the planning process are the clarification of *purpose,* the analysis of the *prospect,* the identification of *problems* or concerns, the listing of *possibilities,* the choice of *projects* or programs, and, finally, the development of a *pattern* of action."[4]

Coming back to the idea of developmental planning more specifically, consider this definition: Developmental planning as it applies to the educational ministry of the church consists of (1) the search for an understanding of the opportunities available, the obstacles to be overcome, the positive potential of the persons to be involved, the resources available; and (2) the decisions which bring these factors together in harmony with God's will to carry out effectively the purpose of the organization over both long and short time frames.

This definition possesses certain implications for educational planners. First, planning allows for the expression of faith. Christianity, while rejecting fatalism, teaches that God's people can have a vital part in shaping the future. Planning demands the element of hope, and hope thrives best on the nourishment of faith. Jesus was critical of those who were so concerned with the future that they filled today with unwarranted worry about tomorrow. He was at least equally chagrined by those who began projects without counting the cost or planning ahead (see Matt. 25:1-13; Luke 14:28-32).

Second, planning identifies with change. Though certain theological truths maintain constancy, change is evident in every area of the Christian's existence. The disciple of Christ ought to be changing more and more into Christ's image. Communities and issues change; family structures change; even ministry and training opportunities change. Planning is a means by which we can discover together the changes called for by our Lord and have a part in making the church more effective through such anticipated change.

Third, planning helps the church to maintain an awareness of purpose. At times individual goals or interests may all too easily take precedence over the church's central purpose. Planning which involves a broad number of members in clarifying and positioning this central purpose helps avoid self-centeredness and aids the church's maturity.

The types of planning needed are rather consistent among all organizations. McDonough calls them long-range, short-range, and operational.[5] Care should be taken in projecting long-range plans too far into the future because of the difficulty of assessing the environment. For educational planning a period of three years and certainly not more than four or five is adequate.

Short-range planning for the educational ministry is planning in detail for one year. This planning transposes the longer-term plans into specific action-oriented plans. Short-range goals, a coordinated calendar, and budget allocations should result from short-range planning.

Operational planning is regular planning occurring quarterly, monthly, and weekly to implement the plans. Examples of this planning are the church council meeting (quarterly or monthly), Sunday School Council, Church Training Council, and the weekly workers' meeting of the Sunday School.

Of course these various levels of planning are interrelated. Consistency with the next higher level of planning should be the goal of each planning group. At times, however, the implementation of shorter-range or operational planning may reveal the need to revise the goals which resulted from the long-range planning. The planning process should always maintain the flexibility which would allow for reasonable revision of goals. For example, if a church reaches in three years its five-year goal to provide special ministries for single adults in its community, some revision should occur when it becomes obvious the goal will be reached early. Goals may need to be revised downward as well—and the system should allow for this.

In any kind of planning there are always certain elements. Drucker lists eight:

1. *Objectives.* What are the overriding accomplishments desired by the planning group? Objectives may be characterized as the church's timeless intention to act.

2. *Assumptions.* These are the possibilities and problems as anticipated by the group making the decisions. What can be counted on to have significant impact on plans made?

3. *Expectations.* These are the things in the future considered likely to result from the implementation of plans.

4. *Alternative courses of action.* Because wrong or less-than-the-best-decisions can be made, other avenues of action should be planned and available.

5. *The decision itself.*

6. *The decision structure.* No decision stands in isolation. Every decision, by the very nature of organizations, is a part of a decision structure. Like bumper cars at a carnival, what one does affects others.

7. *Impact stage.* A decision stays in the arena of good intention unless it leads to implementation. A decision to use total-period teaching in an adult Sunday School department reaches the impact stage when the leadership actually plans for Sunday and then implements those plans in the teaching situation.

8. *Results. What has happened because of planning?*[6]

Principles of Planning

1. *Look out for the powers at work which oppose planning.* Probably the most universal power is people's fears of planned change. Almost all ambitious plans are designed to produce new patterns of thought and action. The truth is—people resist planned change.

A second power opposing planning is the immersion of people in the routine of church to the extent they see no need for planning. Of course, even in the church there is the power of risk aversion. This operates against planning because some kind of important, and perhaps new, commitment to the future will be demanded if new plans are made.

Another power which works against planning is interest protection. Some feel that planned change would lessen their influence, or take away "their" storage cabinet, or hurt their class. Some may feel their own pet project would be passed over and other projects given priority by the planning group.

2. *Encourage as many persons as possible to participate.* A reminder that people like to feel a part of what is going on came to me when attending a professional baseball game in Kansas City. Some fan started batting a beach ball into the air with the intention that others would continue the fun by giving it a solid rap to yet another area of spectators. Until the attendant grabbed the ball, the activity was the center of attention for hundreds of fans, most of whom would have enjoyed getting in one good slug of their own. Anyone catching the ball as though to keep it received hearty boos, especially the attendant hired to help keep order. People like to be in on the action.

A planning group should consciously attempt to involve all the persons it can in developing the plan. Involvement decreases inappropriate resistance and increases commitment. People are much more likely to demonstrate interest in plans they have helped formulate. People may even respond beyond expectation when given a chance to participate in planning. See Figure 1 for a form which may be useful in involving a large number of persons.

3. *Look toward the ultimate destination desired.* Decide where you want your orgainization or project to be when you get there. Knowing this will aid you in determining how to make the trip. This principle applies to all levels of planning, whether designed to lay out a three-year development plan for Sunday School or to prepare for the teaching and learning experiences of next Sunday morning for the children's department.

When objectives are established which are worthy ultimate destinations, then every idea and project may be evaluated and ranked in relation to these objectives. This helps priorities to remain priorities.

4. *Look for potential, not merely problems.* Listing your problems can be very depressing. Considering potential can give new life and self-esteem to a planning group. A church may struggle to maintain a

Church Dreamer's Priority List

Write the potentials and possibilities our church has. Do not limit your dreaming by a lack of such resources as adequate finances or leadership.

I believe our church has an opportunity for increased ministry with these groups of persons or needs:

1.

2.

3.

4.

5.

6.

I am interested in our church giving a priority to number(s) _____.

I am interested in active participation in number(s) _____.

Figure 1

long-established college Sunday School department with few prospects and fail to see the hundreds of noncollege, single adults living all around it as a potential ministry opportunity. For more discussion of problem-based planning versus the potentialities-based approach, see Lyle Schaller's *Effective Church Planning* (Nashville: Abingdon Press, 1979).

5. *Avoid overkill in planning.* A mere casual review of the newsstand will boggle the mind with the number of magazines and books devoted to running. The average person who just wants to get a little exercise may tremble with fear thinking about all he does not know about running. The same principle might paralyze planning in the church. Many books, some very technical, on the subject of planning have come off busy printing presses in recent years. Learn from these but avoid wandering into the quicksand of technicality. Be adaptable and shun despair if things don't go by the book. Keep your planning simple, and thus (maybe) keep it fun!

6. *Look beyond individual agendas to objectivity.* To say that any planning group can maintain complete objectivity would be false. The planning effort probably was born in the first place because at least one person thought change was needed. The difficulty comes when personal agendas remain hidden and are not "officially" recognized. For this reason planning leaders may need to consider giving time early in the process to discovering where the participants are in their thinking. One way to do this is to have persons share with the group such information as who has influenced them most as Christians; what motivated them to take their current position in the church; their greatest fear concerning the project(s) under consideration; and their greatest hope for the experience.

Move beyond these initial feelings to help the group see that their task is not to rubber-stamp any one preconceived plan but to search collectively for the best plan possible.

7. *Maintain the ability to be flexible.* Remember that you are dealing largely with volunteers who cannot be coerced into decisions. Also, unanticipated needs may arise which were not accounted for in earlier planning. New information becomes available. These and other such factors provide evidence that planners and implementers of plans should maintain flexibility. Plans are not unalterable and should be adjusted to meet changing needs. They are always "our" plans not "my" plans.

8. *Evaluate the planning from both process and outcome perspectives.* Evaluation will be discussed later in this chapter.

Guidelines

The Church Council or Cabinet

The church council holds the key planning responsibilities in a church. Its members include the pastor who serves as chairman, church staff members, directors of program organizations, the deacon chairman, and those who chair committees, such as stewardship and missions. Other committee chairmen may be added temporarily or permanently according to need.

Basically, the church council should serve as a forum for a church's leaders in planning, coordinating, and evaluating the total work of the church. The council depends on the various church organizations to implement the church's program according to their assigned tasks. As chairman of the church council, the pastor should be able to lead in the development of a unified program that gives major attention to church priorities. (Additional information concerning the church council and educational organizations is given in chapter 6.)

The principle function, then, is for the council to assist the church to determine its course and to coordinate and evaluate its work. Figure 2 illustrates a planning sheet which may be used by the church council and other planning groups.

Church leaders become members of the church council as a result of election to designated church-leadership positions. They serve correspondingly to their term in the church-elected position.

Specifically, their duties include:

1. Helping the church understand its mission and define its priorities;

2. Coordinating studies of church and community needs;

3. Recommending to the church coordinated plans for evangelism, missions, Christian development, worship, stewardship and ministry;

4. Coordinating the church's schedule of activities, special events, and use of facilities;

5. Evaluating progress and the priority use of church resources.

Program Planning Groups

Each educational organization should have a council group responsible for planning its work. The program director, such as the Sunday School director, serves as the chairman. Other members are the direc-

A Planning Sheet

Project Title:_____

Overall church objective(s) to which this project relates:

_____
_____
_____

Project objective or goal: _____

_____
_____

Possible need(s) to be met: _____

_____
_____

Priority listing of needs: (4) _____
(1) _____   (5) _____
(2) _____   (6) _____
(3) _____   (7) _____

Procedures to meet and reach objective

_____   _____
_____   _____
_____   _____
_____   _____

Assignment of Responsibilities

Person assigned	Action to be taken	Date assigned	Date to be completed	Resources needed	Cost involved

_____

Figure 2

55

tors of the departments, divisions, or units of the organization, as well as the general officers. The director serves on the church council and utilizes his organizational council to help prepare and carry out successfully work related to the church council. The organizational council does not need to report formally to any other group, but should monitor its planning activities for consistency with the church's overall objective(s).

An organization council should evaluate the organization as to its effectiveness; establish goals and actions to fulfill the organization's purpose and tasks; request the needed resources; and coordinate the activities of the organizations. The list in Figure 3 may be used in obtaining the opinions of program workers and leaders.

Unit or Department Planning Groups

When the organization is large enough to have departments or units, planning groups are needed for each entity. For example, an Adult Sunday School department has three possibilities for planning. Since the department engages in a scheduled Bible study session each week, those workers responsible for this work should meet weekly for planning if at all possible. The church-elected director of the department is responsible for leading this planning activity. Other department leaders may fill key roles during the planning sessions.

The department planning group should give the majority of its time to preparation for the upcoming teaching/learning sessions. The group should keep in mind that the entire time alloted for the department meeting on Sunday can be planned to contain learning experiences. For a number of years emphasis on total-period teaching has been given for the preschool, children, and youth departments. As more and more persons with such learning experiences become adults, adult planners will want to consider carefully how they can effectively use the concepts involved in total-period teaching.

Class Leaders' Planning

The teacher, outreach leader, and group leaders should meet monthly or as needed to plan for outreach and ministry. Matters to be included are evaluation of the class's effectiveness in fulfilling its purpose, planning activities growing out of Bible study, and planning for meeting outreach and ministry needs.

Class Meeting

At this monthly or quarterly meeting planning can take place which

A List of Possible Priorities of the Educational Ministry

1. Better training for program leaders
2. Better training for teachers
3. Better visual aids
4. Better physical facilities
5. New buildings
6. Improved adult department periods
7. Better parking facilities
8. More organization-sponsored fellowship
9. More and better volunteer workers
10. More paid educational staff
11. More money for Christian education
12. Better outreach program
13. Stronger missions emphasis
14. More emphasis on the family
15. Enlistment of inactive church members
16. Improved media center (church library)
17. More emphasis on Christian recreation
18. More emphasis on specific ministries by members
19. Study and training classes for the deaf
20. Study and training classes for the mentally retarded
21. Study and training classes for the developmentally disabled
22. Stronger emphasis on prayer
23. More coordination between programs
24. Regular planning by the leaders
25. A better schedule for weekday activities
26. Better food service for the midweek meal
27. Greater punctuality for leaders
28. More participation from members and leaders in curriculum
29. Enlarged Bible teaching program
30. More weekday programs for children
31. More weekday Bible study and training for youth
32. More weekday Bible study and training for adults
33. More programs on political and community awareness
34. An improved Church Training program

Figure 3

involves all the members. Information can be shared, and members can participate in helping improve the departmental organization. Since adults learn better when they help plan the learning experience, it is appropriate to include planning for future lessons in the class meeting.

Evaluating

"But these persons are volunteering their time and efforts," some would say in defending against any kind of formal evaluation in the Christian education program of a church. Indeed, the volunteer aspect weighs heavily when church leaders approach assessing the church's educational ministry.

A fear of evaluation does grow out of a concern that those who staff the program organizations aren't paid (in money) and should not be subjected to the kind of accountability inherent in formal evaluation.

On the other hand, however, our fears may be conditioned by past and mostly inadequate concepts of evaluation. One may recall the feeling when an incorrect answer was given to a question proposed by the teacher in school. The ease with which another student answered that same question may have been even more devastating. One doesn't easily forget such experiences, and they certainly condition thinking relative to evaluation. But it is shortsighted to dismiss evaluation on such grounds or to suggest that it is unimportant in Christian work. Far from being an insult or inappropriate, evaluation properly done may become the greatest favor a church can do for its volunteer workers. (This applies to paid staff persons as well.)

At best it is unthoughtful to ask a person to take a place of responsibility in the church without stating what the church expects from that person, providing resources to do the task, and implementing some means of evaluation to help answer the question any sensitive worker will ask, "How am I doing?" One of the foundational principles of working with adults states that they need feedback on their progress.

Evaluate, according to Webster's *New World Dictionary,* means "to find the value or amount of, to appraise." D. Campbell Wyckoff defined evaluation as "a process of comparing what is with what ought to be, in order to determine areas and directions for improvement."[7]

Evaluation of the Christian enterprise and of those persons who play vital parts in its process is a difficult responsibility. In commenting on this, Adams states:

Any organization, including the church, would be presumptuous to suppose it could deal with the relation to God's standards of a member's work or as yet unrevealed effects of that activity known only to God. Instead, the appraisal is addressed to the Christian's performance in activities designed to accomplish purposes and goals established by the church to which the member has made a commitment in accepting a responsibility.[8]

Ideally evaluation makes a person aware of the quality and kind of his work and furnishes guidance for improvement. Fundamentally, the most important result of evaluation is what happens in and to the persons involved. The church belongs in the people-mending and maturing business; therefore, evaluation should contribute to that process.

William Young enlarges on evaluation in the church by suggesting the context in which it should be considered:

1. Evaluation is a humane process involving an assessment of strengths and weaknesses in the performance of individual human beings.

2. Evaluation is the only way to determine whether the objectives and goals of the education program are being accomplished.

3. Evaluation is a process that, hopefully, will promote an attitude of self-improvement.

4. Evaluation is a process that requires personnel involved in utilizing a variety of assessment techniques to determine levels of accomplishments.

5. Evaluation is a process that enables teachers/leaders and learners to determine the amount of success that each exhibits in the teaching-learning process.

6. Evaluation provides a means whereby the need for and utilization of facilities, equipment, materials, and supplies are seen in relationship to the total education program.[9]

The Purpose of Evaluation

People usually care a great deal about an enterprise in which they invest significant portions of their energy and resources. Because of this care they display keen interest in what they perceive to be the vital signs of that enterprise. The national government is one example. The church is another. Their constituents, as an outgrowth of concern, constantly evaluate such institutions. The evaluation doesn't always bear the marks of fairness or lead to the proper conclusions and implementation of needed change; nonetheless, evaluation does occur.

Because evaluation to some degree takes place constantly, persons in leadership places can profit from understanding the purpose of evaluation. The purpose is basically twofold. First, evaluation speaks to the planning process. Evaluation criteria should be established before the final formulation of plans; and if this is done, then planners can proceed knowing the standards by which their work will be assessed. If ineffectiveness results, the persons responsible can seek improvement in the program, the processes, the facilities, and in other resources which contribute to the overall objective of the educational ministry.

Second, evaluation speaks to learner progress. All the factors listed in the above paragraph exist for the good of the persons involved in the church's educational program. The learner should have some indication of what he does and does not know; what he does and does not do well; his development of attitudes and their value to the Christian life. Properly done, this kind of evaluation helps the learner discover areas of needed growth and become motivated to do something about it.

To further clarify the purpose of evaluation, consider the following:

1. Evaluation should serve to provide a comprehensive view of the educational ministry.

2. Evaluation should assess the consistency of the program with the educational philosophy of the church.

3. Evaluation should provide a chance for a cooperative effort by everyone involved.

4. Evaluation should serve the church continuously as an ongoing part of the planning and implementing process.

5. Evaluation should highlight quality and growth.

6. Evaluation should provide a serious look at teachers/leaders, learners, and the learning process.

7. Evaluation should identify strengths and feed this information into the overall planning process for inclusion when expanded ministries are being considered.

8. Evaluation should identify problems and focus clearly upon them with a view toward proper solution.

9. Evaluation should help clarify good objectives and point out weaknesses in poor ones.

10. Evaluation should provide accurate and relevant information

for those charged by the church with the responsibility for improving the educational ministry.

On What Bases Do We Evaluate?

Standards for evaluation should be determined early in the process before plans are implemented and persons enlisted for places of responsibility. What are some of the standards which may be helpful in assessing the church's education program?

First, the church's objective or purpose statement should provide an overall guideline to help determine if the educational ministry is contributing to the fulfillment of the church's intention. This standard may be used in a formal process of evaluation or simply in regular, ongoing assessment of various programs and activities.

Next, and growing out of the church's objective, an educational objective provides a standard. One such statement reads: "To help persons become aware of God as revealed in Jesus Christ, respond to him in a personal commitment of faith, strive to follow him in the full meaning of discipleship, relate effectively to his church and its mission in the world, live in conscious recognition of the guidance and power of the Holy Spirit, and grow toward Christian maturity."[10]

Additionally, job descriptions or worker covenants formulated (see Figure 4), approved, and shared with workers provide a base for evaluation. Since all good evaluation seeks the development of the person(s) involved, a job description becomes a vital resource. Performances can be measured, and areas for needed improvement become apparent when these clear guidelines exist. This enhances the leader's chance of getting the work done through people, an accomplishment which is more meaningful to all involved.

Furthermore, carefully formulated and tested standards developed by religious education specialists usually connected with one's denomination or publishing house provide criteria for evaluating the organization and the performance of specified tasks. Such standards can be revised and made more specific for a particular church situation.

Another source for standards may be found in the individual worker's own goals developed to be consistent with the church's educational objective and goals. For example an individual might set a personal goal of making so many visits to class members each week or of reading so many books relating to his responsibility. Encouraged and monitored, this type of standard holds promise for individual

Sunday School Worker's Covenant

Believing that the privilege of guiding people in the Christian way of life is worthy of my best, I covenant, as a worker in the Sunday School of _____ Church, to:

Order my conduct in keeping with the principles of the New Testament, and seek the help of the Holy Spirit that I may be faithful and efficient in my work. (Eph. 4:1)

Be regular and punctual in attendance; and, in case of unavoidable absence, give notice thereof as far in advance as possible. (1 Cor. 4:2)

Make thorough preparation of the lesson and for my other duties each week. (2 Tim. 2:15)

Use the Bible with my group on Sunday morning, or other meeting times, and help them to understand and love it. (Psalm 119:16)

Contribute, proportionately and cheerfully, to my church's budget. (1 Cor. 16:2; 2 Cor. 9:7)

Attend the regular planning meetings. (Luke 14:28-30)

Visit prospects frequently and make a special effort to contact absentees each week. (Acts 2:46)

Study one or more books from the Church Study Course each year. (Prov. 15:28a)

Cooperate wholeheartedly in the plans and activities of the church and school. (1 Cor. 3:9)

Be loyal to the program of the church, striving to attend all worship services. (Heb. 10:25)

Make witnessing a major endeavor. (Prov. 11:30)

Seek to discover and meet the needs of those with whom I come into contact, especially fellow church members and prospects for my church. (Gal. 6:2)

Pray regularly for the church, the Sunday School, the officers and teachers, and for the pupils and the homes from which they come. (1 Thess. 5:17)

Apply the teachings of Christ in moral and social issues of my everyday life. (Jas. 1:22)

With the help of God, I will do my utmost to keep this covenant.

Figure 4

improvement and thus organizational and ministry improvement.

The Bible serves as an authoritative standard for all the church does. The standards found there are appropriate, then, for the church's education ministry. One such is found in Colossians 3:17: "And whatever you do, in word or deed, do everything in the name of the Lord Jesus, giving thanks to God the Father through him" (RSV).

Growing out of the biblical teaching is the final standard to be suggested here for use in evaluating the church's educational ministry. The priesthood of all believers, meaning that every believer has equal access to God and a ministry to perform, is vitally related to the measurement of the church's success in reaching and growing persons for Christian discipleship.

Who Are the Evaluators?

The most effective evaluation occurs when it involves active participation by the persons holding stock in it. To be sure, the responsibility for guiding and coordinating the evaluation process belongs to those persons and groups who have major responsibility for the church's religious education program. Somewhere in the total process, however, there should be a place for others who are involved to say what they feel about the program. Such persons included are teachers, leaders, directors, pupils, certain community leaders, and parents of the children and youth.

Caution should be observed at this point. Pushing too hard for formal evaluation may cause more confusion than benefits. Being wise as a serpent and harmless as a dove is good advice in developing an approach to helpful evaluation. Work to include everyone possible and to get them to practice self-evaluation. Encourage the leadership to ask "how am I doing?" type questions. Seek to lead them to measure the organization's effectiveness by the previously agreed upon standards.

Help teachers to study and evaluate their role as learning leaders. Provide guidance and incentives for class or group members to check their performance and growth. Hold up suggested criteria by which they can gauge these matters. Help them to assume responsibility for improvement along with the church-elected leader. Above all, be open to evaluation by others and practice it on yourself. This is simply providing a good model. And everyone needs that.

Getting everyone involved in evaluation has genuine benefits which soon become evident. Hopefully, getting a large number of persons involved helps take the sting out of evaluation, leaving only the honey of improvement for the church to enjoy. Additionally, the people should become more objective in their evaluation through regular practice and by including themselves in the process. They should learn to judge by standards other than their own personal prejudices about programs, and their likes and dislikes of the people involved. Remember, Jesus did not forbid us to judge; he simply stated that we should evaluate using the standards by which we wish to be judged. Getting broad participation means broader ownership by the people involved, a genuine benefit for the church.

In addition to getting broad participation from the church in evaluation, groups such as the staff and church council should feel especially responsible. Tidwell provides these principles for the church council: (1) planners and implementers evaluate; (2) develop evaluation criteria before implementing plans; (3) evaluate qualitatively and quantitatively; (4) time evaluation to get maximum benefit; (5) evaluate processes and results, not personalities; (6) evaluate objectively and subjectively; (7) communicate evaluation findings.[11]

Areas to be Evaluated

Several major areas should be included in a balanced effort to assess the church's educational ministry. It must be recognized that these areas cannot be neatly compartmentalized and stand in isolation from one another. They are all inseparably bound together as a part of an active, living organism which we call the church.

The Curriculum

The curriculum materials used by a church should be chosen to strengthen the church's effort to fulfill its educational objective. Even though curriculum plans and materials are available from one's publishing house, the church still needs to make choices based on its own situation. In doing this, the characteristics of good curriculum become a very basic consideration. Colson and Rigdon suggest seven such characteristics:

> 1. *Biblical and theological soundness* are important to assure that what is taught in the curriculum is genuine Christianity.
> 2. *Relevance* has to do with suiting the teaching to the nature and needs of the learners in their current situation.

3. *Comprehensiveness* means that the curriculum will include all that is essential in the scope and all that is essential to the development of well-rounded Christian personality on the part of learners.

4. *Balance* means that the curriculum will have neither overemphasis nor underemphasis of the various parts that make it up.

5. *Sequence* is the presentation of portions of curriculum content in the best order for learning.

6. *Flexibility* is important if the curriculum is to be adaptable to the individual differences of the learners, adaptable to churches of different types, and adaptable to the varying abilities of leaders and teachers.

7. *Correlation* is the proper relation of part to part in the total curriculum plan.[12]

Certain questions may be asked in evaluating what curriculum materials should be used and how effective they may be in matching the desirable characteristics:

1. Does the curriculum adhere clearly to a set of objectives or goals which aims at comprehensiveness?

2. Are the objectives clearly related to a biblical and church-centered approach?

3. Does the curriculum emphasize an ongoing response to the gospel of Jesus Christ?

4. Does the content help persons encounter the biblical message at the point of their experiences in life?

5. Does the content speak to the needs of the various ages in a comprehensible way?

6. Does the content lead persons to live out a vital faith and to relate to others as a functioning, cooperating member of the body?

7. Does the curriculum incorporate the laws of human growth and development?

8. Is the role of the teacher one of stimulator, guide, and catalyst?

9. Do the materials encourage teachers to think and plan creatively for the learning experience instead of simply transferring information?

10. Is encouragement given for changing attitudes and actions as well as for increasing knowledge and skills?

11. Do the suggestions for teachers/leaders help develop good leadership qualities?

12. Do the suggested methods call for pupils to demonstrate that learning has taken place?

13. Do the procedures cultivate an informal, relaxed atmosphere for learning?

14. Are the suggested activities purposeful rather than simply "activities for activity's sake"?

15. Are supplementary helps suggested which may be secured with reasonable effort?

16. Is each lesson a part of a larger group or unit with suggested objectives, goals, or aims?

17. Are ways given for evaluating pupil progress in appropriating and practicing the principles of Christianity?

18. Are the materials appropriate to the educational level of the pupils?

19. Do the materials provide information and emphasis relative to the denomination or body of churches to which your church relates in a cooperative ministry?

20. Are the materials physically attractive?

Teachers/Leaders

The fact that what happens to the individuals involved is the utmost factor in evaluation has already been stated. Assessing teachers and leaders, therefore, must be done tactfully and with their cooperation.

Bower gives good advice when he states that it is incumbent upon the person who does the work of evaluation to follow the principle of assisting the individual in the most profitable and expeditious use of his gifts, skills, and attitudes. It is not the responsibility of the evaluator to judge or recommend dismissal; rather, it is to encourage, to guide, and to help every member of the church in his God-given ministry, however large or small. It is that of studying personalities with their related skills and then seeking to place them where they can function most effectively for God. Thus, we may transfer a person from one responsibility to another which is more suited to him, but we must not, according to biblical principles, take the attitude that he has no place in the program of God apart from being a passive listener.[13]

That not everyone should be a teacher or leader (leaders are teachers also by how they lead) is common knowledge. It was a problem faced by Paul when he wrote in 1 Timothy 1:7 of those "desiring to be teachers of the law, without understanding either what they are saying or the things about which they make assertions." (RSV). One important function of the educational leader or minister is to help persons who should not be a leader or teacher to avoid the painful experience of being installed in such a position.

Before such a person is ever approached certain questions should be considered. Does the person manifest Christlike characteristics? Does he understand the goals of Christian education, and if not should he be willing to learn and apply them? Can she learn to use proper methods of teaching and leading? Will she participate in outreach? Is he lazy? Does she know the Bible adequately? Can he work with others? Is he willing to use the curriculum materials properly?

Once the person takes a place of service as a teacher or leader, self-evaluation is probably the most effective means of determining strengths, weaknesses, and then planning for improvement. For this to happen the workers need a guide or standard. Perhaps it is a worker's covenant such as the one suggested in Figure 4 which the church has approved and to which the persons involved have agreed. The one closest to the worker in a supervisory relationship could sit down with the person (preferably in the worker's home) and ask some "How are you doing or feeling?" kinds of questions as they relate to the job description or covenant. Out of this exchange should come ways of improvement or even the decision that a person could profit from a change in responsibility.

For a teacher in the Bible teaching program of the church, a checklist such as suggested in Figure 5 can be used quarterly or semiannually. As persons become more aware of the type questions which are appropriate in evaluation, they are likely to become more conscious of the factors on a regular basis. In other words, one is apt to be more aware more of the time of what makes a good teacher. Also, the teacher will benefit from evaluating each session individually and in a group of fellow workers.

Another method of evaluation which can be quite sensitive is observation. The person being observed should be aware of and have agreed to the visit. The results should be shared and carefully assessed with the worker. Lucien Coleman states four principles to be observed in the observation process which help the acceptance of the idea of evaluation by observation: (1) the person doing the evaluating must have the respect of the teacher as someone who "knows what he is doing"; (2) teachers/leaders must enter into the process voluntarily; (3) the evaluative observation must be planned in advance and carried out unobtrusively; and (4) a postobservation conference must be carried out as mutual evaluation.[14]

Although the old idea of "boss" is inappropriate in the church,

Checking Your Bible Teaching

Grade yourself as a teacher by circling beside each question the number which you feel is most accurate. Add up the total of the circled numbers. A score of 85 and above would be an excellent score and 40 and below would be a poor score. In between would range from fair (41-60) to good (61-84).

Preparation

I look through the lesson topics in advance.   Always 5 4 3 2 1 Never
I begin lesson preparation more than one week in
   advance.   Always 5 4 3 2 1 Never
The Bible is the center of my lesson preparation.   Always 5 4 3 2 1 Never
I have a systematic plan of lesson study.   Always 5 4 3 2 1 Never
I keep in mind the specific needs of all my pupils as I
   prepare.   Always 5 4 3 2 1 Never
I write down or have in mind a specific objective for
   each lesson.   Always 5 4 3 2 1 Never
I seek constantly to improve my teaching by general
   reading, by attending workers' meetings, and taking
   training courses.   Always 5 4 3 2 1 Never
I pray regularly about my task.   Always 5 4 3 2 1 Never

Presentation

I am able to stimulate interest from the beginning.   Always 5 4 3 2 1 Never
I seek to have the Bible passages read meaningfully.   Always 5 4 3 2 1 Never
All of my pupils participate in the lesson discussion.   Always 5 4 3 2 1 Never
I use a balanced variety of teaching methods.   Always 5 4 3 2 1 Never
I am able to follow the main subject to a desirable
   conclusion without getting unduly diverted.   Always 5 4 3 2 1 Never
I pace the presentation schedule to give proper
   emphasis to the central truth.   Always 5 4 3 2 1 Never
My pupils and I reach helpful conclusions by the end
   of each lesson period.   Always 5 4 3 2 1 Never

Evaluation

My pupils are stimulated to more Bible study.   Always 5 4 3 2 1 Never
My teaching helps change pupils' moral and social
   standards.   Always 5 4 3 2 1 Never
My teaching contributes to reaching the lost for Christ.   Always 5 4 3 2 1 Never
My teaching helps make pupils more faithful in their
   church relationships.   Always 5 4 3 2 1 Never
My teaching helps make me a better Christian.   Always 5 4 3 2 1 Never

Figure 5

elected leaders have certain supervisory responsibilities to perform. Those persons may find helpful the following questions designed for leader self-evaluation.

(1) Do I have concern for those I lead?

(2) Do I delegate responsibility to my workers?

(3) Do I ask for and respect the opinion of those I lead?

(4) Do I promote loyalty to the entire program and church?

(5) Do I give deserved and specific praise?

(6) Do I keep my workers informed?

(7) Do I include all workers in the planning and evaluation?

(8) Do I deal with problems rather than personalities?

(9) Do I have a checkup system to assure that assignments are followed through to a successful conclusion?

(10) Do I consult those who will be affected by an action before it is taken?

(11) Do I see that a new worker gets proper orientation?

(12) Do I seek to measure up to the standards appropriate to my position?

The Learner's Experience

Included here are the learner and the learning process which combine in the total experience of those who participate as pupils. They must feel that benefit is coming to them in the form of increased knowledge and understanding of the Bible, fellowship and acceptance, opportunities for class participation, and ministry activities in which they feel competent.

The learner needs to be heard from so leaders can know what the learners are learning and how they are making application. Through learner evaluation, needs can be discovered and weaknesses can be improved in the learning process. The quality of instruction can be measured also. Evaluation such as this demands courage for a teacher to open up to others and say, "How am I doing?" It should, however, help the teacher to mature in his leadership role.

There are some easily observable signs available to those seeking to understand the learner's experience. Those signs are the learner's attendance, the learner's attention in class, growth in Christian understanding and character, the learner's comments, and the learner's enthusiasm for reaching new persons.

Tests may be used to help determine learner knowledge and understanding. Such tests may be essay (which usually begin with a word such as *discuss, explain* or *compare);* objective (short answer, based on simple recall and completion); interest and attitude (reaction to a series of statements). Some tests are included in the curriculum material, and others are available from religious publishing houses.

Another effective way to determine learning is to interview individual members of the class or group outside of the regular sessions. The questions should be more open and informal than questions on a written test. This type of evaluation serves to determine a measure of Bible knowledge and to indicate that leaders are serious about the learning experience. Extensive help in evaluating the learner's experience may be found in chapter 6 of H. W. Byrne's book, *Improving Church Education* (Birmingham: Religious Education Press, 1979), pp. 156-229.

Facilities and Equipment

Place is important in Christian education. The physical characteristics of that place contribute significantly to the learning experience. Although many buildings in which Christian education programs are housed do not provide ideal arrangement for classes or groups, evaluation should begin with time-tested standards. Usually denominational offices or publishing houses can provide such help. Age-group program administration books also provide detailed information on the needs for each age group, along with diagrams of rooms showing equipment arrangement. The *Church Property and Building Guidebook,* Lee Anderton, compiler (Nashville: Convention Press, 1973), provides extensive help for use in evaluating educational facilities.

Church workers need to be aware of how much the physical surroundings affect learning. Each time they walk into the room where they work they should observe the physical characteristics with the eye of a stranger. Things such as dirty and unattractive areas, surplus materials out of place, and inappropriate room arrangement can be corrected with little or no money.

A church may find rating scales useful in surveying space and equipment needs. Factors included are room lighting and ventilation, seating, heating, decorations, equipment arrangement, and audiovisuals.

The workers themselves usually can do the best job assessing the facilities in which they teach. They should have the support of the church through a designated committee such as the properties committee or through the use of an outside consultant. When needs are determined which may require expenditures beyond the church's immediate means, then a list of priorities can be made. The church council or cabinet may be used to help establish such a list.

Organization

Organization is the arrangement of the persons and other resources for accomplishing a given task. Because organization can be good and bad, formal and informal, it too should be evaluated. Again, those evaluating can go back to the standards which underlie the current organization. How well are we maintaining those standards? Do the standards still fit our needs? How strong is the formal organization? What is the influence of the informal organization? (Informal organization refers to small groups in the church which may seek to influence policies by use of such as money and position.)

Age-level administration books provide suggested organizational patterns which can be used as evaluation criteria.

Coleman suggests that

> The basic questions in the evaluation of organization and program are these: (1) Do we have enough units, and the right kinds of units, to carry out the work ...? (2) Do we have an adequate corps of workers? (3) Do we have enough of the right kinds of meetings to plan and carry out our Bible study program adequately? (4) Are we making the proper use of resources, including budget, curriculum materials, facilities, personnel, and time?[15]

Using the Evaluation

Evaluation should always maintain the role of a servant, never a tyrant. For it to serve it must be used. Failure to use the results of evaluation at least borders on dishonesty. The same people who helped in planning and conducting evaluation should be included in drawing conclusions and helping decide on what steps to take. Evaluation then serves the people most affected by it.

The process of using evaluation should include: (1) careful examination of the information to determine its validity; (2) determination of the reasons for past success and failure; and (3) the feeding of information back into the planning process for future directions and programs.

Notes

1. Peter F. Drucker, "Long Range Planning: Challenge to Management Science," *The Management Process,* comp. Carroll (New York: MacMillan, 1973), pp. 130 ff.

2. Robert K. Bower, *Administering Christian Education* (Grand Rapids: William B. Eerdmans, 1964), p. 49.

3. Reginald McDonough, *Working with Volunteers in the Church* (Nashville: Broadman Press, 1976), p. 92.

4. Arthur Adams, *Effective Leadership for Today's Church* (Philadelphia: Westminster Press, 1978), pp. 115-116.

5. McDonough, p. 93.

6. Drucker, *The Management Process,* pp. 136-37.

7. D. Cambell Wyckoff, *How to Evaluate Your Christian Education Program* (Philadelphia: Westminster Press, 1962), p. 9.

8. Adams, pp. 158-59.

9. William E. Young, "The Minister of Education as an Evaluator," *The Minister of Education as Educator,* comp. Will Beal (Nashville: Convention Press, 1980), p. 80.

10. Howard P. Colson and Raymond Rigdon, *Understanding Your Church's Curriculum* (Nashville: Broadman Press, 1969), p. 43.

11. Charles A. Tidwell, *Working Together Through the Church Council* (Nashville: Convention Press, 1968), pp. 64-68.

12. Colson and Rigdon, p. 51.

13. Robert K. Bower, *Administering Christian Education* (Grand Rapids: William B. Eerdmans Publishing Co., 1964), p. 132.

14. Lucien E. Coleman, "The Need for Evaluation," *How to Improve Bible Teaching and Learning in Sunday School: Pastor-Director Guide,* comps. Ernest R. Adams and Mavis Allen (Nashville: Convention Press, 1976), p. 38.

15. Ibid., p. 65.

4

How to Organize and Coordinate

Bob I. Johnson

Organizing

Is organization a blessing or a blight? Is it beauty or beast? At times organizing may be pictured as the culprit which stole the attention away from the real task of the church. At other times we recognize the value of organization and may even say, "What we need is to get better organized."

W. L. Howse reminds us that church organizations appeared soon after the early church was established. He recounts: "Evidently it was necessary even in its early days for a church to structure itself in order to conduct its work."[1] Organization is not evil—in fact, it is essential— but it should always be the means by which the church expresses itself as an organism.

Churches sometimes establish organization without adequately deciding what work is to be done. This approach allows the organization to become the end instead of the means. Starting with organization instead of purpose may involve church members in meetings and actions which are less valuable than those dealing with a church's essential work.

At the beginning of the modern era of religious education, the churches reluctantly permitted organizations for teaching and training to come in. Although these organizations met in the church buildings, they were not arms of the church nor designed to represent the churches at work.[2] Failure to recognize these organizations immediately as parts of the organized church led to a crusade for church recognition and support. At times, strong-willed personalities conducted these organizations in opposition to the church program.

In such circumstances competition developed among these organizations, and fragmentation in the churches became easier. What was best for the organization, what would position it favorably, and what would give it prestige and power often became criteria for those who led these organizations.

Today there is an attempt to approach organizational structuring from a different viewpoint. What are the tasks of the church? What does the church plan to do about its God-given assignment? Needed organization should grow from the soil produced by answers to such questions. This makes organizing a means to an end, not an end in itself. It should also minimize competition and enhance cooperation and coordination.

Terminology used to describe important features of organizations has varied both in the literature and in practice. To gain initial perspective for this study of organization, it may be helpful to examine several related terms.

Organizing is the process by which the structure of an organization is created and maintained. This process includes the determination of the specific activities that are necessary to accomplish the objectives of the organization, the grouping of those activities according to some acceptable pattern, and assignment of these grouped activities to a responsible position or person. Organizing (together with other activities such as planning, motivation, communicating, and evaluating) is considered to be a part of the responsibilities of church staff and elected leaders.

Organization is perhaps a broader term, referring to the process of organizing, the structure of an organization, and the processes that occur within an organization. Inquiry about organizations often has been described as the study of organization theory or even the theory of organizations.[3]

Description

At the outset it should be noted that there are three main types of organizational structure which have been prevalent in recent history. These three are found in churches having a distinguishable approach to organization.

The first may be termed the *mechanistic* or executive structure, which is often depicted in charts by titles of job roles contained in a number of separate boxes, some joined by continuous lines to indicate an executive relationship between the roles and some by dotted lines to indicate communications relationships only. The former are termed "lines of command," the latter "lines of communication."

The executive system has been defined as a "system of people in a structure of work roles."[4] This implies that the people may change, but the roles remain the same. The people are thus geared to the roles rather than the roles to the people.

Mechanistic organizations are structured into a hierarchic system of specialist roles or functions. Each individual role carries carefully defined rights and duties and technical requirements. All information is directed to the top of the hierarchy, so the "boss" holds most knowledge of the enterprise's needs and sends down his instructions accordingly to lower levels in the hierarchy. Communications are therefore mostly vertical, that is, between superior and subordinate. Work is carried out according to instructions devised by the head of the hierarchy.

The second structure may be designated by the term *human relations.* Human relations theorists claim that one of the key tasks of management must be to create groups more favorably inclined to the achievement of organizational objectives. Individual incentives should be replaced by group incentives to help workers gain a sense of togetherness. They are to feel themselves a real part of the organization by being allowed to participate in matters relating to their work.

The advocates of the human relations structure claim that organizations should not be depicted as sets of relationships between work roles but rather as relationships between interlocking and interdependent groups. A criticism of the human relations approach is that it can become so engrossed with building up good human relationships among the various interlocking groups that it can neglect the task to be performed.

In the church situation the human relations structure is benevolent, permissive, friendly; everyone is encouraged to be involved. According to W. E. Beveridge in *Managing the Church:* "The church is perceived by its members as a social group alongside other social groupings in the world. Its main concern, like the mechanistic church, is with itself, and its objective is to enlarge its social nexus by bringing in new members."[5]

The third main approach to organization may be thought of as the *organic* structure (also known as the systems approach). Some have viewed the mechanistic and the human relations structures as unable to provide the fulfillment which a person seeks. Purpose, meaning, growth can only be found in an organic structure, some contend.[6]

In the organic structure, knowledge is no longer confined to the top of the hierarchy; it is shared with each member of the organization who needs it for the achievement of his or her task. Work, to be effective, must be coordinated with that of other group members, and this means that communication becomes less a matter of passing down instructions from above and more a matter of sharing information and mutual consultation by the organization members. Communication is both vertical and lateral.

People do not live in little boxes as in the mechanistic structure, but must constantly relate what they are doing to what is being done by everyone else in the organization. The organization is not static, but is in a state of continuous interaction with the environment in which it exists.

To understand something of its intent and approach, contrast the organic (or systems) approach with that of the human relations and mechanistic theories. The mechanistic approach focuses on achieving the organization's goals, while the human relations organization focuses on achieving the goals of its people. Systems theory, however, holds organizational growth and goal achievement, and the growth of persons and the achievement of their own goals within the organization, to be of equal importance.

In considering how we organize in the church, we do well to take into account the differences inherent between work organizations and voluntary organizations. Leslie E. This provides such a list.[7]

Work Organizations	**Voluntary Organizations**
Leader is paid	Leader normally not paid
Followers are paid	Followers are not paid
Followers are interested in advancement	Followers are most interested in achieving organization's goals
Penalties are financial and more severe	Penalties are seldom enforced and are nonmonetary
Leader can "tell" and "sell"	Leader must "sell" and "persuade"
Leader's expertise is important	Leader's personal charisma is important
Authority is derived from above	Authority is derived from followers
Organization prescribes work to be done	Members prescribe work to be done
Leader can direct authoritatively	Leader must direct out of persuasion
Leader is a specialist	Leader is a generalist
Leader is task-oriented	Leader is people-oriented
Leader has work-life tenure	Leader has short tenure
Leader normally is profit-oriented	Leader is service-oriented

Fixed structure	More informal structure
Limits on creativity	Usually open to high creativity
Organization chooses leader	Followers choose leader
Greater risk to economic security	Little or no risk to economic security
Commitment of leader to followers is usually not great	Commitment of leader to followers is great

Principles of Organizing

How to organize is a subject of highest importance for a person in an education ministry leadership role. Here are a few basic principles for consideration.

1. *Let the work to be done provide overall structure.* What the organization is seeking to accomplish, what resources are available to accomplish it, and how much time is available in which to do it are the basic factors which help determine how to organize. Once you have determined, as an overly simple example, that the church ought to be in the Bible teaching business, the next step is to determine the most effective organizational vehicle to accomplish the task.

2. *Group work functions which share important common concerns.* Put together work which is basically similar. The most obvious similarity is skill. So, for example, in a hospital, nurses might be grouped under a director of nursing; in a bank, tellers under a supervisor. In the church there are appropriate ways to group similarly. For example, leadership training should be organized so that a unified thrust is presented and coordinated efforts may be made.

3. *Push decisions as low in the organization as adequate information is available for making them.* You want to do this in order to provide for the maximum growth of the individuals in the organization. Also this leaves the leader as free as possible for his or her own primary responsibility. To help understand the effects of various forms of organization on decision making, pretend that the organization is functioning first on one basis, then another. What decisions are likely to float up to you in each case? In all likelihood the leader will need to provide some thinking as it relates to the whole picture of the total effort, but not need to make every decision for every person involved.

4. *Avoid overorganization.* If you have analyzed needed work and the other factors involved, you have a reasonable idea of the numbers and kinds of persons it will take to get the job done. But keep organization to a minimum. Every additional component and every "layer" of

organization add to the difficulty of communication and increase the need for working time devoted to coordination, relationships, and information exchange. All these things slow down accomplishment, add to inefficiency, and lessen the likelihood that all will feel a partnership in the work and accomplishment of the task. Since the purpose of organization is to establish an easy flow of work and facilitate its successful accomplishment, keep formal structure at a minimum.

5. *Be aware of the span of control factor.* As one thinks about the organization or reorganization of a church institution, he should be aware of the organizational principle called the span of control. The term *span of control* means that for effective administration there is a limit to the number of individuals from whom the top administrator may personally receive reports and with whom he may discuss and determine programs of action.

The observation of this principle is important also for the minister-administrator in either the small or large church. For as soon as one begins to work directly with a large number of persons he reduces his effectiveness. Generally we think of it being far easier to work with three persons than with twenty. This is due to the fact that there are many fewer relationships in the former situation than in the latter.

6. *Seek to understand the informal groups which exist within the formal structures but are not included in an organizational chart.* Robert Bower, referring to such, states:

> These groups may evolve slowly, almost imperceptibly, from within the organization until they become an integral though still informal part of the structure. Some executives have referred to these groups as "kitchen cabinets" because of the policies which they develop on a very unofficial basis. Being closely knit groups they will often meet informally at a group member's home to make plans which ultimately wield a great deal of influence. The term "clique" is frequently applied to such organized bodies. Since they may devise plans of action which catch the administrator off guard, he will be wise to identify and understand the nature of all such groups at the earliest possible time. Should these be broken up? Not always. Cliques and informal groups are not, in every case, detrimental to the welfare of an organization or a church.[8]

Consider a church which is located in a community with a high population turnover and a comparable turnover in the church membership. Cliques and informal groups in this type of situation may form a core of leadership and thereby provide a source of stability and strength for a church in the midst of its changing constituency. Were it not for such groups, churches located in changing communities or in other similar situations might well find themselves deprived of capable leadership.

Another way of expressing this principle is in terms of informal power. The kinds of power used in organizations include physical, economic, knowledge, performance, personality, and ideological power. The leader of an educational ministry exhibits appropriate awareness when he or she considers the informal power structures as programs are organized.

7. *Decide on how you view the persons to whom you relate in the organization.*

The leader's attitude toward and understanding of people will directly affect the organizational approach taken.

Douglas McGregor, in *The Human Side of Enterprise,* popularized the Theory X and Theory Y approaches to organizing people.

Theory X is based on the assumptions that:

1. The average human being dislikes work and will avoid it as far as possible.

2. He is lazy, lacks ambition, is irresponsible.

3. He must be strictly controlled in his work if the objectives of the organization are to be attained.

4. He is gullible and not really to be trusted.

In contrast, Theory Y assumes that:

1. The enjoyment of work is as natural as the enjoyment of games or rest.

2. People will exercise a strong sense of responsibility towards objectives they believe in.

3. If people are given the opportunity, they learn not only to accept but to desire responsibility.

4. The capacity to exercise a high degree of imagination, ingenuity, and creativity is widely and not narrowly distributed among people.

5. Modern industrial life is such that the potentialities of the average man are only partially utilized.

6. In so far as people are passive or resistant to organizational needs, it is because present organizational structures have made them so. People will never learn to become responsible if they are continually treated as if they were irresponsible.[9]

Another approach, called contingency management, has developed as an alternative to the hard acceptance of either Theory X or Theory Y. One illustration, from a secular situation, relates to job enrichment.

It should be recognized that some employees do not want their jobs enriched. Some prefer easier work. Some are troubled by challenge. Others prefer a friendly situation and are not much concerned about job content. Obviously, for the Christian valid questions of theology are involved, such as: How do we view man and his response to Christian commitment?

Reasons for Organization

Negative feelings about organization may arise from the confusion of bad or poor organization with good organization. When organization is right, you are hardly aware of its existence, and the benefits can be experienced by all. McDonough lists the following benefits of good organization.

1. Good organization fixes responsibility.
2. Good organization distributes the work.
3. Good organization pinpoints authority.
4. Good organization establishes proper relationships.
5. Organization creates a team.[10]

Guidelines for Organization

The following actions may serve a church's educational ministry in designing a new organization or in redesigning existing organizations.

1. *Preview the existing situation.* What is the present plan of organization? What has the church stated in its official documents such as its constitution? What, if any, long-range plans does the church have that would involve the educational ministry?

2. *Assess the future in relation to the present and past.* What are the opportunities for the church and what organization is needed to be ready to meet those challenges? What problems existed in the past that can and need to be corrected?

Use the appropriate persons to help determine answers to such questions. Make and retain lists of responses for future evaluation.

3. *Formulate a plan for the organizational needs to be met.* Begin by putting together the structure which seems best. Leave plenty of room in your mind and on the paper for change. Ask if changes in the church's adopted procedures need to be made. Do the constitution and bylaws need to be changed?

Determine when the plan can be put into effect. What are the snags along the way? What can be done to overcome inertia? How much cost is involved?

4. *Prepare a report for information and action.* Depending on where responsibility for development of the plans lies, the church council should review and approve such plans for organizational change and then take them to the church for approval (if the church stipulates that this be the process).

5. *Implement approved plans on an effective schedule.*

Keeping the Organization Up to Date

Setting up the organization is one activity. Keeping it up to date is just as important. Perennial effort to maintain it must be made. At least four things should be done, according to Bob Flegel.

1. *See that visitors and new members are properly classified.* When visitors attend and individuals enroll, they should be led to the proper age or grade, class or department. To fail to classify new members and visitors will soon destroy the work done in setting up the departments and classes.

2. *Study the organization through the year.* Check the ratio of workers to pupils in Preschool and Children's departments. Add workers, if necessary, to maintain a good ratio for growth.

3. *Check the enrollment of classes and departments to see whether they are near or over the suggested maximum enrollments.* Study these units to see whether additional units should be started.

4. *Keep the Sunday School properly graded by observing annual promotion.* Persons who have reached the age or grade for the next class or department should be encouraged to move to that group on the appointed day.[11]

On the last day of the old Sunday School year, recognize members who will be moving to a new unit the next Sunday. Everyone stays in his class or department the whole Sunday School period that day. On the next Sunday, the first Sunday of the church year, each person who is to promote goes directly to his new class and department. In this way, time is not taken on Sunday morning to move groups from room to room.

A church considering Promotion Day on a Sunday other than the last Sunday of September should carefully look at the curriculum plan and determine whether the value of promotion at that time outweighs the interruption of the Bible study plan that the curriculum follows.[12]

Relating to Tradition

A church, like other organizations, develops within a tradition that is an evolving system of assumptions, habits, behavior, and attitudes. This tradition has been shaped by leaders in the past as they dealt with situations inside and outside the organization. As situations change, new leadership may reinforce, reinterpret, or change the tradition. They can never afford to forget the hold on members which the group's history has. Before much time passes a body of people develops momentum. Sudden changes court disaster. Stopping and then starting in a new direction uses up a great deal more time and energy than focusing on elements in the tradition which are allies of biblical imperatives or of responses to new needs.

Thus a church organization that has become a self-centered, mutual-help society may awaken to its evangelistic obligations when the people vividly recall the missionary zeal of its founders and first members. An organization that has been building itself but neglecting its community may begin to show more of the compassion of its Lord when reminded of the priorities he had and how they were carried forth by earlier faithful workers.

Coordinating

Two groups in the church have planned activities requiring the fellowship hall for the same date. Neither checked the calendar or coordinating process, and each learned of the conflict only after significant amounts of time and energy had been invested in preparations. They both had good intentions, but a lack of coordination caused the problem.

This simple reminder points out that the church's educational ministry has unique needs for coordinated, integrated plans and procedures. Since the church is largely dependent on volunteers who see each other for relatively brief times each week, coordination becomes absolutely necessary and at the same time more difficult than in situations where people are together for a regular workweek.

Adams states:

> Organizing is a process going on all the time in any social system, including the church. It involves, among other things, developing in the minds of the members a picture of the group's life together, securing their acceptance of this model, and keeping it up to date. The model may have its tangibility primarily in the words and deeds of leaders and members. It may be embodied in a written statement, such as a constitution or bylaws, or have graphic form in an organization chart. It is useful because it

defines the situation, suggests what particular members should do and expect others to do, and clarifies relationships.[13]

Coordination, then, goes hand in hand with the organizing process and may be defined as the means of bringing together all the parts of an enterprise into a relationship which harmoniously and effectively works toward achieving the organizational goals.

Purpose/Description

According to Alvin Lindgren:

> Sound church administration requires comprehensive, coordinated planning. The church can only achieve its purpose when every segment of it is seen as a part of a larger whole with a single mission. Since the church is the "Body of Christ," all its members and working groups must be united in making a common witness. Our definition of church administration . . . includes "moving in a coherent and comprehensive manner toward providing such experiences as will enable the church to utilize all her resources . . . in the fulfillment of its mission." There must be a mutual supportiveness in all activities if the church is to achieve its mission of making known God's love. This will not take place apart from skillful coordination.[14]

Principles/Reasons for Actions

1. *Basic agreement on the purpose of the organization is necessary for good coordination.* Understanding of purpose must be reached early in the process of organizational relationships so all members of the team can work together. Such understanding must begin with the church's own determination of an overall purpose and then come to maturity as the church's purpose filters into and determines the purpose of each organization.

2. *Planning is essential for good coordination.* Agreement on purpose must be followed by careful planning. By so doing, the overall strategy can be placed before everyone involved. Detailed plans can be made with a minimum of overlapping. Remember that one of the characteristics of coordination is that the lack of it is not often detected until the crisis has arisen.

3. *Good coordination should include all groups involved.* At times church groups tend to exalt their own importance in relation to the whole. Groups may become self-centered and feel that everything must revolve around them. A leader or a group may feel that a room or equipment is exclusive property when in reality it belongs to the larger body, the church. Coordination involving all groups or units

helps maintain a perspective and reminds people of the common task the church is about.

4. *Specific efforts to communicate to the constituency is a part of good coordination.* Communication is essential to effective coordination of activities because the achievement of group purposes is dependent upon dividing the required tasks among the members. Good communication makes options clear and opens the way for wise choices by individuals and groups. It clarifies the relation of actions to the desired results and increases motivation. It makes coordination easier through developing awareness of the actions of others.

Guidelines

1. Use a variety of means.

The Church Council—The church council, as described in the previous chapter, is the key administrative body for planning and coordinating a church's work. The pastor, who serves as chairman, leads this group in maintaining order and relevancy in all phases of church life. Additional information concerning the church council and educational organizations is given in chapter 6.

The church council should meet monthly or often enough to function properly and carry out its task. Members should be encouraged to prepare properly for the sessions so that effective coordination can be accomplished.

Program Councils and Staff—The principle functions of program councils and/or staff are to determine the direction of the program and, of course, to coordinate efforts, and to relate to the church council for overall coordination. Directors of major units in the program become members of the program council and serve for as long as they are in their particular responsibility. For example, the Sunday School council consists either of the age-division directors/coordinators or department directors along with the general Sunday School leadership. See Figure 1 for a suggested monthly agenda for such a council.

Age-division Coordination—Basically age-division coordination is accomplished through either self-coordination, age-division conferences, or age-division coordinators/directors. The complexity of the organization should determine the approach used. In self-coordination, the organization leaders of an age division voluntarily coordinate their work and the use of space, equipment, and supplies. Age-division coordination conferences serve as counseling, advisory, and coordinating groups. Members are leaders of units of a particular age division

Sunday School Council Plan Sheet

Getting Ready for the Meeting	Person Responsible	Date to be Completed
1. Prepare an agenda 2. Mail copy of agenda to all council members one week before the meeting.	Sunday School Director	

Suggestions for the Sunday School Council Agenda

I. Encouragement
Perhaps the pastor could be used to speak briefly.

Pastor or other respected leader

II. Information
Discuss "how" to get the work done.

Division/department Directors

_____
_____
_____
_____

III. Evaluation
Discuss events and activities that have been conducted. Consider how they could be improved or whether they should be held again.

_____
_____
_____
_____

IV. Communication
This period can be used for a progress report on current activities.

_____
_____
_____
_____

V. Preparation
This period is time to schedule, plan, and assign responsibilities for upcoming projects.

_____
_____
_____
_____

After the Meeting
Prepare a summary of the meeting and mail a summary to absent council members.

Adapted from: *Sunday School Leadership* (Nashville: The Sunday School Board of the Southern Baptist Convention, October 1980), p. 28.

Figure 1

(choirs, mission groups, Bible teaching units, and training units). Age-division coordinators/directors counsel age-division leaders and coordinate the work of units within the age division. (Additional information concerning age-division coordination is given in chapter 6.)

Church Calendar—The regularly scheduled activities of the church should be listed for the year and distributed to all officers, workers, staff members, and all members. The cost involved should not be prohibitive and should promote greater effectiveness of the program. A long-range view will recognize the businesslike planning inherent in an annual church calendar and the motivation it will provide for leaders and others to plan their personal programs with the church coming first rather than last in their thinking. A definite process for calendaring should be established through the church council. You are budgeting church resources in dealing with time just as much as in planning how to spend the money the church expects to receive.

Planning Guide—Planning guides are available for every program organization and are available from your denominational bookstore or publishing house. Program leaders should be aware of help available through such a resource and plan work with it in mind.

Written Reports—There will undoubtedly be activities planned which have not been included in the annual church calendar. If reports describing projected activities are submitted to the organizational leaders and/or the church council, this will give sufficient opportunity to coordinate these with the activities already listed in the church calendar. Of course if there is any conflict, the activities scheduled in the annual church calendar should receive preferential treatment.

Organizational Chart—Earlier in this chapter, organizing was discussed. There are values in showing the relationships among persons in leadership positions. A chart of this nature should be distributed to all officers and workers to help them visualize the organization.

If the church distributes a manual to new members, an organizational chart should be included, thereby providing an excellent means for their orientation to the administration of the church. This becomes a coordinating device in that each person knows to whom to go for assistance, rather than moving from one office to another seeking the person with the knowledge and authority pertaining to the matter at hand. See Figure 2 for a checklist which helps in determining strengths and weaknesses in such an arrangement.

Administrative Handbooks—This type of coordinating device should be available to all who function in a leadership capacity. Duties should be defined clearly, procedures for contingency situations explained, and other items of an essential nature should be included. Handbooks which are issued annually for specific groups may include the names, addresses, and telephone numbers of officers and leaders, important activities and their dates, constitution and bylaws, scheduled programs and projects for the year. Some are comprehensive, while others are designed for specific areas of the program.

Workers' Weekly and Monthly Meetings—Regular meetings are absolutely necessary if activities are to be kept coordinated. Examples are: Sunday School Workers' Meeting and Training Leaders Council.

Dominant Idea or Motto—This coordinative device may have value for achieving a sense of unity for a specified period of time. The concept which is used should be directly related to the supreme mission of the church and be emphasized regularly through printed materials, brochures, and other communication media.

Ex-officio Memberships—These are usually extended to persons at the upper levels of organizations so that they can gain information for coordinating the general program. The pastor, an associate pastor, the minister of education, or others may be given ex-officio privileges. This permits them to be members of certain selected committees with or without voting rights, as determined by the group or by the constitution and its bylaws.

Church Bulletins—This is perhaps the most commonly used device for coordinating church activities. It is distributed to all worshipers on Sundays and lists the activities for the coming week. The disadvantage of this method as a coordinating device is that most people plan many of their business, educational, social, and recreational activities a month to three months in advance. Those church bulletins which announce important events for a month ahead are doing the church members a genuine service, but even this cannot begin to take the place of the more efficient method of distributing annual church calendars to the entire membership.

Church Paper—Many churches publish a church paper in addition to a church bulletin. This too may be employed for publicizing and coordinating activities. The problem which most churches find in producing a paper, apart from the financial aspect, is that of recruiting the necessary journalistic talent with sufficient time and dedication to produce it on a regular basis. If a paper is to be started, there should be reasonable assurance that there are persons who are capable of making it a meaningful tool.

Checklist for Coordination Review

1. In your organization have you found:
   (1) Unassigned areas of responsibility? ____ Yes ____ No
   (Describe) _____
   (2) Inadvertent overlapping areas of responsibility? ____ Yes ____ No
   (Describe) _____
   (3) Procedure difficulties between tasks? ____ Yes ____ No
   (Describe) _____
   (4) Fuzzy lines of communication? ____ Yes ____ No
   (Describe) _____
   (5) Other ____ Yes ____ No
   (Describe) _____

2. In your personal contacts with other organizations, have you found:
   (1) Unassigned areas of responsibility? ____ Yes ____ No
   (Describe) _____
   (2) Inadvertent overlapping areas of responsibility? ____ Yes ____ No
   (Describe) _____
   (3) Procedure difficulties between tasks? ____ Yes ____ No
   (Describe) _____
   (4) Fuzzy lines of communication? ____ Yes ____ No
   (Describe) _____
   (5) Other ____ Yes ____ No
   (Describe) _____

3. With respect to your relationship with other persons:
   (1) Is the relationship between your task and overall organization goals clear?
   _____
   (2) Are any of your responsibilities unclear?
   _____
   (3) If you reach all the results planned, will your organization make its full
   contribution to the overall purpose of the church?
   _____
   (4) If the person to whom you look for leadership carries out the planned
   work, will you receive adequate help from him or her?
   _____
   (5) Is the communication channel adequate?
   _____

Figure 2

88

Delegating Responsibilities to a Single Person—This is one of the most important methods of coordination available to the administrator. It permits him to clarify and expect performance of duties assigned to others. Both the one delegating and the one receiving delegation should agree that each understands the other's perceptions of what is involved.

Informal Conferences—In this technique the persons responsible meet on a very informal basis (over cups of coffee, for example) to consider matters of coordination. Through such conferences many of the hindrances to coordination can be minimized or eliminated before they pose any serious problem.

Budget Allotments—The use of budget allotments as a coordinative technique is not often considered. This technique is of value if the activities of a group are funded by the church's budget.

A church may emphasize ministry-oriented budgeting; that is, it may determine the ministries a church should be doing and give priority budgeting to those ministries. Coordination becomes crucial in such a process. What if there isn't enough money (seemingly)? What do we trim? consolidate? reconsider? give precedence to?

Church Mailbox—Using an inhouse mail system can be effective and much less expensive than the regular mail service.

2. Deal wisely with change.

Coordination becomes more acute when dealing with change. Whether dealing with a matter as small as reassigning meeting places for two groups or as large as planning for the years to come when the energy situation becomes ever more serious, change cannot be ignored.

Allow plenty of time for people to think about and reflect on the anticipated changes. If possible keep some of the old with the new so as to make it more acceptable. Be patient with people who react negatively while you keep up the positive pressure for the change.

The environment after change is very important also. Leaders should seek to keep the change effective and to detect any leakage of support and understanding by those involved. Plan to evaluate and encourage. Admit mistakes. Listen to suggestions. Help answer people's questions. Keep a positive, prayerful attitude.

Remember! Too much change too quickly, even if needed, is not good over the long term.

3. Introduce new ideas effectively.

Ideas are the stuff out of which changes are born. How do new ideas

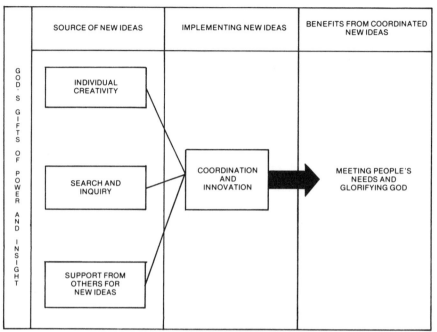

Figure 3

come and how shall they become a part of the coordinating process? See Figure 3 for a diagram of the process.

In any Christian enterprise, God gives his people many gifts—gifts of power, understanding, insight, and knowledge among others. Although some people are more creative than others, we all have the ability to create to some extent. Christian education leaders can become more creative when they are in a supportive atmosphere in which they have an uninhibited opportunity to become aware of the larger number of ideas that rapidly flash into the mind. Free speculation and disciplined reaction to it are important, for there is a persistent force which works against creativity. According to George Prince, "We humans habitually try to protect ourselves even from our own new ideas."[15]

Search and inquiry is another source of new ideas. Thus reading from others is important as well as doing research with the educational ministry.

New ideas should be tried out on some trustworthy persons who are capable of giving an objective viewpoint. Such a person may point out a pitfall not previously considered or make a simple suggestion which not only provides affirmation but perhaps improves the original idea.

4. Deal sensitively with conflict.

Adams reminds us that conflict is evil if it hurts persons without opening possibilities for their redemption or renders it impossible for the church, which is the body of Christ, to carry forward its mission.[16]

While the Bible assures us that God can make the wrath of man to praise him, the family concept of the universe which dominates the Christian revelation places great stress on the blessedness of peace-making. It is the responsibility of the Christian leader to join in the prayer that all may be one (John 17:21) and to do what can be done toward this purpose. Paul, writing to the Corinthians, mourned over the harm done to individuals and to the body of Christ by divisions and quarrels (1 Cor. 1:10-17).

Conflict is inevitable where coordination of the church's education program is attempted. Disagreement that results in open confrontation can be creative and even consistent with Christian commitment. Such conflict may cause both parties to reexamine ideas and procedures.

Conflict which arises when coordination is sought should be handled seriously and objectively. One cannot avoid personality clashes in the church, but as a rule deal with the problem and not with the personality. For more help in this area see Larry McSwain's and Bill Treadwell's book *Conflict Ministry in the Church* and *Church Fights* by Speed Leas.

Notes

1. W. L. Howse, "Understanding Changing Concepts," *Vital Principles in Religious Education,* comp. John Sisemore (Nashville: Broadman Press, 1966), p. 57.

2. Ibid.

3. Herbert G. Hicks and C. Ray Gullett, *Organizations: Theory and Behavior* (New York: McGraw-Hill, 1975), p. 5.

4. A. D. Newman and R. W. Rowbottom, *Organizational Analysis* (New York: Heinemann, 1968), p. 2.

5. W. E. Beveridge, *Managing the Church* (London: SCM Press, 1971), p. 61.

6. Ibid., pp. 60-61.

7. Leslie E. This, *A Guide to Effective Management* (London: Addison-Wesley Publishing Co., 1974), pp. 106-07.

8. Robert K. Bower, *Administering Christian Education* (Grand Rapids: William Eerdmans, 1964), p. 38.

9. Douglas McGregor, *The Human Side of Enterprise* (New York: McGraw-Hill, 1960), pp. 33-57.

10. Reginald McDonough, *Working with Volunteers in the Church* (Nashville: Broadman Press, 1976), pp. 79-80.

11. Bob Flegal, *Sunday School Director's Handbook* (Nashville: Convention Press, 1979), p. 17.

12. Ibid.

13. Arthur Merrihew Adams, *Effective Leadership for Today's Church* (Philadelphia: Westminster Press, 1978), p. 86.

14. Alvin Lindgren, *Foundations for Purposeful Church Administration* (Nashville: Abingdon Press, 1965), p. 226.

15. George Prince, *The Practice of Creativity* (New York: Harper and Row, 1970), p. 9.

16. Adams, p. 106.

5

How to Staff and Motivate
Jerry M. Stubblefield

Purpose

The Christian minister spends considerable time seeking to staff educational organizations. Staffing pressures are usually felt more heavily prior to the beginning of the new church year. The minister should work closely with the church nominating committee (some churches call this the Christian education committee) to staff the educational organizations. Frequently, the nominating committee also has the responsibility for nominating church committees and boards. The minister should endeavor to meet with this committee each time it meets. Time should be spent with the committee chairperson both prior to and following the meetings.

The objectives of this chapter are to suggest practical ideas and guidelines the minister can use in staffing the educational organizations and motivating church leaders. *Every* minister is involved in staffing and motivating whether he is the *only* minister in the church or whether he may be one of several ministers on the church staff.

Good staff leadership must come from an awareness of what each person should be doing in his or her assigned task to assist the church in meeting its stated educational objectives and goals, and of how these contribute to and enhance the church's objectives and goals. The lack of established, clearly defined plans invites distrust, which ultimately leads to poor morale on the part of volunteer workers. The end result is that the church will lose some or all of its potential effectiveness in its ability to reach and develop persons in the church's mission and ministry.

The success and effectiveness of a local church is largely determined by its ability to develop and motivate a staff, whether it be paid or volunteer or a combination of the two. More than 60 percent of the churches in America are small churches. The small church has been characterized as having one full-time paid minister (he may be bi-vocational) and a nondepartmentalized Bible teaching program. These churches have less than 150 enrolled in their Bible teaching programs. These churches will remain one-minister churches due to their size and limited financial resources.

Every minister must have a thorough knowledge both of the educational organizations in a church and also of the educational processes to be used by each age group within the organizations. This is true whether a person is the only minister on the church staff or is the senior minister of a multiple staff church. A minister must be the supervisor of the educational organizations whether working with volunteer leaders or with another professionally trained minister.

The minister who fails to do this will soon discover that the morale among lay leadership is decaying and/or that the educational minister feels that the senior minister does not understand or appreciate what he or she is doing. A wise minister learns all he can about the educational programs of his denomination while in school and continues this practice throughout his ministry. Then he can supervise either volunteers or staff members more knowledgeably and more efficiently.

If a church is to have an effective educational program, it will, of necessity, be heavily dependent upon volunteer workers. This is also true of its programs of mission and ministry. Examine the church where you are a minister or a member. On a sheet of paper list places where volunteers are serving in your church. Your list probably includes Bible teaching activities, choirs, committees, deacon boards, groups of church visitors, shut-in ministries, youth activities, mission projects, etc. The list is endless. A church cannot have a paid staff member to do all of the ministries necessary to carry out the mission of the church.

Some churches have used paid teachers in their Christian education programs. However, these were limited primarily to classes for children and youth. Many of these were professional educators or students training for educational careers. Churches using this approach usually focused upon the *quality* of classroom instruction, with little or no contact outside the classroom. Quality instruction must occur in the classroom, but effective teaching involves the character of the teacher interacting with the learners.

Could your church function without the dedicated corps of volunteers working in *every* facet of its educational program? What would happen without volunteers in the areas of Bible teaching, discipleship training, missionary education and mission activities, youth ministries,

ministries to single adults, senior adult ministries, family life education, and recreation?

This discussion should not be construed to depreciate or minimize the role played by paid church staff members. It simply acknowledges the impracticality and impossibility of a church employing enough persons to minister effectively to persons with whom it has contact and for whom it has responsibility.

For five years I served as minister of education of a church which had nearly two thousand persons enrolled in its Bible teaching program. Even with two other educational ministers, it was impossible for the three of us to minister effectively to that many persons. We worked to equip, train, and enable more than two hundred church-elected volunteers to work directly with the people. In addition, many of the classes and/or departments had other volunteers assisting those elected by the church. The three staff members had personal contact with many of the people, but not to the extent and intensity as that of the two hundred volunteers.

Volunteers are crucial in the day-to-day ministry and functioning of the local church. If the church is to have volunteers, they must be recruited to staff the church's educational organizations. Persons must be inner-directed by the Holy Spirit to perform tasks to the maximum of their ability. This is motivation. How to staff and how to motivate will be described in the remainder of this chapter.

How to Staff

The assumption that the work of staffing the educational organizations of the church is the responsibility of the church nominating committee or the church Christian education committee is basic to this discussion. Responsibility for determining the necessary units and organizational patterns, however, rests within each educational organization or unit, not with the nominating committee. Prior to beginning the staffing process, each organization should submit a written organizational pattern. The task of the nominating committee is to discover and enlist potential leaders as requested by the various educational units, not to determine organizational patterns or needs.

Staffing Principles

Principle 1—Develop a master file of potential church leaders. Several months prior to beginning work, the nominating committee

BIBLE TEACHING PROGRAM

Places I will serve		Places I have served

_____ 1. Outreach Visitor .. _____

_____ 2. Pre-school Tea (0-3) _____

_____ 3. Pre-school Tea (4-5) _____

_____ 4. Child Tea (6-8) . . _____

_____ 5. Child Tea (9-11) . . _____

_____ 6. Youth Tea (12-14) . _____

_____ 7. Youth Tea (15-17) . _____

_____ 8. Adult Tea (18-29) . _____

_____ 9. Adult Tea (30-59) . _____

_____ 10. Adult Tea (60-up) . _____

_____ 11. Dept. Director . . . . _____

_____ 12. Outreach Leader . _____

_____ 13. Vacation B.S. . . . _____

Age Preference . . _____

_____ 14. _____ . . _____

MUSIC

_____ 15. Choir Member . . . _____

_____ 16. Choir Sponsor . . . _____

Age Preference. . _____

_____ 17. Song Leader. . . . . _____

_____ 18. Play Piano . . . . . _____

_____ 19. Other Instruments. _____

What _____

CHURCH TRAINING PROGRAM

Places I will serve		Places I have served

_____ 20. Pre-school Tea (0-3) _____

_____ 21. Pre-school Tea (4-5) _____

_____ 22. Child Tea (6-8) . . _____

_____ 23. Child Tea (9-11). . _____

_____ 24. Youth Lea (12-14). _____

_____ 25. Youth Lea (15-17). _____

_____ 26. Adult Lea (18-25) . _____

_____ 27. Dept. Director. . . . _____

BROTHERHOOD

_____ 28. R. A. Leader . . . . _____

_____ 29. Brotherhood Officer _____

_____ 30. Baptist Men Mem.. _____

MISSIONARY ORGANIZATION

_____ 31. Pre-school Ldr (0-5) _____

_____ 32. Child Ldr (6-11) . . _____

_____ 33. Youth Ldr (12-17) . _____

_____ 34. W.M.S. Chairman. . _____

_____ 35. W.M.S. Member. . . _____

_____ 36. W.M.S. Officer . . . _____

What _____

Figure 1

Places I **will** serve		Places I **have** served
	GENERAL	
______	37. Soul Winning	______
______	38. Visiting Prospects .	______
______	39. Usher	______
______	40. Gen. Office Work . .	______
______	41. Typing	______
______	42. Telephoning	______
______	43. Posters	______
______	44. Carpenter Work . . .	______
______	45. Painting	______
______	46. Rec. Activities . . .	______
______	47. Help Prepare Meals	______
______	48. Help Serve Meals . .	______

ENLISTMENT INFORMATION

As near as possible we would like for all our members to have one place of service. Please sign your name and check the places where you would serve if needed, and the offices you have served in.

NAME ....

DATE CHECKED ....

ADDRESS ....

BIRTHDATE ....

RESIDENT PHONE ....

BUSINESS PHONE ....

Education: High School______; Junior College______;

Senior College______; Business College______.

(over)

(Start With Number One)

Places I **will** serve		Places I **have** served
______	49. Church Nurs. Helper	______
______	50. Library Work	______
______	51. Projector Operator .	______
______	52. Publicity	______
______	53. Flower Arranging . .	______
______	54. Dramatics	______
______	55. Sewing	______
______	56. Radio & Amplifier .	______
______	57. Youth Fellowships .	______
______	58. Give Blood	______
______	59. Are you an ordained Deacon?	______

If you accept one place of service, and only one, what would you prefer?

First Choice ______________________

Second Choice ______________________

CODE 4384-18 BROADMAN SUPPLIES. NASHVILLE, TENNESSEE. PRINTED IN U.S.A.

Figure 2

should see that the church has on file a service record of resident members, showing various positions of responsibility currently and previously held by each member, as well as areas of interest.

Some churches are now using computers to compile this information into a membership profile. The master membership profile indicates those who desire or would be interested in specific tasks as well as positions in which a person has served previously. Information is retrieved either from the service bureau or the church's on-site small computer.

You may be thinking, *You have got to be kidding. My church could never afford a computer.* Cards have been designed that follow the same procedures as the computer but are maintained by hand. The cost is reasonable. One advantage to this method is that the information is readily available and may be secured quickly. See Figures 1 and 2 for a sample of the front and back of an Enlistment Information card which can be filed in the church office.

An even simpler card is the "Christian Service Survey" shown in Figure 3. It provides good information but provides less data about the person than the other two approaches.

It is not my intent to advocate or promote one method over another. You will have to decide which one meets your needs best. No system will be more effective than the membership information it contains. Keep your records current. Be sure to record new service commitments and fill out cards on each new member who joins your church.

Principle 2—Encourage church leaders to suggest potential leaders. The minister and the nominating committee have limited knowledge of persons' spiritual gifts and leadership potential. They cannot know the church's membership in a personal, intimate way. An excellent reservoir of potential church leaders is made of persons known to the present church leadership. Request church leaders to submit the names of persons whom they feel are either ready to assume a place of leadership or are potential church leaders. Potential church leaders can be encouraged to participate in the church's training activities.

It is important for leaders to keep the idea and opportunity of service before their groups. They should not only speak about these possibilities, they should also affirm those who go forth in service. The highest compliment paid to a church leader is not the size of his or her class, but the number of persons from that class who are involved in places of leadership within the church.

CHRISTIAN SERVICE SURVEY

Mr. Mrs. Miss			Date
Residence			Phone
Business Address			Phone

Birth Date: Month___ Day__ Year___; Education: Elem. School___; High School___; College___

Expe-rienced	Will Prepare	SUNDAY SCHOOL	Age Division	Expe-rienced	Will Prepare	W.M.U.		I will assist in:
		General officer				Officer—Baptist Women		Audio-visual Aids
		Teacher						Bus Ministry
		VBS				Baptist Young Women		Dramatics
Expe-rienced	Will Prepare	CHURCH TRAINING	Age Division			Acteens		Flower Arranging
		General officer				Girls in Action		Food service
		Leader				Mission Friends		Library Work
		Leader-training orientation		Expe-rienced	Will Prepare	BROTHERHOOD		Mission Work
						Officer—Baptist Men		Photography
Expe-rienced	Will Prepare	MUSIC MINISTRY				RA Counselor		Poster Making
		Choir: Voice part ___				RA Leader		Recreation
		Instrument(s) played:		I am a		GENERAL AREA		Telephoning
						Tither		Transportation
		Song leader				Deacon		Typing-Office Work
		Graded choirs: Age group(s) ___				Ordained Minister		Ushering
						Nurse: Reg.___; Prac.__		Visitation
		Other: ___				Blood Donor: Type___		Other (see back)

Code: 4384-14, Form 100, Broadman Supplies, Nashville, Tennessee. Printed in U.S.A.

Figure 3

Principle 3—Communicate Christian service opportunities. Requesting volunteers in a worship service usually is an exercise in futility. Public appeals for volunteers are invitations for someone to solve a crisis or emergency. Such needs are seldom presented as a challenge but as a stopgap measure.

Talk about the opportunities for Christian service and the potential rewards or blessings that are inherent in the task should be a common feature of church life. The opportunity for a Christian to grow spiritually while ministering to others through Christian service should be emphasized. Areas of service should be described long before they are to commence.

Recently I visited in three churches. Each minister made his "annual" appeal to staff the church's organizations. Each stressed the idea of doing "one's spiritual duty" (whatever that means) and making the work of the nominating committee easier. No mention was made of the concept of Christian growth, the opportunities to influence and enrich lives, or the idea that one should pray about what God wants him/her to do in the church.

Once a need is identified, it should be communicated to the church. Ask members to pray that God will call one out to meet the need. Once while serving a church, I discovered that we were not reaching the newly weds, primarily because there was not a Bible study class for them. I shared this concern with the deacons. No one responded immediately. Two months later a couple came to me and said, "We have been praying for a place to serve and would like to teach the newly weds." He was a deacon, and they possessed the skills vital to working with this group. Seven years later, they continue to teach the class. God has used them effectively to teach and reach young adults.

Principle 4—Develop written job (position) descriptions. Any task in the church worth doing should have a written job description. Many churches distribute denominationally prepared documents to elected leaders. They are written in broad, general terms. It will take time, energy, and some creativity, but every church should adapt these or develop written job descriptions for every elected position.

Job descriptions should contain the following information:

1. Position title
2. Brief description of the task to be performed
3. Specialized or specific skills essential to effective performance
4. A list of available resources (curriculum items, age group books, additional helps, etc.)
5. Time commitments (regular meeting time, training opportunities, in-service training, etc.)
6. Length of service
7. Objectives and goals of the educational organization (what you are seeking to achieve and how you plan to do it)

See Figure 4 for a sample job description for a Sunday School teacher, and Figure 5 for a sample work sheet.

Principle 5—Emphasize the service to be rendered, not the position or its title.

People are asked to fill many positions in the church. Different skills are necessary for persons to carry out their assignment. For the church adequately to fulfill its mission and ministry challenges, each person contributes through competently completing individual responsibilities. Every task is important. Therefore, magnify the service rendered by each person rather than the position or its title.

Principle 6—Discover the individual's gifts or abilities. It is a tragic waste of spiritual and human gifts when more than 80 percent of the

Sample Job Description
Adult Sunday School Teacher

Tasks to be performed:
1. Understand and use the principles of effective teaching and learning.
2. Prepare for each week's Bible study session with your class.
3. Accept personal responsibility in enlistment and witnessing actions.
4. Share in and encourage your class to participate in ministry actions.
5. Be knowledgeable about the role of the class in the work of the church.
6. Lead the total work of the class.
7. Assist group leaders to minister to members and prospects.
8. Plan regularly with class outreach leader and group leaders.

Essential skills:
1. Ability to communicate effectively.
2. Skill in planning and execution of plans.
3. Leadership—Ability to challenge others to follow your example.
4. Willingness to be a sincere, dedicated student.
5. Willingness to be a learner—from the Bible, the Holy Spirit, and class members.
6. Ability to be a personal visitor.

Available Resources:
The Adult Teacher
Sunday School Adults
Biblical Illustrator
Adult Leadership
Reaching Adults Through the Sunday School
Teaching Adults in the Sunday School
Teaching and Learning with Adults in Sunday School
Basic Adult Sunday School Work

Time Commitments:
1. Be in your classroom fifteen minutes before Sunday School begins.
2. Attend the weekly workers' meeting.
3. Participate in the church's outreach program.
4. Attend Sunday School training sessions.

Length of service:
October 1 to September 30 (unless elected for longer terms).

Organizational objectives:
1. Reach persons for Bible study.
2. Teach the Bible.
3. Witness to persons about Christ and lead persons into church membership.
4. Minister to Sunday School members and nonmembers.
5. Lead members to worship.
6. Interpret and undergird the work of the church and the denomination.

Organizational goals:
Each church must set its own. These are possibilities:
1. Increase enrollment by 10 percent.
2. Increase attendance by 10 percent.
3. Achieve the goal of 50 percent of the class members bringing Bibles and studying the lesson.
4. Win *one* person to Christ.
5. Minister to members and nonmembers as needs occur.

Figure 4

Job Description Work Sheet

(Position Title) Job Description

Tasks to be performed:

Essential skills:

Available resources:

Time commitments:

Length of service (elected for how long):

Organizational objectives:

Organizational goals:

Figure 5

church's leadership positions are filled by 20 percent of the resident membership.

This situation creates two major problems. One, those who are elected to places of responsibility carry more than one major responsibility. Thus, they are not able to do any task well due to the limitation of time and energy. Two, there are many capable, trainable persons within the congregation who are never asked to do anything. Skills can be developed through adequate training and opportunities for service.

God has given each Christian a gift or ability that can be utilized in Christian service; however, not everyone is conscious of such capabilities. The congregation can be used to help its members become aware of their gifts. One such way is through the use of the simulation game called *NEXUS*.[1]

Essential Characteristics of Church Leaders

Many churches have established elaborate criteria for church leaders. So many items are listed that it is impossible for anyone to meet all these qualifications. Rather than describe a list of characteristics, six essential distinctives have been selected for church leaders. Members of each church should take these six factors, put them into their own words, and expand them as needed. *Make them your own.*

1. *Be a Christian.* It seems trite to say that a church leader should be a Christian. All church leaders must have a personal experience with Jesus Christ. Many persons in our churches have equated knowing *about* Jesus with knowing Jesus. Anyone who does not personally know Jesus as Savior and Lord will find it difficult, if not impossible, to lead others to follow Christ in their daily lives.

2. *Be a member of that local church.* All persons filling leadership positions in a church should be members of that church. Any person who is unwilling to join a church, should not be elected to a position of leadership in that church. Nonmembers usually are not as sensitive to the total needs of the church as members. A nonmember may do things in a way that would destroy morale or in direct violation of the church's objectives and goals. Nonmembers are more difficult to supervise than members.

A church should elect only those persons who have demonstrated to that church their commitment to Christ and his church. New church members should become active in various activities of the church's life prior to being elected to leadership positions. One cannot set an arbitrary time limit, but there should be ample opportunity to observe Christian character, Christian commitment, and leadership potential before a new member is asked to serve. Review *principle 1: Develop a master file of potential church leaders.* A church can ask a person to serve too early, or it may wait too long to ask a person to serve.

3. *Be a person who loves people.* The work of the church involves working with people. Ideally, a Christian should love people. Practically, there are many persons who are not people-oriented. They are directed toward the achievement of goals or building a successful organization.

Successful church work involves teamwork. One must know how to deal effectively with people. A leader must have a keen appreciation for the worth and dignity of others. It is incongruous for one to love God and dislike people—God's creation. A church leader must be a person who loves people.

4. *Be a person of aptitude or ability.* Reginald M. McDonough affirms that, "Church leaders should demonstrate aptitude for the work in which they are asked to lead. Genuine interest, flexibility, creativity, initiative, and a sense of purpose are highly desirable characteristics also."[2] Information gained from present church leaders who know the potential worker can aid in determining whether others feel that the person can do the projected task. To enlist a person in a role where successful performance is not highly possible or probable threatens the future growth and Christian usefulness of that person.

5. *Be a person who has demonstrated dependability and responsibility.* Church leaders should be selected from those of the church's membership who have shown that they are faithful, dependable, and responsible to the life and work of the church. A church should expect that its leaders be actively involved in the worship experiences, the Bible teaching program, discipleship training, and that they contribute to the church financially.

6. *Be a person who is willing to learn.* Church leaders should not feel that they presently know all that is necessary to do the task. A leader must be willing to participate in the church's training opportunities that will equip and enable him to do the job effectively and successfully.

A church leader then, should:

1. Be a Christian;

2. Be a member of that local church;

3. Be a person who loves people;

4. Be a person of aptitude or ability;

5. Be a person who has demonstrated dependability and responsibility;

6. Be a person who is willing to learn.

The Enlistment Process

Assume that the nominating committee has decided that a specific person is the right person to do the assigned task. This decision has been made after much prayer. The committee feels led by the Holy Spirit to contact this person. What do they do?

First, a decision must be made concerning who should make the enlistment visit. Usually the person who will work with or supervise this person is asked to do this. For example, a Sunday School teacher should be contacted by the department director in whose department the teacher will teach. However, if the nominating committee feels that there is someone else who is more likely to get a sincere response, then this person should make the enlistment visit. Probably the person who will be the supervisor or under whom the person will work should accompany the person most likely to receive a positive answer.

Before describing the steps to follow in the enlistment process, one additional idea needs to be discussed. Election to serve on the church's nominating committee does not automatically qualify a person to make enlistment visits. The church should train those who will be requested to make an enlistment visit. Included should be members of the nominating committee, the ministers, department directors, committee chairpersons, and others who will seek to enlist persons to staff the church's organizations and committee.

One training technique could be the use of a simulated enlistment visit. Persons skilled in interaction processes should conduct the simulated experience. Guidelines to use in the enlistment effort need to be written down, duplicated, and distributed to each of the trainees. A training model would be to use the approach described below. No one should go out to contact prospective church leaders who has not participated in the training process. This training should be scheduled each year before the nominating committee begins the enlistment effort.

After the nominating committee has determined the contact person, what steps should this person follow in the enlistment process? Eleven steps are proposed:

Step 1—Set a time to talk with the person when you have privacy and adequate time. Persons should *never* be enlisted in the hallways of the church or when pressed for time. Ask to see the person at home, take the person to lunch, or have coffee together. Meet in a friendly, relaxed environment, recognizing the pressures of time.

Step 2—Pray for the leadership of the Holy Spirit as you prepare for the interview. Pray that God will lead you to present the challenge and opportunity of Christian service possible in this task. Pray that God will prepare the person whom you are to visit to be receptive and responsive to the leadership of God.

Step 3—Present the challenge of the position. The prospective worker should be told what the task involves. No one wants to be asked to do a job that is insignificant or that can be achieved with little or no effort. Enlistment must be honest.

Tell the person that this job will call forth the very best that he can give, that it will require time, energy, and prayer. Share the opportunities for personal Christian growth and tell how the prospective leader can influence the lives of others by doing it. Help the person to see that this task is important to the lives of Christians and will benefit the work of Christ and his Church. Share with the prospect your confidence and that of the nominating committee that he can do this job effectively and can expect to have a sense of personal achievement.

Step 4—Prepare and present to the prospective worker a packet of curriculum materials and other available resources. Not every church leader will be in a teaching/training role, but job descriptions, organizational charts, and other materials should be prepared and given to the potential worker. Briefly review and describe the materials you have brought. Share how each item will assist in doing this task. Request that the person study the materials. Point out that you are available to respond to any questions the person has concerning them.

Step 5—Be realistic about the job. Present both the challenges and the problems a person might expect to encounter if this assignment is accepted. The Chinese have a way of looking at a crisis that can help us see this more clearly. "When the Chinese write the word 'crisis,' they do so in two characters, one meaning danger, the other opportunity."[3]

Opportunities for Christian service usually are not crises, but every responsibility has both its positive and negative aspects. In presenting the situation, be realistic rather than idealistic. There are two practical reasons for this approach. One, the person should accept the assignment based upon as much knowledge about it as possible. Two, you must continue to work with and have a relationship with this person. Supervision, morale, and motivation will be more difficult if you have not told this person as much as you should have.

Step 6—Describe scheduled activities for preservice training and also in-service training opportunities. Give the dates when training events have been scheduled. Some tasks in the church require attendance at monthly or weekly planning meetings where additional training is offered. Guide the prospective leader to see that these training activities are planned by the church to provide skills and information so that its volunteers may do a more effective job. Help the prospect see that accepting this assignment will assist his personal growth as a Christian and improve relationships with fellow Christians.

Step 7—Ask the person to pray and study for a week or two before giving you his decision. The prospect will need time to review the materials you have left, and time to pray about this responsibility. Suggest that you will call in a few days to clarify further the role and to answer any questions.

Step 8—Set the date when you will return to receive an answer. Assure the prospective leader that you and other church leaders will be praying with him and for him as he makes this decision. Have a brief prayer asking God to guide and lead him and his family during this time.

Step 9—Call to clarify the role and answer any questions.

Step 10—Return to receive the answer. If it is affirmative, review the training schedule in step 6. Assure the prospect of your continued prayers as he prepares and then begins his new work. Point out how you will be working with him as he begins to function in this new role.

What do you do if the person feels that he should not accept this position? Thank him for his prayerful consideration. Express gratitude for the privilege to become better acquainted. Assure him of your continued prayer support as he seeks to discover what God would have him to do.

Step 11—Follow up. Your task of enlistment is not complete until the person is functioning effectively in his new role. Periodic conferences should be scheduled to see how he feels about what he is doing, to consider any problems he may be encountering, and for encouraging him to continue training and working.

Consider Enlistment for More Than One Year

Churches usually enlist persons to serve on its committees and boards for terms from three to five years. Yet persons asked to serve the educational needs of the church—Bible study, discipleship training, for example—are usually enlisted for one-year terms. Initial enlistment should be for one year; it should then be reviewed and extended in two-or three-year terms, when mutually agreed on by the nominating committee and the worker.

The person's desire to continue in the position should be reaffirmed annually, but the enlistment process described above would not be followed. Thus the staffing task of the church would be simpler and would not require the large amounts of time now usually spent by the nominating committee.

How to Motivate

Several years ago I went to my doctor on Monday morning. In talking about his church and its Sunday worship experience he made this statement, "I really felt sorry for my pastor yesterday." I sat in stunned amazement. His pastor was recognized as an outstanding preacher. Having heard the sermon myself, I felt that he had eloquently communicated his concern for, and the need to minister to, the inner city. His invitation had been a plea for volunteers to go into the inner city and minister there.

Finally, I asked the doctor, "Why did you feel sorry for your pastor?" His reply was that no one had responded to his pastor's invitation to go into the inner city. The doctor believed that the reason no one responded was the minister's inability to motivate the congregation. Many believe that one function of the minister is to motivate others. The truth is that you can motivate yourself; you cannot motivate others.

Many ministers and their congregations believe that the pastor can be a motivator of persons in the same way he can be an administrator. Administration requires the ability to understand certain concepts and procedures—including human nature. However, as McDonough has stated, "To say that one person can motivate another person is a myth. A person's motivation—low or high—is a product of his will, not the leader's."[4] A minister can help establish the climate or environment under which good motivation can happen, but he cannot cause another person to be motivated.

It has been assumed that a person's behavior can be determined from without. However, the opposite is true. One's behavior is determined from *within*. Motivation is internal rather than external. Abraham Maslow has brought together much of the research on motivation, and suggests that motivation is based on the fulfillment of basic needs experienced by the person.[5]

There is no magic formula that a church leader can follow to motivate others. What causes one person to respond positively may generate a negative response from another. Therefore, a minister must know as much as possible about each member of his congregation. He must know at what need level the person is presently responding.

What follows are some motivational principles that have been identified as being significant. Suggestions will be made concerning how to motivate persons in the church.

What Motivates a Person

Persons are motivated by unsatisfied needs. An unmet need causes a person to focus all of his energy and desires on the satisfaction of that need. Until the need is met, it becomes the focus or center of a person's life. Only when one's innate or primary needs are met can he seek to fulfill his secondary needs.

Maslow has classified needs on five levels. The first level is physiological needs, such as food and shelter. These needs must be satisfied before the person begins to respond or react to higher needs.

Once the physiological needs are basically met, then a new set of needs emerges—the safety needs. His behavior is organized around the desire for security, stability, dependency, protection, freedom from fear, freedom from anxiety and chaos, and the need for structure, order, law, and limits.

When the physiological and safety needs are basically satisfied, a new need surfaces—that of love, affection, and belonging. In seeking to meet this need, the person strives for affectionate relationships with people, for a place in his group or family. He seeks to avoid loneliness, ostracism, rejection, friendlessness, and rootlessness. Need satisfaction at this level depends upon his relationship to other persons and his perception of that relationship.

A fourth level of need is for esteem—how he views himself and how he feels others perceive him. A person has a desire to feel good about himself, to possess self-respect or self-esteem, and for the esteem of others. When one's self-esteem need has been met he feels self-confidence, worth, strength, capability, and adequacy, and is aware of being useful and necessary in the world. Such a one feels that he can face life and feels that he can deal adequately with life.

Even when these four needs have been met, one may not feel complete or fulfilled. He may yearn for self-actualization—for self-fulfillment, to become all that he is capable of becoming.[6]

From my perspective, self-actualization is impossible for one who is not a Christian, who has not given his life into the hands of Jesus Christ. McDonough describes the self-actualized person as:

> A person who ... is willing to commit his total resources in the pursuit of his goal. A self-actualized person appreciates group acceptance and ego-building affirmation, but he is not dependent on them for his motivation. At the point of self-actualization, a person's Christian calling becomes very important. A person who understands his gifts and has committed himself to the pursuit of a particular mission is relating to his self-actualization need.[7]

One who desires to help motivate others must be a self-actualized person. Later, a profile of the actualized leader will be described.

Another way to look at needs has been set forth by James K. Van Fleet. He believes that every person has nine subconscious desires which determine or influence behavior: emotional security; recognition of efforts or reassurance of worth; creative outlets; a sense of personal power; a sense of roots—belonging somewhere; immortality; ego-gratification; love in all its forms; and new experiences.[8]

One or more of these subconscious desires is dominant in every person. Remember, once a need or desire has been fulfilled, the person is no longer motivated by it. However, do not assume that a desire or need has been fulfilled for a lifetime. It will resurface many times.

Motivational Principles

What are some motivational principles that will benefit the church leader as he seeks to lead?

Principle 1—Accept the fact that you cannot motivate another person. Motivation comes from within. A person can be led by the Holy Spirit working through his needs, but he, and he alone, can respond to the guidance of the Holy Spirit. McDonough declares, "A Christian leader's role is to build a climate in which a person can fulfill his needs in a way that brings joy and wholeness."[9]

You are not the motivator, except for yourself. Your role is to be the instrument, the facilitator who helps the other person become motivated. Recognize who you are—that you are a servant of God responsible only for yourself. Many leaders ask, "Why didn't I get him to do this or that?" The real question is, "Why didn't he want to do it?" Motivation is internal rather than external. Accept the fact that you cannot motivate another person.

Principle 2—Believe that the person can do the job. Church leaders must have confidence both in the ability of the membership and the equipping, enabling power of the Holy Spirit. You must trust the person to do a good job. Persons accepting new responsibilities in the church may not begin with expertise, but you must believe not only that with proper training, inner motivation, and the energy of the Holy Spirit he can do a good job, but that he will.

Principle 3—Permit each person to work in his own way. You are asking persons to accept an assignment. Allow them to do it their own way. Training sessions tend to teach methods designed to cause each trainee to become a reproduction of the trainer. God has endowed each person differently, so each person will approach the task from his own perspective. He might even discover a better way to do it, particularly if he is a self-actualized person.

Principle 4—Emphasize results, not methods. This is not to say that the end justifies the means. Means should always be consistent with the principles of Jesus Christ. A church elects a person to be a teacher, a committee chairperson, etc. The important factor is that one be an effective teacher, and that the committee does its assigned work. Be sure that the assignment is clear, and then stand back and let the people work.

Van Fleet states, "You can motivate people to do their best for you when you emphasize skill, not rules; results, not methods. To do this, use *mission-type orders*. (A mission-type order tells a person what you want done and when you want it, but it doesn't tell him how to do it. The 'how to' is left up to him.) A mission-type order opens the door wide so people can use their imagination, initiative, and ingenuity to do the job for you."[10]

Keep your attention focused on the end result, not the techniques used to get there.

Principle 5—Rule people by work; do not work people by rules. This keeps all eyes focused on the job to be done—the mission and ministry to be accomplished. Give people something worthwhile and meaningful to do. This keeps people physically as well as mentally occupied. They will be happy and contented with their work.[11]

Creating a Climate for Self-Motivation

If motivation comes from inside a person, why consider factors that help a person motivate himself? To help volunteer leaders in the church to be motivated, the minister must seek to develop an atmosphere where the volunteer can be motivated under the guidance of the Holy Spirit. McDonough explains, "A leader's role in motivation is to be sensitive to the needs and gifts of persons, to help persons understand their needs and gifts, and to help them live out their Christian calling in satisfying and fulfilling ways."[12]

If the minister is to become a self-actualizer, he must develop some specific skills. He must himself be self-actualized and practice a leadership style characterized by the following:

1. *He must be genuinely interested in other people.* People yearn for attention from others. Everyone wants to feel that his ideas and opinions are heard. The desire for attention is present in all of us. People need to be important to someone else. If you wish to be a self-actualizer, become truly interested in other persons and their problems. You must place more emphasis on others' problems than on your own. What is needed is an attitude of complete unselfishness.

2. *He must learn to listen.* You must put aside your own interests, your own pleasures, and your own preoccupations. You must learn to listen with your eyes as well as your ears. Changes of facial expressions are significant communicators. Learn to be a good listener.

3. *He must practice patience.* In working with others, do not criticize or offer snap judgments. Learn to make allowances for inexperience. Do not expect perfection.

4. *He must never take another person for granted.* Regardless of how faithful the worker is, express gratitude and appreciation for the work being performed. A word of praise serves as a significant self-motivator. People will work harder when they feel appreciated—knowing that what they do really makes a difference. The parable of

the talents contains a well-known affirmation, "Well done, thou good and faithful servant" (Matt. 25:21, KJV).

5. *He must be concerned about others.* A minister's heart must be filled with compassion toward others. Feelings of concern or genuine interest in others cannot be faked. Attention to others must be accompanied by honest concern for them. A person cannot do this unless he is really willing to share another's pain and help solve personal problems.[13]

6. *He must treat each person as an individual.* Recognize that what stimulates one person to action may not be appropriate in another situation. It might have the opposite effect. Do not develop a bag of motivational tricks. Self-actualizers are motivated from within. Help each person to discover that which makes him a self-actualized person.

7. *He must create team efforts.* The work of the church depends upon effective teamwork. Every task is important to the church's achievement of its mission and ministry. McDonough notes that "Teamwork relates to the need to belong and to be loved . . . . A team relationship enables a person to receive and give affection."[14]

Three keys to creating team efforts, are: (1) a team must have a reason for being to which all members are committed; (2) a team cannot function without good communication, since teamwork is interdependent work; and (3) teams must have openness and trust.[15]

8. *He must generate excitement about the mission.* Excitement and enthusiasm are contagious. For persons to be self-actualized motivationally, they must believe that what they are doing has meaning and purpose. They must feel that they really do make a difference. Excitement must be genuine. A minister who has no excitement about what is happening in and through the church has himself ceased to be a self-actualized person. The achievement of objectives and goals brings a sense of exhilaration and expectancy to church leaders. Being involved with God in his work should generate excitement.

9. *He should be willing to share responsibility and authority.* Volunteer leaders should be given authority commensurate with their responsibilities. To ask a person to assume a place of leadership without authority leads to potential failure of the project and poor morale. No one wants to do only the mechanics. McDonough concludes, "A person's motivation will soar when he realizes he has been entrusted with decision-making responsibility."[16]

10. *He must get the right person in the right job.* Many people accept volunteer leadership positions in a church out of a sense of

duty or loyalty to the person who asks them. A person must feel that he has the skills necessary to do a job well. In doing the task there should be a sense of accomplishment, and the job should be pleasurable. The person should be worked with until he is in a position that brings personal satisfaction.

11. *He must keep working toward goals.* "A goal-oriented environment is a motivating environment," affirms McDonough.[17] Organizational objectives and goals must be magnified. This is the why and the what for which volunteer leaders are enlisted. Each person should be led to establish personal goals which will give him a sense of achievement and satisfaction. Periodic review of objectives and goals are key motivational factors. Goals should be realistic and attainable, yet challenging, to call forth the best from the person.

12. *He must challenge persons to become involved in a mission.* When the volunteer leader sees his task as a mission he is in the process of becoming a self-actualized person. There is a reason for what he does which becomes an energizing force for him. He is in pursuit of a goal. He will not be satisfied until that goal is reached. It must call forth the very best in him. What joy comes to a person who is engaged in a mission! Once this challenge has been successfully met, he is ready for new, more challenging experiences.[18]

Qualities of a Motivator

Every minister faces the danger of becoming a manipulator. In actuality, there is an extremely fine line between manipulation and persuasion. For the minister to become a *motivator* rather than a manipulator, he must become a facilitator of human resources. Use the following descriptions provided by McDonough to evaluate your effectiveness as a motivator.[19]

1. *He is committed to a specific task.* The self-actualized minister has focused his attention on the achievement of a goal—the equipping and enabling of the people of God for ministry. His sense of mission causes others to capture a vision of what the church is all about. He assists others to high levels of commitment to achieve their assigned tasks.

2. *He concentrates on concerns outside of himself.* The self-actualized minister seeks the realization of goals not for himself but for others—the church, Christ, and the kingdom of God. He helps others see beyond themselves, to be unselfish in service, time, and energy.

3. *He is capable of meaningful relationships.* He is capable and willing to share much of himself with others. His relationships with others are characterized by self-confidence and trust of others. He helps those with whom he works to concentrate on the mission before them. Through this relationship he calls forth the best effort from others.

4. *He perceives issues clearly.* He is astute in solving problems. His healthy self-image protects him from being easily threatened. His keen perception aids his ability to see and challenge the potential in others. He sees what people can become in Christ, not what they are now.

5. *He is spontaneous and direct.* There is a sense of authenticity about him. He has freedom both in expression and in his own personhood. He is not trying to impress others. Followers know where he stands on issues. His spontaneity makes others feel comfortable around him. He shares opinions about issues, not final decisions. His leadership style encourages others to respond naturally and honestly.

6. *He is courageous in the face of opposition.* Because of his sense of security and self-esteem, opposition does not paralyze him. He is open to new ideas. Followers feel open and free to exchange viewpoints. He perceives conflict as healthy and normal, not something to be shunned or avoided at all costs. His sense of security aids the development of healthy self-esteem in his followers.

7. *He has self-confidence.* Others see his strength of character. He feels good about himself. Little energy is spent in defense mechanisms or in second-guessing. His dedication and commitment to the task before him move him forward with great objectivity. It is easy for others to capture his spirit of self-confidence, thus stimulating themselves to do more effective work.

8. *He has a positive attitude toward life.* He majors on the positive. He is happy and transmits this happy, joyous attitude to others. He encourages others to be optimistic about life. Others are captivated by this positive attitude.

9. *He is capable of deep spiritual experience.* The self-actualized minister not only has had a deep spiritual experience but also continues to maintain a close, personal relationship with God. He assists those with whom he works to have similar experiences with God and with each other.

Notes

1. *NEXUS* (Nashville: Convention Press, 1974).

2. Reginald M. McDonough, *Working with Volunteer Leaders in the Church* (Nashville: Broadman Press, 1976), p. 30.

3. Philip Kotler, *Marketing for Non-profit Organizations* (Englewood Cliffs: Prentice-Hall, Inc., 1975), p. 55.

4. McDonough, p. 50.

5. Abraham H. Maslow, *Motivation and Personality* (New York: Harper and Row, 1970).

6. Maslow, pp. 35-47.

7. McDonough, p. 58.

8. James K. Van Fleet, *Power with People* (West Nyack: Parker Publishing Co., Inc., 1970), p. 40.

9. Reginald M. McDonough, *Keys to Effective Motivation* (Nashville: Broadman Press, 1979), pp. 78-79.

10. Van Fleet, p. 73.

11. Ibid., pp. 108-10.

12. McDonough, *Working with Volunteer Leaders,* p. 58.

13. Van Fleet, pp. 145-58.

14. McDonough, *Keys,* p. 80.

15. McDonough, *Working with Volunteer Leaders,* pp. 59-60.

16. Ibid., p. 63.

17. Ibid., p. 64.

18. Ibid., pp. 58-65.

19. McDonough, *Keys,* pp. 125-28.

6
Administering Church Educational Organizations
Bruce P. Powers

As described earlier, education in a church is a support function that enables a congregation of Christians to make disciples, help members grow, and develop spiritual power in the lives of members. Education, along with the other church functions of worship, proclamation, and ministry, become the distinguishing characteristics of a New Testament church. Whereas the other functions have value in and of themselves, however, education must always exist to serve, functioning as a midwife to enable persons to learn.

So it is with educational organizations. They are a *means* for achieving the mission or purpose of a church—they are not ends in themselves. Each organization exists in order to achieve a specific purpose, or portion of a church's educational ministry. And each one, theoretically, should be the most effective structure to achieve the purpose for which it exists.

Organizational Distinctions

Due to rather basic objectives among evangelical churches—making disciples, enabling members to grow and mature, and developing spiritual awareness and power in the lives of believers—similar structures have evolved among denominations to enable churches to do their work. For example, most churches have organizations to facilitate Bible study, discipleship development, mission activities, and worship experiences. Although names of these may vary, such as Sunday School, Bible School, and Church School, the functions and general organizational principles for such organizations are remarkably similar from denomination to denomination.

Basic Church Programs

These structures or organizations are the primary channels for the ongoing, functional education provided by a congregation. Educational experiences are usually graded according to the ability and/or need level of participants. Basic church programs are designed to help a church achieve its objective *and*, at the same time, to meet the general needs of persons in the congregation.[1]

As an example, Southern Baptists through their denominational organizations have chosen to establish six basic programs, each with a cluster of tasks which are believed to be essential, continuing, and of primary importance to the work of a church. (See Figure 1.)[2]

Five of these programs are essentially educational and exist in some form in many evangelical churches; thus they will be covered in this chapter. The sixth, pastoral ministries, focuses primarily on administration, proclamation, and ministry concerns and is included below only for reference.

Other organizations are necessary to provide effective Christian education in a church, but these are primarily service-oriented such as media/library services; or are oriented toward specialized activities for a subgroup in a congregation, such as a club for senior adults. Subsequent chapters will deal with each of these categories under the headings of "Administering Educational Support Services" and "Administering Specialized Educational Activities."

Determining Organizational Structure

The essential elements in determining how to organize an educational program include
- Identifying the specific purpose of the organization.
    Ask questions such as: Why does (should) it exist? What is its unique contribution to the church? What would happen if we didn't have this organization?
- Determining the best way to achieve the stated purpose.
    Ask questions such as: What resources (leaders, facilities, denominational assistance, financial support, and such) are available? What are the priorities within and among the educational organizations? What structures will provide efficient and effective team work among leaders as well as facilitate the achievement of educational objectives?
- Defining clear areas of responsibility and decision making in order to achieve maximum effectiveness in the total educational ministry, as well as in each component.
    Ask questions such as: What is the distinct responsibility for each position? What decisions should the person in each posi-

Basic Church Programs

There are six established church programs. Each of the six has a cluster of tasks that are basic, continuing, and of primary importance to the total work of a church. Each has significant organization and seeks to involve the total church in its work. These programs form the foundation of church structure. They are now referred to as basic programs.

Listed below are the tasks which have been grouped for assignment to each of these six programs:

Bible Teaching
1. Reach persons for Bible study.
2. Teach the Bible.
3. Witness to persons about Christ and lead persons into church membership.
4. Minister to Sunday School members and nonmembers.
5. Lead members to worship.
6. Interpret and undergird the work of the church and the denomination.

Church Training
1. Equip church members for discipleship and personal ministry.
2. Teach Christian theology and Baptist doctrine, Christian ethics, Christian history, and church polity and organization.
3. Equip church leaders for service.
4. Interpret and undergird the work of the church and the denomination.

Music Ministry
1. Provide musical experiences in congregational services.
2. Develop musical skills, attitudes, and understandings.
3. Witness and minister through music.
4. Interpret and undergird the work of the church and the denomination.

Brotherhood
1. Engage in missions activities.
2. Teach missions.
3. Pray for and give to missions.
4. Develop personal ministry.
5. Interpret and undergird the work of the church and the denomination.

Woman's Missionary Union
1. Teach missions.
2. Engage in mission action and personal witnessing.
3. Support missions.
4. Interpret and undergird the work of the church and the denomination.

Pastoral Ministries
1. Lead the church in the accomplishment of its mission.
2. Proclaim the gospel to believers and unbelievers.
3. Care for the church's members and other persons in the community.
4. Interpret and undergird the work of the church and the denomination.

Figure 1

119

The Church Council

The church council serves as a forum for a church's leaders to guide planning, coordination, conducting, and evaluation of the total work of the church. The council depends on the various church organizations to implement the church's program according to their assigned tasks. As chairman of the church council, the pastor is able to lead in the development of a unified program that gives major attention to priority needs.

Principal function: to assist the church to determine its course, and to coordinate and evaluate its work

Method of election: church leaders become members of the church council as a result of election to designated church leadership positions

Term of office: corresponds to term of office in church-elected position

Members: pastor (chairman), church staff members, program directors, deacon chairman, stewardship committee chairman, missions committee chairman, and other committee chairmen as needed

Duties:
- Help the church understand its mission and define its priorities
- Coordinate studies of church and community needs
- Recommend to the church coordinated plans for evangelism, missions, Christian development, worship, stewardship, and ministry
- Coordinate the church's schedule of activities, special events, and use of facilities
- Evaluate progress and the priority use of church resources.

Figure 2

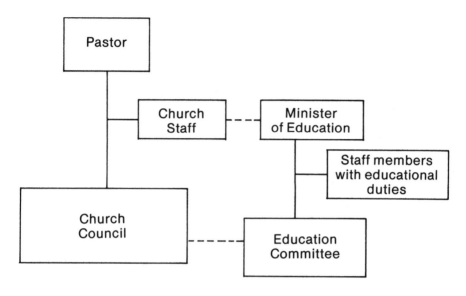

Figure 3

tion be able to make without consultation? What are the positions that link each level (or unit) with the larger body for purposes of communication, planning, evaluation, and such? Do all leaders have someone to whom they are responsible?

General Coordination

An effective organizational structure would include a church council or education committee, which would be charged with planning, coordinating, and evaluating a church's educational activities. (Information about a church council is given in Figure 2.)

In most churches, this group would be chaired by the pastor and would include church staff members, leaders of all church programs and service organizations, leader of the deacons (or church board), and chairpersons of key committees (those closely related to the work of church program organizations, such as missions, stewardship, and nominating committees).

In larger churches with a full-time minister of education, educational activities might need to be planned, coordinated, and evaluated

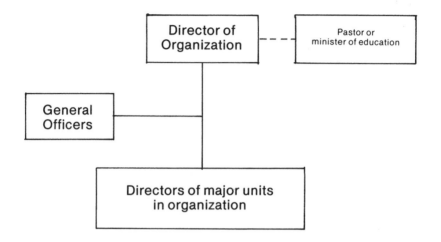

Figure 4

through a specialized group composed of leaders representing the various educational components, church staff personnel with educational duties, and age-group coordinators, if used, as illustrated in Figure 3.

Similarly, each program organization would have an administrative council or staff to guide the work for which it is responsible, as shown in Figure 4. (Information about a program council/staff is given in Figure 5.)

Age-Division Coordination

Whereas most administration is handled *within* programs, a need often exists to link persons working with similar age groups in different organizations in order to facilitate their work and provide mutual support. This can be achieved through age-level coordination.

The simplest approach is when leaders of a particular age division voluntarily coordinate their work and the use of space, equipment,

Program Council and/or Staff

Principal functions: to assist the program to determine its course, to coordinate program efforts, and to relate to the church council for overall coordination

Membership and method of election: Directors of major units/age divisions in the program become members of the program council as a result of election by the church to program leadership positions. If there are no age division directors, the leader of each department represents his or her group.

Term of Office: Corresponds to term of office in church-elected position

Report: As a program, to the church; director serves on church council, or other general coordinating body.

Duties:
- Help the program understand its mission and define its priorities in the light of church priorities
- Conduct studies of church and community needs related to program tasks
- Coordinate the program's activities and schedules
- Evaluate progress, effectiveness, and the priority use of church resources

Figure 5

Age-Division Coordination

Age-division coordination may be accomplished in three ways: self-coordination, age-division conferences, or age-division coordinators/directors. The approach used by a church is determined by the complexity of the organization within the age division.

Self-coordination

Self-coordination exists when organization leaders of an age division voluntarily coordinate their work and the use of space, equipment, and supplies. It is the simplest and most effective. It is particularly suited for small churches and age divisions with few workers.

Age-division coordination conferences

Principal function: to serve as a counseling, advisory, and coordinating group when self-coordination is not adequate

Members: leaders of departments, choirs, and other organizational units of a particular age division

Convener: one of the members of the group elected by the group

Age-division coordinators/directors

Principal function: to counsel age-division leaders and coordinate the work of units within the age division, as assigned

Age-division coordinators are elected by the church and responsible to the pastor or minister of education as designated by the church. The pastor leads in developing procedures for providing consultative and advisory services to the minister of music and other staff members as needed.

Duties:

- Consult with department leaders to resolve philosophical, procedural, and scheduling problems
- Give assistance in classifying and enrolling new members
- Consult with department leaders to coordinate the use of program materials, supplies, equipment, and space
- Give individual guidance to department directors and workers
- Work with church program leaders to provide training opportunities for department leaders and workers
- Work with director of recreation to provide appropriate services
- Give assistance as needed to department directors in discovering and enlisting department workers
- Coordinate age-division visitation
- Encourage and provide assistance to leaders in planning and evaluating their work
- Serve as ex officio members of program councils

Figure 6

and supplies. This is the most effective approach for small churches and age divisions with few workers.

Another approach is to schedule periodic conferences for age-division coordination, the purpose being to deal with issues of common concern among leaders within each age group. Persons in each group could elect a convener to facilitate meetings and channel messages.

In large churches, age-group coordinators (or directors) often will be necessary. Their principle function is to facilitate the work of all programs within the age division on behalf of the total educational ministry. Coordinators should serve on the education committee, or church council. (Descriptive information concerning age-division coordination is given in Figure 6.)

Grouping of Persons

There are three general approaches to dividing congregations for educational purposes: age, compatibility, and interest. To a lesser extent, some churches choose to create additional subgroupings by using distinctives such as gender and marital status.

Age. Age grouping, or grading, is used most often when trying to match developmental needs of individuals with the educational experiences provided. This is the approach usually recommended by denominational program leaders in order to facilitate an ongoing, systematic study of curriculum materials by all ages. Under this plan, educational groupings follow a general pattern, but often are adjusted when subgrouping to allow for compatibility and/or interest grouping. For example, the "Organization Planning Chart," Figure 7, lists the major divisions, suggested maximum enrollment per unit, and worker-pupil ratio for preschool and children's departments. By completing the chart, you can determine the number of classes/groups/departments needed as well as the approximate number of workers.

In a small church with few rooms, try to have at least two departments for preschoolers (ages 0-3 and 4-5) and two for children (grades 1-3 and 4-6). Only if space is not available should all preschoolers, or grades one through six be together.

If space and leaders are available, set up three groups for preschoolers—birth—1; ages 2 and 3; and ages 4 and 5. Also, provide three groups for children—grades 1 and 2; grades 3 and 4; and grades 5 and 6.

Provide at least two classes for youth, if space and leadership are available and there are sufficient participants for each group (six or

ORGANIZATION PLANNING CHART

DIVISION	Member Classification Age (Grade)		Pupil Possibilities Enrollment M	F	Prospects M	F	Total Possibilities M	F	Departments Suggested Maximum Enrollment	Departments Needed	Classes Suggested Maximum Enrollment	Classes Needed	Workers Suggested Worker/Member Ratio	Approximate No. of Workers Needed
			2		3		4		5	6	7	8	9	10
PRESCHOOL	Birth-1	Cradle Roll							50		x	x	1/6	
		Baby							12		x	x	1/3	
		Creeper							12		x	x	1/3	
		Toddler							12		x	x	1/3	
	2								15		x	x	1/4	
	3								20		x	x	1/4	
	4								20		x	x	1/4	
	5								20		x	x	1/4	
CHILDREN	Special Education								20		x	x	1/4	
	6 (Grade 1)								30		x	x	1/7	
	7 (Grade 2)								30		x	x	1/7	
	8 (Grade 3)								30		x	x	1/7	
	9 (Grade 4)								30		x	x	1/7	
	10 (Grade 5)								30		x	x	1/7	
	11 (Grade 6)								30		x	x	1/7	
YOUTH	12 (Grade 7)								40-60		10-15		x	
	13 (Grade 8)								40-60		10-15		x	
	14 (Grade 9)								40-60		10-15		x	
	15 (Grade 10)								40-60		10-15		x	
	16 (Grade 11)								40-60		10-15		x	
	17 (Grade 12)								40-60		10-15		x	
ADULT	18-29 (College)								125		25		x	
	18-29 (Single)								125		25		x	
	18-29 (Married)								125		25		x	
	30-39 (Single)								125		25		x	
	30-39 (Married)								125		25		x	
	40-49								125		25		x	
	50-59								125		25		x	
	60-69								125		25		x	
	70-up								125		25		x	
	Sunday Workers								125		25		x	
	Adults Away								75		6	x	x	
	Homebound								75		8	x	x	
Fellowship Bible Classes									x	x	x		x	
New Sunday Schools									x		x		x	
General Officers			x	x	x	x	x	x	x	x	x	x	x	
Totals									x		x		x	

Figure 7

126

more enrolled). Divide older and younger youth, possibly using the same grading system as your local public school—junior high and senior high.

If possible, provide a class for every twenty-five adults enrolled. Begin by dividing younger and older (using some midpoint age) or by having a class for women and a class for men. Additional classes might be graded as indicated in the "Organization Planning Chart," or formed according to compatibility or interest.

Larger churches would add additional classes/groups/departments for each of the age groups according to enrollment and the availability of leaders and space.

Compatibility. Grouping according to compatibility is practiced in many churches, particularly among adults, in order to allow persons who have the most in common to study together. Persons tend to gravitate toward each other due to factors such as preferred learning style, or fellowship needs, and these preferences are established as a regular part of the organizational structure.

Often, this grouping approach is used in combination with age grading and may be seen, for example, in a men's Fellowhip Bible Class, or in a class of persons who have chosen to remain together despite suggestions that they "promote" to another age-group class.

Interest. Interest grouping is used when persons are free to select the most appealing study or activity. These groups exist as long as the particular study or activity is provided; consequently, this approach is used primarily with short-term educational activities and special emphases.

In some churches, all three approaches to grouping persons will be used; however, age-group divisions remain the foundation. Additional groups can be organized as necessary or appropriate to meet the needs of persons and to achieve the purpose of the organization.

Choosing a Pattern

Ultimately, every church has to make its own decisions concerning the best way to organize and administer its work. The guidelines and options which have been described will help you assess possibilities, but you in consultation with other church leaders will have to choose the most appropriate arrangement.

As an additional resource, a list of possible patterns for church organization (Figure 8) is included. By studying these options you may be able to clarify how best to proceed with any adjustments needed in your church.

Guidelines For the Administrator

Here are ten guidelines that will enable you to give effective and strong leadership to church educational organizations.

1. Determine the purpose and organizational structure for each educational program. Prepare a chart listing every position and unit, and the name of every officer and teacher. Place this information at the front of a reference notebook/folder devoted to educational administration.

2. Use, or establish, a church council or committee of key leaders to plan, coordinate, and evaluate the church's total educational ministry. Meet at least monthly. (Suggestions for forming such a group are included in chapter 3.)

3. Prepare job descriptions (following guidelines in the previous chapter) for all positions giving duties, decision-making authority, and person to whom responsible.

4. Use the above materials when enlisting and orienting new leaders, planning for enlargement, determining organizational problems, and other similar administrative duties.

5. Make annual plans for each organization. Following the enlistment of officers for a new church year, schedule a *planning workshop* to develop goals and make plans for the next twelve months. Prior to the meeting distribute the appropriate purpose and organizational statements to each leader along with suggested areas for evaluation and goal setting. Ask each organizational leader to consult with his or her coordinating group for orientation, evaluation, and to develop proposed goals and plans to be considered at the planning workshop. (See Figures 9 & 10.)

6. Budget for regular expenses such as curriculum materials, and for all special items in the annual plan. Delegate to organizational leaders as appropriate.

7. Maintain a *master calendar* listing all plans, person(s) responsible, and budget provisions if any. Use this to monitor educational activities, record progress toward goals, as a diary of your reactions concerning educational activities, and as a guide in planning with the church staff.

8. Maintain a complete record system for each organization listing persons involved, contact information, officers, and attendance records. This information is needed for communication purposes and for planning. Additional information on record keeping is given in the following chapter.

Church Organization

Organization is grouping persons in a way that enables individuals and groups to accomplish their goals. In organization, activities and responsibilities are assigned to individuals and groups. In organization, working relationships are established. In organization, responsibility and authority are delegated to enable individuals and groups to use initiative in their work.

I. Choosing an Organizational Pattern

    A. Possible Organizational Components
       There are many organizational components a church can design to perform its work. Components commonly found in Southern Baptist churches include staff, deacons, church officers, church committees, coordinating units (councils), Sunday School, Church Training, Music Ministry, Woman's Missionary Union, Brotherhood, Media Services, and Recreation Services.

    B. Effective Organization
       An effective organization grows out of an understanding of the church's mission, resources, and tradition. No one pattern is best for all churches or even all churches of a similar size. A church must develop its own organization. Church objectives, priorities, tradition, availability of leaders, needs and numbers of people, availability of space and equipment, and availability of schedule time will influence decisions on the organizational patterns adopted by the church.

    C. Possibilities for Church Organization
       The following chart shows some possibilities for church organization. Each church will choose its own patterns.

Figure 8a

II. Possibilities for Church Organization

Type of Unit Position	Suggested Units or Positions				
	Churches with Fewer than 150 Members*	Churches with 150 to 399 Members	Churches with 400 to 699 Members	Churches with 700 to 1,499 Members	Churches with 1,500 or more Members
Staff	Pastor Music Director[1]	Pastor Music Director[1] Secretary[2] Custodian[2] Pianist/Organist[1]	Pastor Minister of Music and Education Secretary Custodian Organist[1] Pianist[1]	Pastor Minister of Music Minister of Education Secretaries[3] Custodians[3] Organist[1] Pianist[1] Age-Division Ministers[3]	Pastor Associate Pastor Minister of Education Minister of Music Business Administrator Minister of Recreation Evangelism/Outreach Minister Age-division Ministers Organist-Music Assistant Family Life Minister Secretaries[3] Custodians[3] Hostess Food service personnel[3]
Deacons	Deacons (1 deacon per 15 family units; minimum of 2 deacons)	Deacons (1 deacon per 15 family units)	Deacons (1 deacon per 15 family units)	Deacons (1 deacon per 15 family units)	Deacons (1 deacon per 15 family units)
Church Officers	Moderator (Pastor) Trustees Clerk Treasurer	Moderator Trustees Clerk Treasurer	Moderator Trustees Clerk Treasurer	Moderator Trustees Clerk Treasurer	Moderator Trustees Clerk Treasurer
Church Committees	Nominating Stewardship Missions Evangelism	Nominating Property and Space Stewardship Ushers Missions Preschool[4] Evangelism	Nominating Property and Space Stewardship Personnel Missions Preschool History Ushers Weekday Education[4] Public Relations Evangelism	Nominating Property and Space Stewardship Personnel Missions Preschool Food Service History Ushers Weekday Education[4] Public Relations Evangelism	Nominating Property and Space Stewardship Personnel Missions Preschool Food Service History Ushers Weekday Education[4] Public Relations Evangelism Other committees as needed
Service Programs	Media Services Director	Media Services Director (up to 3 workers) Recreation Director	Media Staff Recreation Staff	Media Staff Recreation Staff	Media Staff Recreation Staff

Special Ministries	Senior Adult Ministry	Senior Adult Ministry, Singles Ministry	Senior Adult Ministry, Singles Ministry	Senior Adult Ministry, Singles Ministry	Senior Adult Ministry, Singles Ministry, Intergenerational Activities
Coordination	Church Council	Church Council, WMU Council, S.S. Council, Brotherhood Council	Church Council, S.S. Council, C.T. Council, Music Council, WMU Council, Brotherhood Council, Division Coordination Conferences	Church Council, S.S. Council, C.T. Council, Music Council, WMU Council, Brotherhood Council, Division Coordination Conferences	Church Council, S.S. Council, C.T. Council, Music Council, WMU Council, Brotherhood Council, Media Services Council, Division Coordination Conferences
Bible Teaching	General officers and organization for each age division	Departments for each age division	Multiple departments as needed	Multiple departments as needed	Multiple departments as needed
Church Training	Church Training Director, Age-group leaders[4]	Member training groups and departments for each age division, Equipping Centers, New Church Member Training	Member training groups and departments for each age division, Equipping Centers, New Church Member Training	Member training groups and departments for each age division, Equipping Centers, New Church Member Training	Member training groups and departments for each age division, Equipping Centers, New Church Member Training
WMU	WMU Director, Age level organizations as needed	Age level organizations as needed	Age level organizations as needed	Age level organizations as needed	Age level organizations as needed
Brotherhood	Brotherhood Director	Baptist Men, Royal Ambassador groups as needed	Baptist Men, Royal Ambassador groups as needed	Baptist Men, Royal Ambassador groups as needed	Baptist Men, Royal Ambassador groups as needed
Music Ministry	Music Director[5], Organist, Church Choir or Ensemble, Age-division choirs when possible	Age-division choirs, Instrumental groups as needed	Fully developed Music Ministry	Fully developed Music Ministry	Fully developed Music Ministry

[1]Volunteer or part-time
[2]Part-time
[3]As needed
[4]If needed
[5]Person serves as program leader and staff member

• NOTE: It is important to encourage, in any way possible, churches of 150 members or less to have choir, recreation, and other needed ministries even though directors or other leaders for that activity might not be listed in column one of this chart.

Figure 8b

9. Evaluate periodically and annually. Spend time prior to each church council or education committee meeting assessing the effectiveness of the church's educational ministry. Look at records, review your master calendar, and check any information you have received or gained from your contact with classes, departments, or committees. Discuss current needs with other leaders and adjust the annual plan as necessary. Prepare annually an extensive evaluation to present to the church and to the planning workshop; use this in developing future goals and plans.

10. Follow the basic principle of working with, for, and through people in administering church educational organizations. The three "I's" will be your best guide:

- *Inform*—Communicate specifically what is happening and why; seek a clear understanding of all plans and procedures; provide opportunities for open discussion of pertinent issues; keep in touch with key leaders in the educational organizations.
- *Inspire*—Minister to and motivate the persons with whom you work. Whatever you are as a leader will be the most powerful influence on those through whom you must work. Administration is not doing the work yourself, but eliciting, combining, and guiding the resources of the congregation. What you cause to happen will be multiplied through others.
- *Involve*—Share leadership duties widely among responsible persons. This requires giving major attention to (1) equipping leaders to perform their tasks, delegating to them responsibility, and supporting/encouraging them as they do their jobs: and (2) involving persons in making decisions which will affect their organization.

How To Relate to Organizational Leaders

Administration, as explained earlier, focuses on working with and through people. It does not mean that you make all the decisions, attend all the meetings, or do all the work yourself. In administering educational organizations, remember that your job is to enable and guide many areas of work rather than to immerse yourself in the details of one or two organizations. This requires serving as a *primary leader in one group* and as an advisor to several others.

The church leader responsible for educational ministry (minister of education, pastor, or other designated person) is the chairman of or

Goal Planning Work Sheet

Use the following when exploring and planning goals for your committee/work group/church.

---

1. **Proposed Goal:**

---

2. What we hope to accomplish by this goal is to . . .

6. We will feel we have made progress toward this goal when:

3. This goal is related to the following objective(s):

7. Major obstacles we see in implementing this goal:

4. What is already being done related to this goal?

8. Major resources needed to begin:

5. Specific age or interest group(s) to which goal is related.

Decision regarding proposed goal:

_____Approved
_____No decision at this time.
_____Hold for further discussion/ development.
_____Develop action plan(s).
_____Secure input from_____
_____Other:

Figure 9

133

Sample Format for Planning Report

Page __ of __

Program,
Organization,
or Officer _____ Date Prepared_____

Objective:

Goal:

Action Plan #____:

Action	Person Responsible	Completion Date	Estimated Budget

Figure 10

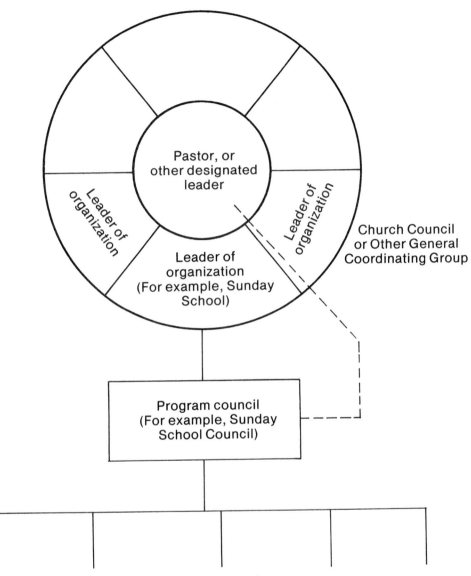

Organizational Units
(For example, age divisions, departments, and classes)

Figure 11

staff to the general body that plans, directs, and evaluates all *educational* activities sponsored by the congregation. This person then serves in an *advisory* capacity (or as a general officer) to the leader and administrative council for each educational organization. In this way, thorough coordination can be maintained while spreading the load of responsibility and decision making.

Thus the educational leader would have direct, administrative responsibility for *one* group, and would serve as advisor to the members of that body as they, in turn, lead their respective organizations. This organizational arrangement is illustrated in Figure 11.

Starting New Educational Units

The following steps can be followed to begin a new unit in any educational organization or, if necessary, to begin a new program.

1. *Determine the Need.* Examine prospect files and membership rolls for the educational program or church to determine possibilities. Review attendance patterns and determine growth potential. Consult with the appropriate leadership council.
2. *Decide on the Organization Needed and Provide Facilities.* Using the guidelines given earlier for appropriate number of members and leader-member ratio, choose the best organization for your situation or the setup you would like to work toward. Provide appropriate facilities.
3. *Enlist and Train Leaders.* Find persons who are enthusiastic, and willing to start new work. Give careful orientation to the job expectations and provide the necessary training, materials or supplies, and personal support. Involve them in making subsequent plans for starting the new unit.
4. *Secure Materials and Supplies.* When a beginning date is set, plan to have available a sufficient supply of study materials and supplies for the largest number of persons expected.
5. *Promote the New Unit and Enlist Members.* General promotion through posters, announcements, and bulletin articles will be helpful. These will not, however, take the place of enlistment activities—visits, phone calls, notes, and other personal contacts—to secure new members. (For assistance, see the chapter "Guiding Outreach and Enlistment.")

Extra attention and support should be given the new unit and its leader(s) until it has been fully integrated into the larger organization.

Resources for General Administration

On the following pages you will find basic information concerning programs. This is not intended to be exhaustive nor to stand in place of guidebooks for directors of church programs. Rather, you will find general reference and administrative helps useful in providing overall guidance for your church's educational ministry.[3]

In each case, a brief overview of the organization is given, including definition and a statement of its purpose and scope of work. An organizational chart follows showing a typical arrangement; descriptions are given for the major jobs listed. Additional items which might be helpful for instructional purposes or in preparation for meetings are included for your convenience.

Note that many of the aids located in the "Bible Teaching Program" section are useful in other organizations; you will want to draw and adapt from them as appropriate.

Bible Teaching Program

Definition:

The planned educational activities provided by a local church for the primary purpose of involving persons in Bible study.

Purpose and scope of work:

The purpose of the Bible teaching program is to facilitate Bible study at an appropriate level for all persons who will respond to a church's invitation. This usually includes a weekly study period following a prescribed curriculum, as well as periodic extra studies devoted to specialized topics. Bible classes and informal study groups often are provided away from a church building in members' homes or in other settings in order to reach additional persons.

The Bible teaching program is considered the primary means for facilitating outreach and witnessing for a congregation.

Key Resource:

Piland, Harry M. *Basic Sunday School Work*. Nashville: Convention Press, 1980.

Sunday School Organization

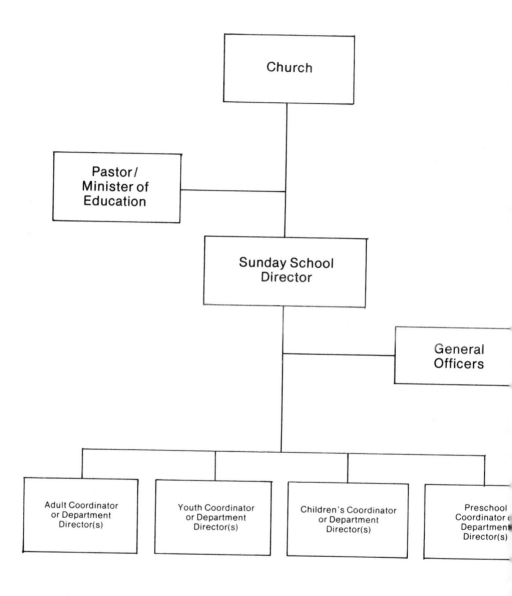

Figure 12

Job Descriptions

General Officers

The pastor and the minister of education.

The pastor has the responsibility for final policy decisions related to Sunday School work. However, if a church has a minister of education he/she would share the following responsibilities with the pastor.

1. Lead the church to have a challenging program of Bible study and to provide adequate resources for it.
2. Interpret to the congregation the biblical basis for Bible study, outreach/witness, and ministry.
3. Lead the church to have an aggressive program for reaching persons for Bible study, salvation, and church membership.
4. Lead the church to use organizational plans and curriculum resources that best meet the needs of its membership.
5. Assist in making available adequate training for all workers; lead in training activities as appropriate.
6. Assist the Sunday School director in annual planning.
7. Share information about potential workers; lead the church to adopt adequate leadership standards for teachers and officers.
8. Participate in Bible teaching projects as appropriate.
9. Lead the church council to involve the Sunday School in stewardship education, stewardship promotion, and subscription of the church budget.

Sunday School Director

The Sunday School director is responsible to the church for planning, conducting, and evaluating the work of the Sunday School. He will look to the pastor (and to the minister of education, if there is one) for counsel and leadership in the Sunday School. The director will, in turn, give leadership to the work of the Sunday School council. Ordinarily, he will serve as chairman of the group. He has the following major responsibilities:

1. Lead in determining the Sunday School organization needed to reach and teach effectively.
2. Give direction to the enlisting of workers for the Sunday School.
3. Give support and guidance to other general officers in accomplishing their work.
4. Give specific assistance to each department director in accomplishing his work.
5. Help all workers see the importance of involving people in effective Bible study.
6. Help in leading all workers to become effective witnesses to lost persons.
7. Develop and support the outreach program of the Sunday School.
8. Determine training needs of the workers and develop a comprehensive training plan.
9. Develop and maintain a weekly workers' meeting.
10. Give direction to planning and conducting Bible teaching projects.
11. Lead workers in setting challenging but reachable goals.
12. Give direction to the selection and proper use of all curriculum materials.
13. Determine financial and physical resources needed for the Sunday School and recommend these needs to the church.

14. Maintain and use records for the Sunday School.

15. Keep the Sunday School leaders informed concerning the work of the church and the denomination.

16. Report periodically to the church on the progress of the Sunday School.

17. Lead in evaluating the work of the Sunday School.

Sunday School Assistant Director

Some churches elect an assistant director. The assistant director is responsible to the Sunday School director for performing duties assigned to him by the director. These duties may include any combination of the following:

1. Assist in determining the Sunday School organization needed to reach and teach effectively.

2. Assist in enlisting workers for the Sunday School.

3. Assist in developing an ongoing outreach program through the Sunday School.

4. Assist in determining training needs of the workers and planning special training to meet these needs.

5. Assist in publicizing the Sunday School.

6. Assist in maintaining records for the Sunday School.

Sunday School Bible Teaching Projects Director

This officer is responsible to the Sunday School director for planning, directing, and coordinating Bible teaching projects of the Sunday School (such as VBS, January Bible Study, Bible conferences, and others).

1. Lead in determining additional types of Bible teaching projects that could be conducted by the church.

2. Determine the organization needed to conduct each project.

3. Recommend and enlist workers required for each proposed project.

4. Review and recommend curriculum for each project.

5. Cooperate with the outreach director in reaching appropriate persons for each project.

6. Maintain records for evaluating each project.

7. Report on each project to the Sunday School director.

8. Represent the needs of the Bible teaching projects on the Sunday School council.

9. Determine financial and physical resources needed for the projects and recommend these needs to the Sunday School director.

Sunday School Director of Teaching Improvement and Training

This director is responsible to the Sunday School director for improving the effectiveness of Bible teaching in the Sunday School. This worker's duties would include the following:

1. Assist in directing the improvement of teaching in the Sunday School.

2. Work with the director of the Sunday School in determining the necessary organization, schedules, and approaches needed for effective teaching in the Sunday School.

3. Assist in developing and maintaining a weekly workers' meeting.

4. Assist in giving direction to the selection and proper use of all curriculum materials.

5. Work with the department directors in determining resources needed for effective teaching.

6. Assist in determining training needs of Sunday School workers and developing a comprehensive training plan.

7. Work directly with department directors in developing plans to improve Bible teaching.

8. Assist the director in evaluating the teaching ministry of the Sunday School.

Sunday School Outreach Director

The outreach director is responsible to the director of the Sunday School for planning, conducting, and evaluating efforts for reaching persons for Sunday School enrollment and for Christ and church membership. These duties are as follows:

1. Assist in directing the outreach efforts of the Sunday School.

2. Cooperate with the director in determining the organization needed to reach people for Bible study through the Sunday School.

3. Assist department directors and outreach leaders in developing outreach and evangelism plans.

4. Assist the director in helping all workers in the Sunday School see the importance of involving people in effective Bible study and reaching them for Christ and church membership.

5. Provide outreach and evangelism training opportunities.

6. Suggest outreach and evangelism training resources to department directors and department outreach leaders.

7. Maintain an up-to-date file of prospects.

8. Lead in assigning prospects to departments and classes for ongoing visitation and in procuring and interpreting reports.

9. Assist in developing a regular program of visitation of Sunday School prospects.

10. Assist the department leaders in regular absentee contacts.

Sunday School Bus Director

If a bus director is needed, this person is responsible to the Sunday School director for planning, promoting, and evaluating efforts to reach persons for Bible study, for Christ, and for church membership through bus outreach.

1. Lead in identifying, surveying, and establishing routes.

2. Lead in enlisting a bus captain for each route.

3. Interpret assignments and responsibilities to the bus captains and secure their commitments.

4. Promote bus outreach through the church.

5. Lead bus captains in evaluating their work.

6. Maintain records and report to the Sunday School council monthly.

7. Coordinate Sunday morning schedule of buses, including parking and guidance of riders to appropriate departments to avoid confusion.

8. Prepare and submit budget requests annually in cooperation with the church plan.

9. Coordinate expenditures of budgeted funds according to the plan of the church.

10. Meet with transportation personnel as needs arise.

11. Lead bus captains to share appropriate information with Sunday School workers in departments in which bus riders are involved.

Sunday School Secretary

The secretary is responsible to the Sunday School director for compiling and evaluating records of the Sunday School.

1. Guide enrollment procedures for the school.
2. Maintain a master enrollment file on all phases of the Bible teaching program.
3. Assist department secretaries in maintaining department records.
4. Compile requests for literature and other resources from the departments and submit to the Sunday School director.
5. Record the minutes of the Sunday School council and share copies with council members.

Adult Department Leaders

The following job descriptions are for Adult department officers and class officers:

Department Director

1. Develop the organization.
2. Enlist and train leaders.
3. Administer the work of the department.
4. Assist class leaders.
5. Lead department meetings.
5. Lead teachers in their planning for Bible study. In some churches, one of the teachers or a department teaching leader, if one is elected, is assigned this responsibility.
7. Encourage members to worship, witness, minister, and apply Christian principles to all areas of life.
8. Encourage members to have a part in other Bible study activities (Vacation Bible School, Fellowship Bible Classes, Bible conferences, family Bible study).

Department Outreach Leader

1. Relate to the Sunday School outreach director in planning the department's enlistment and witnessing actions.
2. Interpret enlistment and witnessing programs to classes and individuals and guide them in outreach.
3. Set an example as visitor, witness, and faithful church member.
4. Plan training sessions for individuals and classes to help them to become better visitors and witnesses.
5. Promote a spirit of love within the department and direct fellowship activities.
6. Lead in expressing concern for people by ministering to the physical and spiritual needs of members, prospects, and others.

Department Secretary

1. Master the records system used by the department and interpret it to department and class leaders and members.
2. Process records and reports, and submit reports to the department outreach leader and general secretary.
3. Confer with department director on literature needs. Give department's literature order to the person who orders Sunday School materials.

Class Teacher

1. Understand the class's role in the work of the church.
2. Lead the total work of the class.
3. Head the team of class outreach leader and group leaders by knowing their duties and training them for their work.

4. Seek to understand and to use effectively the principles of teaching and learning.
5. Guide in Bible study.
6. Serve as friend, sensitive and helpful, to the many needs of class members.
7. Accept personal responsibility in enlistment and witnessing actions.
8. Share in and encourage participation in ministry actions.
9. Plan regularly with the class outreach leader and group leaders.

Class Outreach Leader
1. Lead in outreach by working with the teacher to organize the class into groups for maximum effectiveness in ministry and enlistment.
2. Interpret to group leaders their duties.
3. Assign prospects to proper group for outreach and help group leaders learn how to cultivate, to enlist, and to witness to prospects.
4. Communicate general Sunday School programs and enlist group participation.
5. Minister and enlist class members in ministering to needs of members, prospects, and others.

Class Group Leader
1. Encourage regular attendance of group members.
2. Challenge members to be consistent participants in Bible study.
3. Respond with sympathetic understanding to members' needs and concerns.
4. Assume responsibility for enlisting unsaved adults in Bible study and leading them to Christ.
5. Seek to meet all the ministry needs of group members in the spirit of Christian concern.
6. Lead group members to minister to members and others.

Class Secretary
1. Compile the class report each Sunday.
2. Secure Registration Record on all visitors and new members, if this is not done by the department or general secretary.
3. Provide copy of class report to the class outreach leader.
4. Provide the department (or general) secretary with class report.
5. Follow church's guidelines for enrolling and removing names from the class roll.

Youth Department Leaders

The following job descriptions are for Youth department and class officers:
Department Director
1. Lead in determining the organizational pattern which best fits the needs of the youth of the church and community.
2. Examine available information regarding curriculum and, in conference with other Youth workers, determine which to use.
3. Take the initiative in learning about possible ways of teaching the biblical revelation more effectively and lead workers to the highest degree of effectiveness.
4. Organize the department to reach unchurched and unenlisted youth and youth who attend Sunday School only spasmodically.
5. Seek to discover ways to help workers and youth develop solid Christian habits and attitudes of living.
6. Direct the Sunday morning sessions, keeping the concept of total period teaching in mind.
7. Be responsible for weekly and/or monthly planning meetings.

8. Present workers and youth with information concerning the work of the church and of the denomination.

9. Evaluate department's effectiveness in carrying out the functions of the church (worship, witness, educate, minister).

10. Relate the work of the department to the families of members and prospects.

11. Provide vocational guidance to leaders and members.

Department Outreach Leader

1. Be responsible to the department director for planning the efforts of the department in outreach.

2. Maintain an up-to-date prospect file or list and make assignments to classes.

3. Secure and compile records and reports on attendance, outreach activities, and on the involvement of youth in putting Christian principles into practice.

4. Be on hand on Sunday morning to guide in enrolling youth in Bible study.

5. Work with class leaders in planning and directing fellowship activities of the department.

6. Enlist youth to visit on a regular schedule determined by the church.

Class Teacher

1. Be responsible to the department director for carrying out the total work of a class.

2. Assume responsibility for the attendance of all members of the class and for reaching prospects assigned to the class.

3. Work with the department outreach leader in developing a plan of outreach which involves the entire department.

4. Cooperate with department leaders in planning, setting goals, and in discovering ways to meet those goals.

5. Assume the task of guiding youth in their study of the biblical revelation.

6. Lead youth to put into practice what they have learned.

7. Provide new class members with all information necessary to make them feel a part of the group.

Class Leader

This is a member who may be elected by the class or appointed by the teacher to serve for a unit of study, a project, or for a longer period of time. His duties are:

1. Work with the teacher to correlate and implement all class activities, such as those related to learning, outreach, outgrowths of lesson study, and fellowship.

2. Represent the class in planning activities which involve the whole department.

3. Sometimes work with department leaders in planning various projects. May be elected or appointed.

Children's Department Leaders

Department Director

1. Discover, recommend, and enlist workers for the department.

2. Secure literature and other resources needed for use in the department, if designated to do so by general director.

3. Lead the workers to make the best use of curriculum materials and other resources.

4. Enlist workers and guide them in weekly planning for the ongoing work of the department.

5. Represent the department on the Sunday School council or to the division director (if there is one).

6. Give general direction to the Sunday sessions of the department.

7. Guide large-group learning activities.

8. Guide pupils in spiritual growth, including conversion as the Holy Spirit directs.

9. Involve department workers in the cultivation of members and their families.

10. Lead the department workers in discovering prospects for the department, cooperating with all prospect-discovery projects and activities conducted by the Sunday School.

11. Encourage the outreach leader to involve all department workers in discovering and enrolling prospects for the department. This responsibility includes maintaining an up-to-date prospect file for the department.

12. Make requests for and use appropriately the money, equipment, and space designated for the department in accordance with church policy.

13. Secure and maintain weekly records and reports on department workers and children. (The director may assign this responsibility to the outreach leader or to the secretary, an optional officer.)

14. Guide the workers in using and maintaining department supplies and equipment.

15. Maintain up-to-date information and evaluate periodically the department's progress.

16. Determine activities and study which will improve the skills of the workers in the department.

17. Regularly evaluate worker and pupil needs, growth, and development in light of the department's responsibilities in these areas.

Department Outreach Leader

1. Assist the department director in the total work of the department. Coordinate department outreach plans with those of the outreach director of the Sunday School.

2. Lead the department workers in discovering prospects for the department.

3. Encourage the department workers to cooperate in all prospect-discovery projects and activities conducted by the Sunday School.

4. Participate in weekly workers' meeting held for the department.

5. Involve department workers in the cultivation of prospects and their families, maintain an up-to-date prospect file, and make assignments to workers.

6. Engage in activities and study which will improve effectiveness in all areas of work.

7. Serve as a teacher (younger and middle children) or as a substitute teacher (older children).

8. Guide pupils in spiritual growth, including conversion as the Holy Spirit directs.

9. Help the department director with records if requested.

Department Teacher

1. Guide a small group in the planning and developing of a Bible-learning project during each unit of study. Assist individual learning activities as needed.

2. Assist the director in large-group learning activities as appropriate.

3. Cooperate with the department director or outreach leader in discovering and cultivating prospects and their families.

4. Participate in the weekly workers' meeting held for the department.

5. Through regular visitation, cultivate the members and their families assigned to his group.

6. Engage in activities and study which improve his effectiveness.

7. Guide pupils in spiritual growth, including conversion as the Holy Spirit directs.

8. Assist the department director in planning, performing, and evaluating the work of the department.

Department Secretary

1. Secure and maintain weekly records and reports on department activities, and involvement in performing church functions.

2. Use records in helping the department director in evaluating the work of the department.

3. Secure literature and other resources needed for use in the work of the department.

4. Assist the department director in planning, performing, and evaluating the work of the department. (For instance: Guide a small group in absence or tardiness of a teacher and assist in large-group activities as appropriate.)

5. Guide pupils in spiritual growth, including conversion as the Holy Spirit directs.

6. Cooperate with the department director or outreach leader in discovering and cultivating prospects and their families.

7. Cooperate with the department director in cultivating members and their families.

8. Engage in activities and study which improve effectiveness.

Preschool Department Leaders

Department Director

1. Discover, recommend, and enlist workers for the department, and, where appropriate, extended session assistants.

2. Direct Sunday sessions and guide group-time learning activities in departments for threes, fours, or fives.

3. Give general direction to the extended sessions (if the department has one) and teach when scheduled.

4. Secure and distribute literature and other resources for teachers and arrange for distribution of periodicals for parents and preschoolers.

5. Initiate and encourage regular department planning and evaluation (preferably weekly).

6. Lead workers to make optimum use of the curriculum materials and resources used in the department.

7. Make request for and use appropriately the money, furnishings, and space designated for the department in accordance with church policy.

8. Engage in activities and study which improve his effectiveness in all areas of his work.

9. Determine activities and study which will improve the skills of the workers in the department.

10. Represent the department on the Sunday School council, or to the Preschool division director.

11. Cooperate in achieving necessary and/or desirable coordination with other organizations serving preschoolers.

12. Represent the department on the Preschool committee if not represented by a Preschool division director.

_____**Council Roster**

	POSITION	NAME	ADDRESS	PHONE
GENERAL OFFICERS	Director			
	Assistant Director			
	Secretary			
STAFF	Pastor			
	Minister of Education			
DEPARTMENTS AND DEPARTMENT/DIVISION DIRECTORS				

Figure 13

147

Division Organization Guidelines

Preschool Division Organization

Preschool Possibilities	Enrollment Guidelines	Ideal Provisions
Cradle Roll—Babies (birth through 1 year)*	1 department for each 50 members	1 visitor-teacher for each 6 homes
Birth through 5 years—where projected enrollment is less than 8.	One department *only* if the church cannot provide leadership and space for more	At least two departments (birth through 2 years; 3 through 5 years) if the ages are distributed widely across the age range
Babies (birth through 1 year)*	1 department for each 12 members	Infants, creepers, and toddlers separate if enrollment justifies
2- or 3-year-olds	1 department for each 20 members	Separate departments for 2- and 3-year-olds if enrollment justifies
4- and 5-year-olds	1 department for each 25 members	Separate departments for 4- and 5-year-olds if enrollment justifies

*New babies born into the homes of members or prospects are considered prospects for Cradle Roll and Preschool Departments.

Children's Division Organization

Children's Possibilities	Enrollment Guidelines	Ideal Provisions
Children (6-11 years or grades 1-6)—where projected enrollment is less than 10.	One department *only* if church cannot provide leadership and space for two.	Two departments (ages 6-8 and 9-11) if the ages are distributed widely across the age range
Children (6-11 years or grades 1-6) where projected enrollment is more than 10.	One department for each 30 enrolled (including workers)	Two departments (ages 6-8 and 9-11) if enrollment justifies OR three departments (ages 6-7, 8-9, and 10-11) if enrollment justifies. Provide a separate department for each year (or grade) if enrollment justifies. Larger churches will need more than one department for each year or grade.

Youth Division Organization

Youth Possibilities	Enrollment Guidelines	Ideal Provisions
Youth 12-17 years (or grades 7-12) where the projected enrollment is less than 15	One class *only* if leadership and space are available for only 1 class	A class for boys and class for girls or class for boys and girls 12-14 and class for boys and girls 15-17.

148

Youth 12-17 years (or grades 7-12) where projected enrollment is 15 and above	A department for each 2 to 6 (and not more than 8) classes; maximum enrollment of department not to exceed 50 for younger youth and 60 for older youth	At least two departments in the division if at all feasible in light of projected enrollment.
	Maximum enrollment for classes: 10 for younger youth and 15 for older youth.	

Adult Division Organization

Adult Possibilities	Enrollment Guidelines	Ideal Provisions
Young Adults (18-29)	40 to 125 in departments; 15 to 25 in classes	Separate provision for single, married, and college whenever possible. Also separate provision for older and younger ages in age span.
Adults (30-55 or 60)	40 to 125 in departments; 15 to 25 in classes	Wherever possible, the age span for a department should not exceed ten years, and the age range for a class should not exceed five years.
Senior Adults (56 to 61 up)	40 to 125 in departments; 15 to 25 in classes	Wherever possible, the age span for a department should not exceed ten years, and the age range for a class should not exceed five years.
Adults who work on Sunday—weektime departments and/or classes	25 in classes	Department (designated as Adult III, IV, etc.) if enrollment justifies. If not, relate class organizationally to an existing Adult department.
Adults who are physically unable to attend—*Homebound Department**	8 members for each visiting teacher	Fewer than 8 members for each visiting teacher
Adults away from home temporarily—*Adult Away Department**	4 members for each correspondent	

*As an alternate approach for churches that cannot provide Homebound and Adult Away Departments, classes may assume responsibility for teaching and ministry.

Figure 14

149

13. Lead workers to minister to members and their families.

14. Maintain an up-to-date prospect file for the department and lead the department workers in discovering prospects for the department. Cooperate in all church prospect-discovery projects and activities.

15. Plan for and participate in regular communication between parents and teachers (visitation, individual conferences, and parent-worker meetings).

16. Maintain up-to-date information and evaluate periodically the department's progress.

17. Assist in enlisting and training substitute teachers.

18. Arrange for a teacher to be in charge of the department when necessary.

19. Help to meet social needs of teachers by providing fellowship opportunities.

20. Regularly evaluate workers' and preschoolers' needs, growth, and development in the light of the department's responsibilities in these areas.

21. Secure or assign responsibility for department records and reports.

Department Teacher(s)

1. Assist the department director in planning, performing, and evaluating the work of the department.

2. Guide individuals or small groups in learning activities.

3. Assist as appropriate during group time (in departments for threes, four, and fives).

4. Cooperate with the department director or outreach leader in discovering and ministering to prospects and their families.

5. Guide teaching activities on scheduled Sundays during extended sessions if the department provides them.

6. Visit and minister to assigned members and their families.

7. Engage in activities and study which improve one's effectiveness.

8. Upon request, assist the department director in securing and maintaining weekly records and reports.

9. Notify the department director in time for a substitute teacher to be contacted when absence is necessary.

Department Outreach Leader

1. Assist the department director in planning and evaluating the work of the department.

2. Lead department workers in discovering prospects for the department, cooperating in all prospect discovery projects and activities conducted by the Sunday School.

3. Involve department workers in enlisting prospects and ministering to their families and in maintaining an up-to-date prospect file.

4. Guide individuals and small groups in learning activities, assist in group time as appropriate, and teach in the extended session if the department has one.

5. Cooperate with the department director in ministering to the children and their families assigned to him.

6. Engage in activities and studies which improve effectiveness in all areas of his work with preschoolers.

7. Upon request, serve as department secretary and assist the department director with the records and reports.

8. Participate in planning meetings held for the department.[4]

Work Sheet for Listing Enrollment, Prospects, and Total Possibilities By Ages

Age	Enrolled Now	Number of Prospects	Total Possibilities
0-1			
2			
3			
4			
5			
6 (or grade 1)			
7 (or grade 2)			
8 (or grade 3)			
9 (or grade 4)			

Age	Boys	Girls	Boys	Girls	Boys	Girls	Total
10 (or grade 5)							
11 (or grade 6)							
12 (or grade 7)							
13 (or grade 8)							
14 (or grade 9)							
15 (or grade 10)							
16 (or grade 11)							
17 (or grade 12)							
18							
19							
20							
21							
22							
23							
24							
25							
26							
27							

Age	Enrolled Now		Number of Prospects		Total Possibilities		
	Men	Women	Men	Women	Men	Women	Total
28							
29							
30							
31							
32							
33							
34							
35							
36							
37							
38							
39							
40							
41							
42							
43							
44							
45							
46							
47							
48							
49							
50							
51							
52							
53							
54							
55							
56							

Age	Enrolled Now		Number of Prospects		Total Possibilities		
	Men	Women	Men	Women	Men	Women	Total
57							
58							
59							
60							
61							
62							
63							
64							
65							
66							
67							
68							
69							
70							
71							
72							
73							
74							
75							
76							
77							
78							
79							
80							
81							
82							
83							
84							
85-up							

Figure 15

153

Workers Needed Work Sheet

General Officers
Sunday School director_____
Assistant director_____
Outreach director_____
Secretary_____

Cradle Roll Department*
Director_____
Visitor-teachers_____
_____
_____
_____

Preschool Department* (Baby—age __)
Director_____
Outreach leader_____
Teachers_____
_____
_____
_____

Preschool Department* (Ages __)
Director_____
Outreach leader_____
Teachers_____
_____
_____
_____

Preschool Department* (Ages __)
Director_____
Outreach leader_____
Teachers_____
_____
_____
_____

Children's Department* (Ages __)
Director_____
Outreach leader_____
Teachers_____
_____
_____
_____

Children's Department* (Ages __)

Director_____

Outreach leader_____

Teachers_____

_____

_____

_____

Youth Department* (Ages __)

Director_____

Outreach leader_____

Teachers_____

_____

_____

_____

Youth Department* (Ages __)

Director_____

Outreach leader_____

Teachers_____

_____

_____

_____

Adult Department* (Ages __)

Director_____

Outreach leader_____

Secretary_____

Teachers_____

_____

_____

_____

Adult Department* (Ages __)

Director_____

Outreach leader_____

Secretary_____

Teachers_____

_____

_____

_____

*Note: Fill in ages as appropriate for your organization.

Figure 16

Determining Space in Age-Division Rooms

Organization and Space Needs for Division Grouping and Grading

Division	Age	For Each Department			For Each Class			Suggested Floor Space Per Person			
		Maximum Enrollment Attendance$_a$	Average Attendance$_a$	Capacity of Space$_b$	Max. Enrol.	Aver.$_a$ Attend.	Cap. of Space$_b$	Department Assembly		Classroom	
								Minimum$_c$	Recommended	Minimum$_c$	Recommended
Preschool	B-1	12	5-8	7-10	Not applicable			20 sq. ft.	25 +	None	None
	2-3	20	9-13	12-16							
	4-5	25	11-16	15-20							
Children	6-8 9-11$_d$	30	14-20	18-24	Not applicable			20 sq. ft.	25 +	None	None
Youth	12-14	50	23-33	30-40	10	5-7	6-8	8 sq. ft.	10	10 sq. ft.	12
	15-17	60	27-39	36-48	15	8-10	9-12	8 sq. ft.	10	10 sq. ft.	12
Adult	18-up	125	56-81	75-100	25	12-16	15-20	8 sq. ft.	10	8 sq. ft.	12

Space is provided for each person expected to be in the rooms of the building. Determining the number for which to plan this space is a result of a careful analysis of projected enrollment, organization, and attendance.

In determining the total number of square feet of educational space required, the church should add to the floor space mentioned above enough space for offices, corridors, stairways, restrooms, storage, service space, and other accessory areas. This will require a total square footage from 35 square feet to 45 square feet per person in the educational building. Many churches provide even more space.

a Average attendance in churches ranges from 45% to 65% of enrollment.

b Capacity space to provide is figured at 60 to 80 percent of enrollment to be adequate for high expected attendance. Percentage to be used should be determined by the individual church's record of enrollment and attendance.

c Minimum square footage may sometimes be necessary in smaller churches and mission buildings.

d Existing assemblies with classrooms may sometimes be used by departments in the Children's Division. Provide additional tables, chairs, and chalkboards as needed.

Church Architecture Department, The Sunday School Board of the Southern Baptist Convention, Nashville, Tennessee

Figure 17

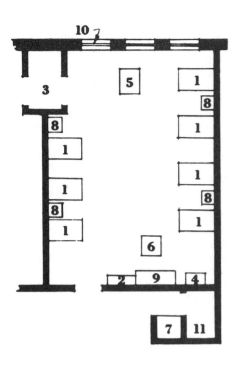

Department for Babies and Creepers

1. Beds (hospital cribs, 27 by 42 inches)
2. Diaper bag shelf
3. Diaper rinsing provision (with flush bowl)
4. Record player
5. Rocker (adult)
6. Safety chair
7. Sink-refrigerator combination (28 inches wide, 30 inches long, 40 inches high)
8. Tables (utility)
9. Wall supply cabinet (mounted 50 inches from floor)
10. Windows (clear glass; sills 22 to 24 inches from the floor)
11. Adult toilet

Note: In the Creeper Department it will be desirable to have fewer beds and substitute a playpen.

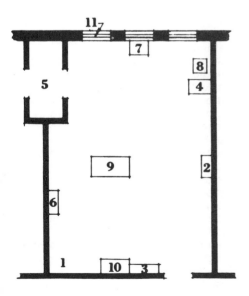

Department for Toddlers

1. Area for cardboard blocks
2. Bookrack with slanting shelves (11 inches deep, 28 inches long, 27 inches high)
3. Diaper bag shelf
4. Doll bed (16 inches wide, 28 inches long, board supporting mattress 8 inches from floor)
5. Adjoining toilet (child-size fixtures)
6. Open shelves with closed back (26 inches high, 30 inches long, 12 inches deep)
7. Record player
8. Rocker (child size)
9. Rocking boat and steps
10. Wall supply cabinets (mounted 50 inches from floor)
11. Windows (sills 22 to 24 inches from the floor)

157

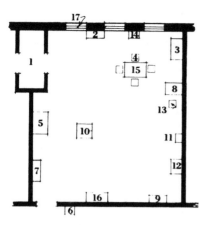

Department for Two–and Three–Year Olds

1. Adjoining toilet (child-size fixtures)
2. Bookrack with slanting shelves (11 inches deep, 28 inches long, 27 inches high)
3. Cabinet sink (32 inches high, 34 inches wide, 18 inches deep, 24 inches from floor to top of work surface)
4. Chairs (seat is 10 inches high)
5. Clothes drying rack (for wet paintings)
6. Coatrack (for adults, outside room)
7. Coatrack (for children; 40 inches high, 40 inches wide, 14 inches deep)
8. Doll bed (16 inches wide, 28 inches long, board supporting mattress 8 inches from floor)
9. Open shelves with closed back (26 inches high, 30 inches long, 12 inches deep)
10. Painting easel (45 inches high with 25 by 20 inch painting surface)
11. Puzzle rack
12. Record player
13. Rocker (child size)
14. Stove (24 inches high, 18 inches wide, 12 inches deep)
15. Table (24 inches wide, 36 inches long, 20 inches from floor)
16. Wall supply cabinet (mounted 50 inches from floor)
17. Windows (sills 22 to 24 inches from floor)

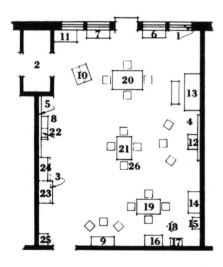

Department for Four–and Five–Year Olds

1. Windows (clear glass; sills 22 to 24 inches from the floor); draperies and blinds not necessary, unless needed to prevent glare
2. Restroom may serve two adjoining departments for four- and five-year-olds; two commodes 10 inches high; two lavatories, faucets 24 inches from floor; desirable to have drinking fountain attachment on one faucet
3. Wall supply cabinet units hung on wall side by side (bottom 50 inches from floor; picture file desk and rack for children's wraps under supply cabinet)
4. Picture rail (about 6 feet long, near middle of longest unbroken wall)
5. Tackboard (not as essential as some other items; beginning 20 inches from floor; 8 to 12 feet long; 18 to 24 inches wide; on wall other than front wall)
6. Block shelves (30 inches wide, 26 inches high, 12 inches deep)
7. Nature shelves
8. Art shelves
9. Bookrack (with slanting shelves, 14 inches deep, 33 inches high, 36 inches wide)
10. Painting easel (45 inches overall height, 25 inches wide, painting surface 20 by 25 inches)
11. Small clothes drying rack (for drying paintings)
12. Record player (three-speed with turntable visible to children and

easily operated by them) or table cabinet (for record player and recordings; 24 inches long, 18 inches wide, 20 inches high)

13. Piano (studio type, approximately 44 inches high)
14. Cabinet-sink (34 inches wide, 24 inches to working surface, 18 inches deep, 32 inches overall height)
15. Stove (18 inches wide, 24 inches high, 12 inches deep)
16. Doll bed (16 inches wide, 28 inches long, 16 inches high, board supporting mattress 8 inches from floor)
17. Chest of drawers (for doll clothes and dress-up clothes, 18 inches wide, 12 inches deep, 24 inches high)
18. Child's rocking chair (seat is 12 inches from floor)
19. Table for home living (24 by 36 inches)*

20. Art table (30 by 48 inches)*
21. Puzzle table (24 by 36 inches)*
22. Puzzle rack (9 inches wide, 12 inches long, 9 inches high)
23. Picture file desk (for teaching pictures and reports; 38 inches long, 22 inches wide, 30 inches high)
24. Rack for children's wraps (40 inches wide, 40 inches high, 14 inches deep)
25. Rack for adult wraps (18 inches wide, 60 inches high, 14 inches deep)
26. Chairs (wooden; formfitting; two horizontal back slats; seat 10 inches high for four-year-olds; 12 inches high for five-year-olds or for fours and fives together; one chair for each child and each worker; same chairs used for activities and group time)

* All tables are ten inches higher than the seats of the chairs; plastic tops are desirable.

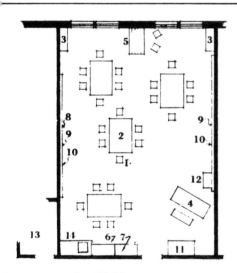

Department for Children

1. Chairs (one chair per child for largest organization using the room; seats are 12 inches high for ages 6 and 7; 14 inches high for ages 8 and 9; 16 inches high for ages 10 and 11)
2. Tables (waterproof tops; 36 by 54 inches or 30 by 48 inches; height is 10 inches above chair seat height; one table for every six children)
3. Two or three portable shelves with closed backs (42 to 46 inches high, 3 feet wide, 4 feet long, 12 inches deep, 12 to 14 inches between shelves)
4. Piano (studio size)

5. Bookrack (slanted shelves on one side and flat shelves on other side; 42 to 46 inches high, 2½ feet wide, 3½ feet long)
6. Coatracks (portable; 4 feet, 4 inches high for children; 5 feet, 8 inches high for adults)
7. Storage cabinets (18 inches deep; hung on wall; adequate size for material and for separate storage needed by each organization using the room)
8, 9, & 10. Combination chalkboard, tackboard, and picture rail may be permanently installed so as to make the surface tilt with the top against the wall and the bottom about six inches from the wall; (lengths for younger ages would be minimum of 6 feet of chalkboard and 18 feet of tackboard, both 30 inches high and mounted with the bottom 28 inches above floor; lengths for older ages would be a minimum of 8 feet of chalkboard and 24 feet of tackboard, both 30 inches high and mounted 28 inches above the floor)
11. Cabinet (for pictures—12 by 18 inches; for posters—24 by 36 inches)
12. Record player (3 or 4 speed; record storage cabinet 26 inches high, 24 inches wide, 14 inches deep)
13. Restrooms nearby on hall for all children
14. Sink

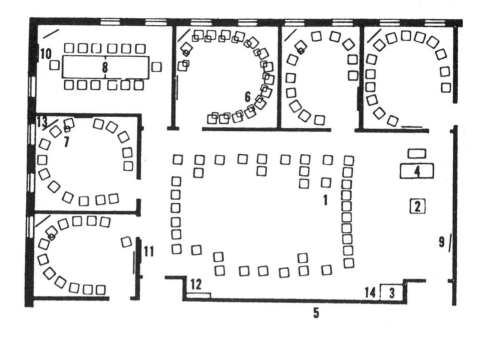

Department for Youth or Adults
1. Movable chairs (stacking or folding; seats are 18 inches from floor)
2. Small table (or lecturn) for use by director
3. Table for secretary or outreach leader
4. Piano (studio size)
5. Movable rack for coats and hats
6. Chairs with tablet arms (folding arms recommended)
7. Small table and/or tablet-arm chair for teacher
8. Folding tables (30 by 72 inches; for class members to sit around or Royal Ambassador program)
9. Movable chalkboard (freestanding)
10. Chalkboard-tackboard (fixed to wall)
11. Tackboard (fixed to wall)
12. Shelves (open and adjustable; for Bible study aids, books, etc.)
13. Easel
14. Wastebasket

Figure 18

Church Training Program

Definition:

The planned educational activities provided by a local church to (1) equip church members for discipleship and personal ministry; and (2) equip church leaders for service.

Purpose and scope of work:

The purpose of the Church Training program is twofold: to enable church members to live distinctively Christian lives and to prepare persons to assume a leadership responsibility within the congregation. The former involves short-term studies for integrating new members into the life and faith of the congregation as well as an on-going curriculum-guided study oriented around themes such as Christian theology, doctrine, ethics, history, and church polity. Additional areas of study which may be provided within the established curriculum or on a short-term basis include just about any topic that would help a person apply biblical teachings to everyday life.

General training for discipleship, personal ministry, and interpersonal effectiveness is part of the ongoing training curriculum as well as the foundation for leadership development. In addition, specialized training is provided at appropriate times during the year for committee members, teachers, group leaders, church visitors, and other similar positions.

Key Resource:

Edgemon, Roy T., compiler. *Equipping Disciples Through Church Training.* Nashville: Convention Press, 1981.

Patterns of Organization:

Each church should provide a comprehensive program of training for its members. Such a program should include appropriate training opportunities for all church members and their families. It should also include special training activities for new church members and for church leaders. One possible pattern of organization is suggested in Figure 19. Each church should adapt or adjust this pattern in order to develop its own practical approach to training.

Church Training Organization

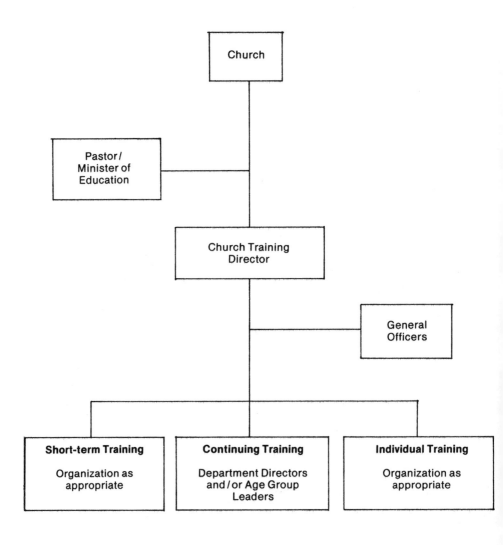

Figure 19

Job Descriptions

General Officers

The number and the classification of general officers depends upon the size and comprehensiveness of the training program which a church may have. Included in the group of general officers are church training director, church training secretary, director of enlistment, director of new church member training, director of church member training, and director of church leader training.

1. Personal Qualifications

General officers in the Church Training program should be:

• Mature Christians

• Sincerely committed to training

• Knowledgeable regarding the training program, or willing to become knowledgeable

• Skillful in areas of work for which they are responsible, such as administration, communication, enlistment, record keeping, and so on.

2. Duties

Church Training Director

1. Represent all Church Training needs and plans as a member of the church council.

2. Conduct the Church Training council meetings to plan, conduct, and evaluate the church's training program.

3. Lead all Church Training leaders to improve their leadership skills through participation in appropriate training activities.

4. Develop and recommend the budget for the Church Training program.

5. Plan and coordinate special training projects, such as Baptist Doctrine Study.

6. Assist Church Training organizational leaders with work related to planning, maintenance, and enlistment.

7. Work with the directors of each type of training—new church member training, church member training, and church leader training—to plan, conduct, and evaluate the training activities in their respective areas.

8. *Note:* If the director also serves as director of one or more of the types of training, the duties recommended for that director become a part of his specific duties.

Church Training Secretary

1. Serve on the Church Training council and assist with record keeping as assigned.

2. Compile general records and reports needed by the Church Training director, and by other leaders in the training program.

3. Compile requests for literature and supplies needed in the various training units, and order those items as needed.

4. Distribute literature and supplies to training units.

5. Assist secretaries in the various training units with proper maintenance of records.

6. Handle the classification and enrollment of new members, remove names from rolls, and otherwise maintain records of all kinds of training completed by groups and by individuals, according to the plan adopted by the church.

Director of Enlistment

1. Serve on the Church Training council to represent a continuing concern for reaching more people for training.

2. Maintain up-to-date lists of prospects for all kinds of training activities.

3. Suggest assignments and enlistment approaches to organizational units in the training program.

4. Plan and promote a total approach for contacts with absentees and prospects.

5. Conduct periodic surveys of the church membership to determine kinds of training activities needed.

6. Assume duties of Church Training director in his absence, as requested.

Director of New Church Member Training

1. Serve on the Church Training council to represent the continuing concern of the church to provide a comprehensive training program for its new members.

2. Work with new church member training leaders (sponsors, counselors, instructors, and so on) in planning and conducting their work.

3. Recommend budget for literature and supplies to be used in training new church members.

Director of Church Member Training

1. Serve on the Church Training council to help plan, conduct, and improve the training activities provided for church members and their families.

2. Work with leaders of age-group departments and training groups in planning, conducting, and improving their training activities.

3. Recommend the budget for literature and supplies to be used in training church members and their families.

Director of Church Leader Training

1. Serve on the Church Training council to help plan, conduct, and improve the training activities provided for leaders of the church.

2. Lead the church to discover its leader training needs.

3. Lead in planning, conducting, and improving general leader training.

4. Lead in planning, conducting, and improving training for prospective and potential leaders.

5. Recommend the budget for literature and supplies to be used in training church leaders.

Department Officers

Each department should organize so that certain essential functions are carried out. These functions include: presiding, planning, training, maintaining records, and enlisting. The department director is responsible for all of these functions, either directly or by delegation and assignment to others.

The duties of department officers are listed in the paragraphs to follow. No one list is exhaustive. Under each officer heading there are listed a number of duties which are common to all department officers, regardless of the age group in which they work.

Department Director

1. Preside over department meetings.

2. Represent the department on the Church Training council.

3. Plan and lead department worship periods when they are held.

4. Lead in enlisting and providing training for other department and training group leaders.

5. Assure that literature and supplies are available for use in the department and training groups.

6. Work with department and training group leaders in enlisting church members and their families in appropriate training units.

Department Secretary

1. Maintain enrollment and attendance records for members of the department and training groups.

2. Assist department director as needed.

3. Confer with department and training group leaders regarding absenteeism of group members.

4. Maintain current prospect lists for the department and training gr ups.

Optional Officers

(If, or when, department worship periods are held, these officers would function.)

1. *Song Leader*
   a. Select music and lead singing for each department meeting.
   b. Arrange for special music as needed.
   c. Serve as a member of a training group or as a training group leader.

2. *Pianist*
   a. Play for all meetings of the department.
   b. Serve as a member of a training group or as a training group leader.[5]

Church Training Council

Who is involved?—The Church Training council is made up of church elected officers who are responsible for the Church Training program. These officers include:

1. The director who serves as chairman
2. All other general officers, such as the director of enlistment and general secretary
3. Directors of the three types of training—new church member, church member, and church leader
4. Age-group coordinators for churches that have these officers
5. Pastor and appropriate staff members
6. Age-group department or training group leaders for churches with only a member training program

What do they plan?—This group is concerned with an overall planning process as it relates to Church Training. Planning done is within the context of total church planning developed in the church council. That which evolves from this group should undergird the church plan and provide specific training to equip members in achieving church goals.

Thus the Church Training council *plans, coordinates,* and *evaluates* a church's training program. This includes church and program goals, organization, activities, projects, and emphases.

In planning the complete Church Training program, the director, through the training council, accepts responsibility for these administrative planning actions:

1. *Establish objectives and goals.*—Determine the answer to, What do we want to accomplish within this period of time? Normally this will be annual planning, though

short-term or project planning needs clearly defined objectives.

2. *Determine priorities.*—If we cannot do everything, either because of time or resources, what ought to be given top billing?

3. *Plan actions.*—Now that we have determined what we ought to do, how do we go about getting it done?

4. *Determine organization.*—Not people—just places or positions of responsibility which are necessary.

5. *Enlist and train personnel.*—They go together—you should not have one without the other.

6. *Assign and define responsibilities.*—Persons selected and trained should have clearly defined responsibilities.

7. *Allocate resources.*—These include equipment, space, curriculum materials, books, finances, and so on.

8. *Maintain communications.*—Two-way give-and-take are important. A system to provide this should be considered.

9. *Evaluate results.*—Find out what worked, what did not work and why; then incorporate newfound knowledge in future planning.

This or some version of this process should be used by a Church Training council in accomplishing its planning task. What specifically is the scope of the council work?

It is to develop a comprehensive program of training for the church and seek ways to gain awareness of, commitment to, and involvement in its work. This includes providing training of three types: new church member, church member, and church leader.

Accomplishing this objective involves organizing, planning actions (continuing and short-term), allocating resources, assigning responsibilities, and developing schedules. Coordination and evaluation are vital functions of the Church Training council.

The value of the planning process can easily be identified in the planning work of the training council.

Suggested Planning Agenda for the Church Training Council

A suggested planning agenda for the Church Training council could be:

1. Devotional period of Scripture reading and specific prayer
2. Noting of attendance
3. Evaluation, study of records, reports, results, and so on. Such questions as: What have we accomplished? What are we doing or not doing? How can we do better?
4. Look at schedules, special projects pending—finalize plans—tie up loose ends. Look ahead three months.
5. Preview church calendar—consider recommendations from church council pertinent to the training program—plan actions if necessary.
6. Determine needs, problems, goals, and so on. Questions might include: What are our greatest needs? Where are our problem areas? What could we be doing? Do this with item 5 in mind.
7. Assign responsibilities and provide for reporting—who is going to do what, and when, and how will the council know results?[6]

CHURCH TRAINING INREACH SURVEY

CHURCH: _____

CHURCH TRAINING ATTENDANCE: _____ Resident Membership _____
(Average for Past Quarter)

DIVISION	AGE	S. S. Enrollment NOW	C. T. Enrollment NOW	Prospects for Training *NOW	DEPTS. NOW	ADD'L. DEPTS. NEEDED	TRAINING GROUPS NOW	ADD'L TR. GROUPS NEEDED	WORKERS NOW	ADD'L. WORKERS NEEDED
PRESCHOOL ONGOING TRAINING	BIRTH-1									
	1									
	2									
	3									
	4									
	5									
CHILDREN ONGOING TRAINING	6 (Grade 1)									
	7 (Grade 2)									
	8 (Grade 3)									
	9 (Grade 4)									
	10 (Grade 5)									
	11 (Grade 6)									
YOUTH ONGOING TRAINING	12 (Grade 7)									
	13 (Grade 8)									
	14 (Grade 9)									
	15 (Grade 10)									
	16 (Grade 11)									
	17 (Grade 12)									
ADULT ONGOING TRAINING *	18 College									
	Singles									
	Married									
	29 Young Adult									
	30 59 Adult									
	60 up Senior Adult									
EQUIPPING CENTERS*	Group Study									
	Individual Study									
Other Short Term Training	Adult									
	Youth									
Church Leader Training	Group Study									
	Individual Study									
New Church Member Training	Adult									
	Youth									
	Children									
Hold File										
General Officers										
TOTALS										

*Determine if adults are prospects for ongoing training. Equipping
Centers or church leader training.

Figure 20

Music Ministry Program

Definition:

The planned educational, worship, and witness activities provided by a local church to develop musical skills, attitudes, and understandings that can contribute to worship, witness, and Christian living.[7]

Purpose and scope of work:

The purpose of the Music Ministry program is to develop appreciation for and ability to use musical experiences that will enhance specifically the worship and witness areas of church experience, and generally, all dimensions of a Christian's life.

Musical experiences extend from congregational singing and choral anthems to participation in graded choirs for all ages. A structured curriculum often is provided for younger choirs, focusing on music skills and appreciation. Youth and adult choirs, on the other hand, spend most of their time learning and performing music. Although sometimes considered more of a worship and witness means rather than an educational function of the church, the Music Ministry program nevertheless significantly influences lives of those who are not performing, and teaches those who are.

Key Resource:

Reynolds, William J., compiler. *Building an Effective Music Ministry.* Nashville: Convention Press, 1980.

Job Descriptions

A basic commandment of good organization is "define responsibilities." If a Music Ministry is to function properly and accomplish its mission, the music leaders must know what their jobs are. To assist you in communicating clear descriptions of responsibilities to your music leaders, we are including examples of statements of duties or job descriptions. These are examples to be studied and redesigned to fit your organizational needs and work. Do provide your leaders with written descriptions of their responsibilities. Don't just copy the ones listed here. The examples are grouped by Music Ministry size.

Small Music Ministries

A description of responsibilities for music leaders is important even in a small church. The following are listed to provide a source of ideas. Each church will need to write descriptions of the specific work of their leaders. One approach is to add to or delete from the guidelines given here.

Small Music Ministry

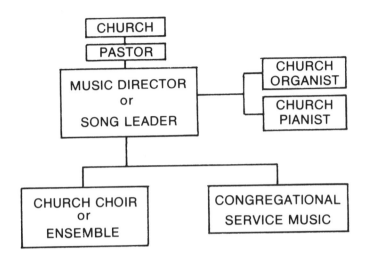

Medium-Sized Music Ministry

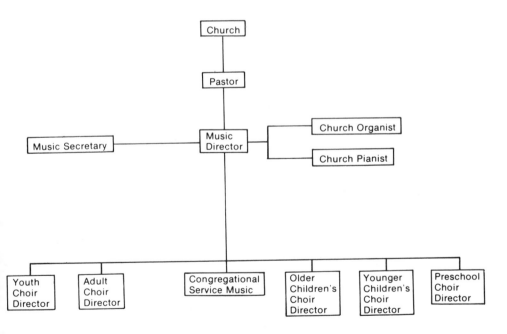

Large Music Ministry

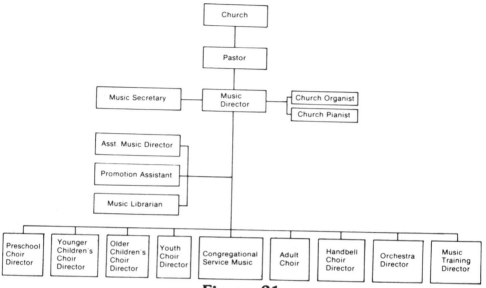

Figure 21

Church Music Director
Principal Function

The music director is responsible to the pastor and to the church for planning, conducting, and evaluating congregational music and activities of the church choir.
Responsibilities

1. Assist the pastor in planning congregational services and be responsible for the selection of music.

2. Direct music groups and congregational singing.

3. Be responsible for enlisting and training leaders for the Music Ministry in cooperation with the church nominating committee.

4. Supervise the work of all music leaders in the Music Ministry.

5. Supervise maintenance of the music library.

6. Cooperate with associational, state convention, and Southern Baptist Convention leaders in promoting activities of the denomination and the church.

7. Prepare and administer the Music Ministry budget.

8. Serve on the church council.

Church Organist
Principal Function

The church organist is responsible to the music director for playing for congregational services, weddings, funerals, and serving as accompanist for the church choir.

Responsibilities

1. Play for all services of the church.

2. Assist in planning congregational services, choir rehearsal, and special music events.

3. Maintain a regular schedule of organ practice, special studies, reading, and self-improvement.

4. Supervise the use of the church organ by persons other than the organist.

5. Provide for proper maintenance of the organ.

6. Plan, maintain, and use a complete list of music for preludes, offertories, and postludes in the congregational services.

7. Serve as accompanist for choirs, ensembles, and soloists in regular and special rehearsals and services.

8. Serve as accompanist for soloists and groups for appearances outside the church.

Church Pianist

Principal Function

The church pianist is responsible to the music director for playing for congregational services and special services as assigned.

Responsibilities

1. Play for services of the church as assigned.

2. Assist in planning congregational services, choir rehearsals, and special music events as requested.

3. Maintain a regular schedule of piano practice and self-improvement.

4. Assist in training pianists for church organizations.

5. Plan, maintain, and use a complete list of music for church soloists.

6. Serve as accompanist for choirs, ensembles, and soloists as assigned.

Medium-Sized Music Ministries

Church Music Director

Principal Function

The music director is responsible to the pastor and to the church for planning, conducting, and evaluating the Music Ministry.

Responsibilities

1. Direct the planning, coordination, and evaluation of the Music Ministry.

2. Serve as chairman of the Church Music council; coordinate the Music Ministry with the calendar and emphases of the church.

3. Lead in maintaining a Church Music council; train members of the council and all music leaders; guide the council in determining Music Ministry goals, organization, leadership, facilities, finances, and administrative procedures.

4. Assist the pastor in planning congregational services of the church and be responsible for the selection of music.

6. Direct congregational singing and music groups.

6. Be responsible for enlisting and training leaders for the Music Ministry in cooperation with the church nominating committee.

7. Supervise the work of all music leaders in the music program.

8. Coordinate the performance schedules of music groups and individuals in the functions of the church.

9. Give direction to a Music Ministry plan of visitation and enlistment.

10. Supervise maintenance of and additions to the music library.

11. Cooperate with associational, state convention, and Southern Baptist Convention leaders in promoting activities of the denomination and the church.

12. Be informed of denominational goals, emphases, publications, materials, policies, and plans for employing them as they relate to the local church.

13. Prepare and administer the Music Ministry budget.

14. Serve on the church council.

Church Organist

Principal Function

Be responsible to the music director for providing all organ music for congregational services and for accompanying rehearsals of designated choral groups, ensembles, and soloists.

Responsibilities

1. Play for all services of the church.

2. Assist in planning congregational services, choral rehearsals, and special musical events.

3. Assist, when requested by the music director, in planning and directing a training program to develop future organists.

4. Teach classes as assigned in hymn and service playing for the training of organizational pianists.

5. Maintain a regular schedule of organ practice and self-improvement.

6. Supervise the use of the church organ by persons other than the organist. Be responsible for overseeing the regular maintenance of the organ.

7. Plan, maintain, and use a complete list of solo music for preludes, offertories, and postludes.

8. Serve as accompanist for choirs, ensembles, and soloists in regular and special rehearsals and services.

9. Serve as accompanist for soloists and groups for appearances outside the church.

10. Serve on the music council.

Church Pianist

Principal Function

The church pianist is responsible to the music director for playing for congregational services and serving as accompanist for performing musical groups as assigned by the church music director.

Responsibilities

1. Playing for services of the church as assigned.

2. Play for, and be available to advise concerning choice of instrumental music for weddings, funerals, special occasions, and other events upon request or by assignment.

3. Assist in planning congregational services, choir rehearsals, and special music events, as requested.

4. Assist the church music director as requested in appraising and selecting music and in a preliminary study of new materials as requested.

5. Assist, when requested by the music director, in planning and in directing the training program to develop future pianists for the church.

6. Teach classes as assigned in hymn and service playing for the training of organizational pianists.

7. Maintain a regular schedule of piano practice, special studies, reading, and self-improvement.

8. Assist the music director as requested in teaching, rehearsal activities, and general duties.

9. Supervise the use of church pianos. Be responsible for overseeing the regular maintenance of church pianos.

10. Plan, maintain, and use a comprehensive appropriate repertoire for the piano for use in congregational services.

As accompanist:

1. Serve as accompanist for choirs, ensembles, and soloists in regular and special rehearsals and services, as assigned.

2. Serve as accompanist for soloists and groups for appearances outside the church, upon invitation or by assignment and with the approval of the music director.

Large Music Ministries

Church Music Director
Principal Function

The music director is responsible to the pastor and the church for planning, conducting, and evaluating the Music Ministry.

Responsibilities

1. Direct the planning, coordination, operation, and evaluation of a comprehensive Music Ministry.

2. Serve as chairman of the Church Music council which coordinates the Music Ministry with the calendar and emphases of the church.

3. Lead in maintaining a Church Music council. Train members of the council. Guide the council in determining music program goals, organization, leadership, facilities, finances, and administrative procedures.

4. Assist the pastor in planning congregational services of the church and be responsible for the selection of the music.

5. Be aware of weddings and funerals to be held in the church. Be available to counsel. Arrange and provide music for special projects, ministries, and other church-related activities in cooperation with appropriate individuals or groups.

6. Direct music groups and congregational singing.

7. Be responsible for enlisting and training leaders for the Music Ministry in cooperation with the church nominating committee.

8. Supervise the work of all music leaders in the music program, delegate work and responsibility as needed.

9. Work in cooperation with appropriate persons including the nominating committee in selecting, enlisting, training, and counseling with song leaders, accompanists, and other musicians who serve in church program organizations.

10. Coordinate the performance schedules of music groups and individuals in activities of the church.

11. Give direction to a plan of visitation and enlistment.

12. Supervise maintenance of and additions to music library. Provide music mate-

rials, supplies, instruments, and other music equipment for use in the church's program.

13. Be aware of current music methods, materials, promotion, and administration, utilizing them where appropriate.

14. Cooperate with associational, state convention, and Southern Baptist Convention leaders in promoting activities of the denomination and the church.

15. Coordinate the training and use of instrumentalists and vocalists in groups or as individuals.

16. Be informed of denominational goals, emphases, publications, materials, policies, and plans for employing them as they relate to the local church and its welfare.

17. Prepare and administer the Music Ministry budget.

18. Fulfill personal responsibility to witness and counsel in music-related opportunities.

19. Serve on the church council.

Church Organist

Principal Function

The church organist is responsible to the music director for playing for congregational services, weddings, and funerals and serving as accompanist for performing musical groups as assigned by the music director.

Responsibilities

1. Play for services of the church as assigned.

2. Play for weddings, funerals, special occasions, and other events upon request or by assignment. Be available to advise concerning choice of appropriate instrumental music.

3. Assist, as requested, in planning congregational services, choir rehearsals, and special music events.

4. Assist the music director, when requested, in reviewing and selecting music.

5. Assist, when requested by the music director, in planning and directing a training program for organists.

6. Teach classes as assigned in hymn and service playing for the training of organizational pianists.

7. Maintain a regular schedule of organ practice, special studies, reading, and self-improvement.

8. Assist the music director, as requested, in teaching, rehearsal activities, and general duties.

9. Supervise use of the church organ by persons other than the organist (practicing students, guest organists for weddings).

10. Plan, maintain, and use an appropriate repertoire for preludes, offertories, and postludes for congregational services.

11. Serve as a member of the Church Music council.

As an accompanist:

1. Serve, as assigned, as accompanist for choral and instrumental groups and soloists' rehearsals and services.

2. Serve, when assigned, as accompanist for soloists and music groups for appearances outside the church.

Church Pianist

Principal Function

The church pianist is responsible to the music director for playing for congregational services and serving as accompanist for performing musical groups as assigned by the music director.

Responsibilities

As church pianist:

1. Playing for services of the church as assigned.

2. Play for, and be available to advise concerning choice of instrumental music for weddings, funerals, special occasions, and other events, upon request or by assignment.

3. Assist in planning congregational services, choir rehearsals, and special music events as requested.

4. Assist the music director as requested in reviewing and selecting music.

5. Assist, when requested by the music director, in planning and in directing the training program for pianists.

6. Teach classes as assigned in hymn and service playing for the training of organizational pianists.

7. Maintain a regular schedule of piano practice, special studies, reading, and self-improvement.

8. Assist the music director as requested in teaching, rehearsal activities, and general duties.

9. Supervise use of the church pianos. Be responsible for overseeing the regular maintenance of church pianos.

10. Plan, maintain, and use a comprehensive appropriate repertoire for the piano for use in congregational service music.

11. Serve as a member of the Church Music council.

As accompanist:

1. Serve as accompanist for choirs, ensembles, and soloists in regular and special rehearsals and services as assigned.

2. Serve as accompanist for soloists and groups for appearances outside the church upon invitation or by assignment and with the approval of the church music director.

General Music Secretary

Principal Function

To assist the music director by keeping enrollment and attendance records and preparing reports of the work of the Music Ministry

Responsibilities

1. Maintain an up-to-date membership roll for the Music Ministry.

2. Receive and record attendance reports from the various groups or divisions.

3. Prepare monthly and annual reports for the Music Ministry.

4. Purchase record and report forms used in the music records system.

5. Guide music group secretaries in keeping records and making reports.

6. Keep the council minutes.

7. Serve as a member of the music council.

Church Music Librarian

Principal Function

Be responsible to the music director for setting up and maintaining the music library.

Responsibilities

1. Maintain an up-to-date card index file of all music and equipment available in the music library.

2. Obtain music supplies and equipment for the Music Ministry as authorized by the music director.

3. Provide the music leaders of the church with a regular listing of all music, supplies, and equipment.

4. Catalog and file music and equipment.

5. Repair and reorder music, supplies, and equipment as needed.

6. Work with the church library in properly relating materials of the two libraries.

Enlistment Assistant

Principal Function

To assist the music director in enlisting persons in the Music Ministry.

Responsibilities

1. Lead in discovering prospects for choir and instrumental groups.

2. Maintain an up-to-date music program individual prospect file by music group. Provide a prospect list to each director every month.

3. Lead in Music Ministry enlistment activities.

4. Serve as a member of the music council.

Promotion Assistant

Principal Function

To assist the music director in publicizing and promoting the activities of the music program.

Responsibilities

1. Publicize and promote the activities and projects of the Music Ministry.

2. Develop and produce promotion materials for the Music Ministry according to plans approved by the music director.

3. Develop and pursue actions designed to improve public relations of the Music Ministry.

4. Serve as a member of the music council.

Instrumental Coordinator

Principal Function

To assist the music director in developing and coordinating the instrumental music groups of the Music Ministry

Responsibilities

1. Evaluate all phases of instrumental training in the church, working in cooperation with the music director and other appropriate persons to provide instrumental training opportunities.

2. Conduct specific instrumental training actions.

3. Lead in providing instrumental literature to appropriate persons.

4. Assist the church organizations by enlisting pianists and other instrumentalists as requested.

5. Assist age-division directors, as requested, with instrumental activities.

6. Coordinate instrumental actions where they cross age-division lines.

7. Direct instrumental group.

8. Serve as a member of the music council.

Age-Division Coordinator (Preschool or Children)

Principal Function

The age-division coordinator is responsible to the music director for planning and coordinating the work of his age division.

Responsibilities

1. Administer the planning, conducting, and evaluating of the work in the division.

2. Study and recommend to the music director organization, leadership, curriculum, and schedules for the division.

3. Make recommendations concerning space, equipment, materials, literature, and other resources.

4. Lead in promoting specialized training actions for the age division.

5. Use planning and evaluation achievement guides.

6. Recommend and assist in enlisting and training music leaders within the division.

7. Assist the music director in providing music and musicians for the church worship services and program organizations as requested.

8. Coordinate the training and use of instrumentalists and vocalists.

9. Encourage the use of music in the home.

10. Encourage the use of music in family worship.

11. Lead family members to minister to other families' needs through music.

12. Serve as a member of the music council.

13. Communicate to the music director and the music council matters pertaining to his division which require council action or leadership.

14. Communicate to leaders and members of his division those administrative council actions which affect the division.

Handbell Coordinator

Principal Function

The handbell coordinator is responsible to the music director for planning and leading the handbell music groups of the Music Ministry.

Responsibilities

1. Administer, plan, conduct, and evaluate the work of handbell ensembles.

2. Plan and conduct specific training for future handbell choir directors and prospective handbell choir members.

3. Lead in determining organization, leadership, curriculum, and schedules for handbell work within the framework of the church and the Music Ministry.

4. Make recommendations concerning space, equipment, materials, literature, and other resources.

5. Recommend and assist in enlistment of leaders for handbell choirs.

6. Assist the music director in providing music and musicians for church worship services and other meetings as requested.

7. Serve as a member of the Church Music council.

Preschool and Children's Choir Directors

Principal Function

A Preschool or Children's choir director is responsible to the music director, or in those churches which have one, a choir coordinator, and is the single most important person in the success of the choir.

Responsibilities

1. Plan and direct the work of the choir.

2. Lead in planning the curriculum units and in the evaluation of the teaching done in each session.

3. Guide the work of the accompanist and teachers.

4. Encourage and guide teachers to improve the quality of their work.

5. Give overall supervision to the rehearsal sessions and personally direct large-group activities.

6. Provide and direct appropriate sharing and/or performance opportunities for the choir.

7. Maintain adequate communication with parents to inform them of the various activities of the choir.

8. Be responsible for a plan to discover and enlist new members.

9. Encourage the use of music in the home.

10. See that appropriate social and recreational activities are provided.

11. Assist leaders in other church program organizations with music as needed.

12. Participate in an on-going plan of study and skill development.

13. Serve on the Age-Group Division music planning group (if there is one).

14. Serve on the Church Music council if the Music Ministry does not have a choir coordinator.

Preschool and Children's Choir Accompanist/Teacher
Principal Function

The accompanist/teacher is responsible to the director and assumes the responsibilities assigned by the director. The primary task is keyboard accompaniment.
Responsibilities

1. Provide accompaniment for rehearsals, performances, and sharing activities.

2. Assist the director in the planning of curriculum and in the evaluation of the teaching done in each session.

3. Accept an appropriate share of the responsibility for planning and leading small-group activities.

4. Assist the director with large-group activities as needed.

5. Participate in an on-going plan of study and skill development.

Preschool and Children's Choir Teacher
Principal Function

The teacher is responsible to the director and assumes the responsibilities assigned by the director.
Responsibilities

1. Assist the director in the planning of curriculum units and in the evaluation of teaching done in each session.

2. Accept an appropriate share of the responsibility for planning and leading small-group activities.

3. Assist the director with large-group activities as needed.

4. Participate in a continuing plan of study and skill development.

5. Assist the director in developing and implementing a plan to discover and enlist new members.

6. Assist the director in providing appropriate social and recreational activities.

Guidelines for Organizing Adult and Youth Choirs

The number of Adult choirs is determined by worship service requirements and then by the availability of singers for each voice part. Churches with one Sunday morning worship service usually have one Adult choir. The growing practice of holding two or more morning worship services has produced a need for two or more Adult

Guidelines for Organizing Preschool and Children's Choirs

Division	Age Grade	Average Attendance Range	Number of Choirs	Number of Workers Needed	Space Needed	Span	Leader Member Ratio	Space Ratio
Preschool Choir	4 years to	8-18	One Choir	2 to 3	450 sq. ft. approx. 15' x 30'	2 yrs.	1-6	25-35 sq. ft. per person
	5 years	18-24	Two Choirs	4 to 6	2 Rooms 450 sq. ft. each	1 yr.	1-6	
		24-54	Three Choirs	6 to 9	3 Rooms, 450 sq. ft. each	6 mo.	1-6	
Children's Choir	Grades 1 thru 6	6-12	One Choir	2 to 3	300 sq. ft. approx. 15' x 20'	6 Grades	1-7	25 sq. ft. per person
Younger Children's Choir	Grades 1-3	6-21	One Choir	2 to 3	450 sq. ft. approx. 15' x 30'	3 Grades	1-7	25 sq. ft. per person
		18-42	Two Choirs	4 to 6	2 Rooms approx. 450 sq. ft.	1½ Grades	1-7	
		42-54	Three Choirs	6 to 9	3 Rooms approx. 450 sq. ft.	1 Grade	1-7	
Older Children's Choir	Grades 4-6	6-48	One Choir	2 to 6	450 sq. ft. to 1,200 sq. ft. 2 Rooms	3 Grades	1-8	25 sq. ft. per person
		48-100	Two Choirs	6 to 13	App. 1,200 sq. ft. (30' x 40') 3 Rooms	1 to 2 Grades	1-8	
		100-150	Three Choirs	13 to 19	Approx. 1,200 sq. ft. ea	1 Grade	1-8	

Figure 22

choirs in those churches. On special occasions these choirs can be combined with extraordinary results.

Youth choirs are primarily performance choirs providing music for congregational services. They frequently take their music into the community. The impact of a Youth choir is made strong by quality choral work and by satisfying needs for belonging, love, and esteem.

A second Youth choir may be set up to meet the special needs of the adolescent voice and may be organized when there are sufficient members, prospects, leaders, space, and equipment to provide rewarding experiences for both Youth choirs. This second Youth choir is usually a Junior High School or Middle School choir, depending on how the local school system is organized. The first choir then becomes a High School choir.

Important intangible factors in organizing a second Youth choir are interest and commitment from members, leaders, and parents that will hold both groups together.

Four measurable factors will encourage or limit the growth of Youth and Adult choirs: space, leader-member ratio, attendance, and rehearsal time.

Sixteen square feet of rehearsal space per person is recommended. When attendance reaches the capacity indicated by the space ratio for a room, then attendance will level off or drop.

A favorable leader-member ratio is one worker for every eight members. Growth can be encouraged by lowering that ratio. Choir officers will be considered as workers for the purpose of figuring this ratio.

At least one rehearsal hour per week without conflicts for choir members should be provided for Adult and Youth choirs. This is the means by which those choirs provide satisfactory experiences for the members and for the congregation.

Brotherhood

Definition:

A church organization for men and boys devoted to equipping and involving members in Christian service.[8]

Purpose and scope of work:

The major purpose of this organization is to inform, motivate, and involve men and boys in praying, studying, enlisting, giving, ministering, and bearing witness to Christ where they live as well as cooperatively throughout the world. Great emphasis is placed on developing a style of Christian living and personal ministry that is a natural part of one's life.

Age-graded leadership and study materials often are used to provide guidance for groups of members ranging from first graders through adults.

This organization should not be confused with the fellowship-

Brotherhood Organization

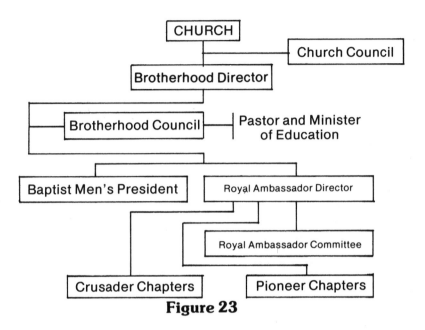

Figure 23

oriented meetings for men held in some churches. The Brotherhood program is a serious, ongoing educational organization whose concern is much broader.

Key Resource:

Belew, Wendell. *The Purpose and Plan of Baptist Brotherhood.* Memphis: Brotherhood Commission, 1979.

Job Descriptions

The Pastor

What the Brotherhood is able to do in accomplishing its tasks will to a great degree depend on the attitude, support, relationship, and assistance given by the pastor.

The pastor is one of the major officers of Brotherhood work. He stands alongside the Brotherhood Director in setting directions and leading the work. Brotherhood work will be supportive and complementary to the goals and work of the pastor as he leads the church. The pastor as an officer can influence and work through the Brotherhood to accomplish the work of the church in missions.

The pastor's responsibilities as officer are extremely important: (1) He works with the church nominating committee to select and have elected qualified and effective leaders. (2) He is a member of the Brotherhood council and actively plans with the other officers the goals and work of Brotherhood. (3) Through the varied avenues available to him, the pastor also encourages the involvement of all men and boys in missions work.

The Minister of Education

Brotherhood is a part of the total education program of a church. The minister of education, therefore, has a leadership and cooperative role along with the pastor.

The minister of education has a particular role as the educational leader in the church. He relates to Brotherhood work as he does to Sunday School and other church organizations. Working with the Brotherhood Director and pastor, the minister of education assists in enlisting and training leadership, helps Brotherhood to accomplish its educational function, and relates Brotherhood work with other church educational programs.

Other staff members, such as youth director or recreational director, relate to age groups, needs of units, and activities as appropriate to their job assignments.

The Brotherhood Director

Brotherhood leadership begins with the director. He is elected by the church through its nominating committee as are directors of Sunday School, Church Training, and Woman's Missionary Union. He is responsible to the church for his work.

A Brotherhood Director should be elected regardless of the type of work to be started, whether it would be the mission action unit, prayer unit, Royal Ambassador chapter, or other kinds of approaches.

The Brotherhood Director is to lead in providing organization, leadership, and resources to carry out Brotherhood work. Total Brotherhood work includes Crusader and Pioneer Royal Ambassadors and Baptist Men.

The Director:

1. Leads total Brotherhood planning, coordination, and evaluation.
2. Leads in establishing Brotherhood age-division units.
3. Serves as leader of each unit until he secures additional leadership.
4. Works with Brotherhood leadership in discovering mission needs and in discovering and channeling member gifts in ministry.
5. Leads men and boys to participate in mission learning experiences and mission activities in age-division units and churchwide activities.
6. Develops a plan for training Brotherhood workers.
7. Recommends Brotherhood budget, policies, and procedures.
8. Leads in coordinating the selection of mission areas to be taught and the ordering of Brotherhood curriculum materials and supplies.
9. Reports the progress of Brotherhood work to the church and church council regularly, working with the Brotherhood secretary.
10. Leads in implementing special projects of the church as assigned and in helping members to understand the work of the church and denomination.
11. Works with WMU director in planning and conducting churchwide projects such as graded series mission studies, weeks of prayer, mission offerings, mission action.
12. Leads church to participate in World Mission Conferences as they are planned by the association.

13. Serves on the Search Group for Lay Renewal.

14. Represents Brotherhood on the church council.

In summary, the Brotherhood director performs his duties in four areas, planning, delegating, coordinating, and evaluating.

The Brotherhood Secretary

The Brotherhood secretary is a general Brotherhood officer, along with the director, pastor, and minister of education. He should be selected through the church nominating committee process, with the director taking the lead role in his selection.

The secretary's role is important in maintaining and coordinating the records and reports of all units and groups.

1. Maintains the master membership role in the church office.

2. Works with each of the units in maintaining correct membership records.

3. Prepares monthly reports to the church and annual reports for the Uniform Church Letter to the association.

4. Keeps minutes and records of the Brotherhood Council meetings.

5. Orders or coordinates the ordering of resources and materials for Brotherhood work.

The Brotherhood Council

The Brotherhood Council is the moving force of Brotherhood leadership. It brings together the strategists for mission planning, coordinating, and evaluating.

Brotherhood Council membership usually includes the Brotherhood Director, Brotherhood secretary, Baptist Men's presidents, Royal Ambassador Director, the pastor, and minister of education.

' Other Baptist Men officers, Royal Ambassador committeemen and counselors may attend meetings if a coordinated planning session is followed or if business is related to their area of work.

The Brotherhood Council usually meets quarterly with the Brotherhood Director serving as chairman. The Brotherhood secretary serves as secretary of the council.

Baptist Men's Work

Baptist Men is a fellowship of men, members of the church, eighteen years of age and older, who are organized to involve men in mission learning experiences, witnessing and ministering, and missions support.

Officers and Duties

The officers' duties are:

President

1. Initiates and coordinates planning committee meetings.

2. Presides at Baptist Men's meetings.

3. Assigns responsibility to the officers.

4. Directs training of the officers.

5. Represents unit on Brotherhood Council.

6. Presents needs of unit to Brotherhood Director.

7. Communicates information on denominational programs.

8. Authorizes budgeted funds.

9. Serves on the church council to represent Brotherhood work when a Brotherhood Director has not been elected or when the Royal Ambassador Director is not designated as representative.

Vice-President
1. Serves on Planning Committee
2. Builds attendance
3. Increases enrollment
4. Publicizes meetings
5. Promotes fellowship
6. Presides in absence of president

Secretary
1. Serves on Planning Committee
2. Keeps accurate records
3. Reports records and minutes
4. Checks attendance at unit meetings
5. Compiles and makes reports
6. Prepares and maintains accurate mailing list
7. Participates in planning committee meetings
8. Orders *World Mission Journal, Baptist Men's Handbook* (for officers), and *Brotherhood Builder*
9. Handles miscellaneous funds

Mission Study Leader
1. Serves on Planning Committee
2. Helps plan unit meeting agenda
3. Leads in presenting the mission study (program) at unit meetings
4. Provides other opportunities for mission study, such as World Missions Conferences
5. Reports participation of men in mission study to secretary
6. Organizes mission study groups requiring service of Mission Study Group Leader
7. Encourages individual mission study

Mission Activity Leader
1. Serves on Planning Committee
2. Assists in conducting survey for mission action needs
3. Organizes for ongoing mission action and forms mission action and mission support groups
    (1) Consider the interest and abilities of men
    (2) Enlist individuals
    (3) Select mission action group leaders, mission support leaders, and project leaders
4. Coordinates ongoing mission action groups
5. Plans and coordinates mission projects
6. Reports participation of men to secretary
7. Reports progress of mission action groups at unit meeting
8. Leads men to support missions through prayer activities
9. Leads men to support missions through giving activities
10. Directs special projects assigned by the church.

Royal Ambassador Work

Royal Ambassadors is a missions program for boys in grades 1-12. Royal Ambassadors has two age-graded divisions:

Crusaders for boys in grades 1-6

Pioneers for boys in grades 7-12

Royal Ambassadors seeks to carry out its purposes by working with boys through chapter meetings, advancement, mission activities, meaningful relationships, and interest activities.

Royal Ambassadors capitalizes on what boys enjoy doing and contributes to their spiritual, physical, mental, and social growth.

Officers and Duties

The Royal Ambassador Director's duties are:

1. Works with the Brotherhood Director and the church nominating committee to enlist committee members and have them elected by the church

2. Makes assignments to committee members

3. Orients the committee concerning Royal Ambassador work and their committee duties

4. Works with committee in the selection and enlistment of counselors

5. Calls monthly meeting of the committee and plans meeting agendas

6. Serves on the Brotherhood Council and reports to the council and church on Royal Ambassador work

7. Serves on the church council to represent Brotherhood work when a Brotherhood Director has not been elected or when the Baptist Men's president is not designated as representative

The Royal Ambassador Committee's duties are:

1. Learn the requirements for the task

2. Provide opportunity for all interested boys in the church and community to be Royal Ambassadors

3. Enlist counselors

4. Train counselors

5. Assist in planning total Royal Ambassador program in the church

6. Provide direct assistance to the counselors for regular chapter meetings, as needed

7. Assist with outdoor and other activities

8. Keep the church informed about Royal Ambassadors

The Counselor's duties are:

1. Trains for his job

2. Handles chapter detail, such as chapter record book, reports, physical room arrangements, contact with boys

3. Develops chapter organization

4. Leads in planning chapter meetings and events from the standpoint of yearly plans, weekly meetings, and boys' participation

5. Works with individual boys in advancement, and in personal and spiritual growth

6. Meets with Royal Ambassador Committee for planning, as necessary

Woman's Missionary Union

Definition:

A church organization for women, girls, and preschool children devoted to teaching, promoting, and supporting missions.[9]

Purpose and scope of work:

The major purpose of this church program organization is to lead persons to explore with growing understanding the nature, implications, and evidences of God's missionary purpose, and to respond in personal commitment and active participation.

Personal witnessing, participation in mission projects, and support of missionary efforts through prayer, study, and contributions are activities usually associated with this group.

Age-graded leadership and study materials often are used to provide guidance for groups of members ranging from older preschoolers through adults.

Key Resources:

Martin, Mickey. *Woman's Missionary Union Manual (Birmingham: Woman's Missionary Union, 1981).*

Sorrill, Bobbie. *WMU—A Church Missions Organization* (Birmingham: Woman's Missionary Union, SBC, 1981).

The Organization of Woman's Missionary Union

These principles of organization are considered when Woman's Missionary Union begins in a church, and as it continues to work. Woman's Missionary Union is made up of age-level organizations in four divisions. These are:

• Adult Division for women eighteen through twenty-nine years (Baptist Young Women) and for women thirty years and up (Baptist Women)

• Youth Division (Acteens) for girls twelve (grade 7) through seventeen (or high school graduation)

• Children's Division (Girls in Action) for girls six (or grade 1) through eleven (grade 6)

• Preschool Division (Mission Friends) for boys and girls birth through five years (or school entrance)

Within any of these divisions there may be multiple age-level organizations.

WMU Organization Guidelines

One Officer but No Organization (Pattern 1)

Woman's Missionary Union work in a church can begin with one WMU officer, the WMU director. Her election by the church is considered the beginning point in organizing a WMU. She works with the pastor in developing the WMU organization needed. Sometimes her first responsibility will be to lead the church in churchwide missions projects, such as study of graded series books, weeks of prayer and missions

PATTERN 1. WMU without age-level organizations.

A possible variation in this pattern would be one age-level organization in a church with no WMU director. In such a case, the leader of the organization would be substituted for WMU director.

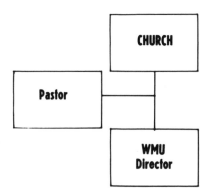

Figure 24a

offerings, until age-level organizations can be started.

A church should consider this kind of beginning for WMU work when there is no WMU organization and if no age division in the church has as many as three prospects; also if age-level organizations seem unwise because of lack of leadership or geographical distribution of members. There might be times when a church is new and small and needs to spend its major resources in building the fellowship and in outreach. This usually is temporary, and the WMU director will know the appropriate time to begin age-level work.

With One Age-level Organization

Woman's Missionary Union may also begin in a church with one age-level organization even when there is no WMU director. In this case, the leader of the age-level organization is responsible directly to the church. In all other ways she will operate from suggestions appropriate for her age-level organization.

The church should be sensitive to the needs for even a small number of prospects to have missions experiences. One foreign missionary tells of growing up in a small church with only one other girl in her age group. One woman began working with them when they were preschoolers. She continued with the two of them throughout their school years. This missionary says, "That's some kind of success! Who else can say that one half of the youth with whom she worked became foreign missionaries?"

Expanding the Organization (Pattern 2)

The organization of Woman's Missionary Union expands when the second WMU

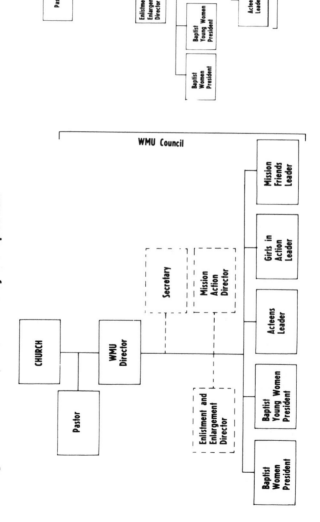

PATTERN 2. WMU with one organization each in one or more age levels

Mission action director, enlistment and enlargement director, and secretary are optional.

WMU Council

CHURCH

Pastor

WMU Director

Enlistment and Enlargement Director

Secretary

Mission Action Director

Baptist Women President

Baptist Young Women President

Acteens Leader

Girls in Action Leader

Mission Friends Leader

Note: Broken line indicates optional officer.

Figure 24b

PATTERN 3. WMU with more than one organization (and with age-level councils) in one or more age levels

WMU Council

CHURCH

Pastor

WMU Director

Secretary

Mission Action Director

Enlistment and Enlargement Director

Baptist Women President

Baptist Young Women President

Acteens Director

Acteens Leader

Acteens Leader

Acteens Council

Girls in Action Director

Girls in Action Leader

Girls in Action Leader

Girls in Action Council

Mission Friends Director

Figure 24c

188

leader is elected by the church. This person is the leader of the age-level organization that is formed. As organizations are begun for other age levels and their leaders elected by the church, these leaders join the WMU council. As needed, WMU officers such as a mission action director, enlistment and enlargement director, or secretary are elected and added to the WMU council. The WMU council, led by the WMU director, is responsible for planning, coordinating, and evaluating WMU work in a church. When there is only one organization in an age level, the organization leader serves on the WMU council. The pastor, or a staff member he appoints, is an ex officio member of the WMU council.

When a church desires to provide age-level missions experiences in addition to churchwide emphases, and when there are enough prospects to form one or more age-level organizations, that church uses organization Pattern 2.

Adding Age-level Directors and Age-level Councils (Pattern 3)

When there are two or more organizations within an age level, an age-level director is added. This is an additional enlargement. An age-level director leads in coordinating the work of organizations within the age level. She serves on the WMU council representing the leaders with whom she works. When an age-level director is added, an age-level council is formed. The members of the age-level council are the age-level director, the age-level leaders (or presidents), assistant leaders, and teachers. The director is chairman.

Age-level directors can be added one at a time as there is need. In age levels where there is only one organization, the leader continues to serve on the WMU council. When age-level directors are added, a WMU probably has need for a mission action director, enlistment and enlargement director, and secretary.

When a church has some age levels with multiple organizations and other age levels with only one organization, the WMU council takes on a different look.

Other WMU officers are added whenever a need is felt for a secretary, a mission action director, and an enlistment and enlargement director. A secretary is usually added when age-level directors are added. Churches choose a large organization pattern when any one or all of these factors are present:

• When there are enough members and prospects to form more than one organization in an age level

• When closer grading of an age level will improve the teaching of missions and involvement in missions

• When circumstances such as interests, home location, and time schedules seem to call for several organizations within an age level.

WMU leaders always should remember that organization will vary from church to church. Some churches have only one officer, the WMU director. In others there will be many officers and leaders. A church determines the kind of organization it needs to do its work well, but a WMU should have only the minimum organization necessary.

Duties of WMU Officers

(These officers make up the WMU council.)

WMU Director

The WMU director is responsible to the church for leading in planning, conducting, and evaluating the work of WMU. She will:

1. Serve on the church council and work with the pastor

2. Lead the WMU council

3. Confer with WMU council members; assist them in their work

4. Work with Brotherhood director in planning and conducting joint work of the two organizations, including churchwide missions projects

5. Interpret the work of the church and denomination to WMU; encourage participation in total work of the church

6. Assist the WMU leadership committee in selecting WMU officers and leaders

7. Report the progress of WMU work to the church regularly.

WMU Mission Action Director

The WMU mission action director is responsible to the WMU director for guiding mission action and direct evangelism efforts of WMU. (If there is no mission action director, the WMU director fulfills these duties.) She will:

1. Serve on the WMU council

2. Lead in discovering total possibilities for mission action and direct evangelism by the church

3. Lead in evaluating and using information about church members' skills and interests which might be used in WMU-related mission action

4. Keep possibilities for mission action and direct evangelism before the church and WMU organizations; provide for organizations an up-to-date list of mission action needs; be a resource person for WMU leaders wanting to help to plan mission action projects or group work

5. Correlate WMU-related activities aimed at the same target groups or issues

6. Continually evaluate the total mission action and direct evangelism work of the church to see that WMU-related activities are making the most significant contribution possible

7. Work with organization leaders to make definite suggestions about work to be accepted by organizations for projects for adult mission action groups

8. Lead the church in churchwide mission action and direct evangelism projects for which WMU has initiative

9. Work with Brotherhood director in beginning joint mission action groups; work with organization leaders in assigning WMU-related joint groups to an organization

10 Work with Brotherhood director to coordinate mission action

11. As requested, assist organizations and groups in developing budget requests related to mission action and direct evangelism

12. Lead in providing mission action and direct evangelism training activities when more than one age level is involved or when training is to be provided for churchwide mission action for which WMU is responsible; encourage and assist age-level, organization, and group leaders in providing mission action and direct evangelism training for their members

13. Be a liaison between WMU and community resources used in mission action.

WMU Enlistment and Enlargement Director

The WMU enlistment and enlargement director is responsible to the WMU director for guiding in enlisting persons in WMU and enlarging the organization of WMU as needed. (If there is no enlistment and enlargement director, the WMU director fulfills these duties.) She will:

1. Serve on the WMU council

2. Lead in conducting an enlistment survey and in discovering prospects in other ways

3. Lead in devising a plan for initial enlistment contact with new church or Sunday School members

4. Provide an up-to-date list of prospects for each age-level organization

5. Lead in conducting enlistment activities involving more than one age level

6. As requested, assist organization and mission group leaders in planning enlistment activities for organizations and groups

7. In annual planning, lead in reviewing organizational patterns to determine the need for new age-level organizations; review needs throughout the year

8. Assist in beginning new age-level organizations as needed

9. As requested, assist adult organizations in determining need for additional study and prayer groups.

WMU Secretary

The WMU secretary is responsible to the WMU director for keeping records. (If there is no secretary, the WMU director fulfills these duties.) She will:

1. Serve as secretary of the WMU council

2. Keep accurate records of work

3. Assist with financial records according to church plan

4. Order WMU magazines for all age levels and WMU council; keep subscription lists up-to-date.

Age-Level Directors

(Baptist Women director, Baptist Young Women director, Acteens director, Girls in Action director, Mission Friends director)

The age-level director is responsible to the WMU director for coordinating the work of organizations within the age level. She will:

1. Serve on the WMU council

2. Lead the age-level council

3. Confer with organization leaders; assist them in planning, conducting, and evaluating their work

4. Interpret the work of the church and denomination to organization leaders; encourage participation in total work of church

5. Assist in selecting organization leaders (presidents of Baptist Women and Baptist Young Women, leaders of Acteens, leaders and assistant leaders of Girls in Action, leaders and teachers of Mission Friends)

6. Work with persons in other church programs to coordinate the church's work in that age level

7. Report progress of age-level work to WMU director regularly.

Duties of WMU Leaders

These leaders (except assistant GA leader and Mission Friends teacher) serve on the WMU council if there is only one organization in the age level. If there are two or more organizations in an age level, they serve on the respective age-level council.

Baptist Women or Baptist Young Women President

The Baptist Women or Baptist Young Women president is responsible to the Baptist Women or Baptist Young Women director (or to the WMU director, if there is no Baptist Women or Baptist Young Women director) for leading in planning, conducting, and evaluating the work of a Baptist Women or Baptist Young Women organization. She will:

1. Serve on the Baptist Women or Baptist Young Women council (or on the WMU council, if there is no Baptist Women or Baptist Young Women council)
2. Lead the officers council
3. Confer with the other officers; assist them in their work
4. Preside at organization meetings
5. Interpret the work of the church and denomination to officers and members; encourage participation in total work of the church
6. Report progress of organization to Baptist Women or Baptist Young Women director (or to WMU director, if there is no Baptist Women or Baptist Young Women director) regularly
7. If there is no Baptist Women or Baptist Young Women director, work with persons in other church programs to coordinate the church's work in the adult division.

Acteens Leader

The Acteens leader is responsible to the Acteens director (or to the WMU director, if there is no Acteens director) for leading in planning, conducting, and evaluating the work of an Acteens organization. She will:

1. Serve on the Acteens council (or on the WMU council, if there is no Acteens council)
2. Participate in WMU annual planning
3. Guide the organization in planning, conducting, and evaluating its work; share leadership with officers to extent of their maturity
4. Plan with organization officers; assist them in their work
5. Interpret the work of the church and denomination to officers and members; encourage participation in total work of the church
6. Plan for training of officers and members
7. Plan ways to enlist prospects and contact absentees
8. Visit in the homes of members
9. Keep records of organization work, including budget
10. Report progress of organization work to the Acteens director (or to the WMU director, if there is no Acteens director)
11. Work with the Acteens council, or WMU council in securing literature and supplies and in securing and maintaining furnishings and equipment
12. If there is no Acteens director, work with persons in other church programs to coordinate the church's work with youth.

Girls in Action Leader

The Girls in Action leader is responsible to the Girls in Action director (or to the WMU director, if there is no Girls in Action director) for leading in planning, conducting, and evaluating the work of a Girls in Action organization. She will:

1. Serve on the Girls in Action council (or on the WMU council, if there is no GA council)
2. Participate in WMU annual planning and lead assistant leader(s) in annual and regular planning
3. Work with assistant leaders to develop a specific list of duties for each assistant leader
4. Interpret the work of the church and denomination to members; encourage participation in total work of the church in ways appropriate to the age group

5. Plan for training of members

6. Plan ways to enlist prospects and contact absentees

7. Visit in the homes of members

8. At organization meetings, lead one or more small-group activities and the large-group activity

9. Keep records of organization work, including budget

10. Report progress of organization work to Girls in Action director (or to WMU director, if there is no GA director)

11. Work with Girls in Action council (or WMU council) in securing literature and supplies and in securing and maintaining furnishings and equipment

12. If there is no Girls in Action director, work with persons in other church programs to coordinate the church's work in the children's division.

Girls in Action Assistant Leader

The Assistant GA leader is responsible to the GA leader for helping to lead the organization. By agreement with the leader, she may assume some or all of the duties listed below. (If there is more than one assistant leader, divide the duties; if there are no assistant leaders, the leader fulfills these responsibilities also.) She will:

1. Participate in WMU annual planning and in regular planning

2. Assist in training members

3. Assume responsibility for contacting some prospects and absentees

4. Assume responsibility for visiting in homes of a portion of the members

5. At organization meetings, lead some of the small-group activities and help with the large-group activities as needed

6. Assume responsibility for particular missions projects appropriate to the age group

7. Keep records of work

8. Assume other duties as assigned

9. Serve on the Girls in Action council, if assistant leaders are to be included in the council.

Mission Friends Leader

The Mission Friends leader is responsible to the Mission Friends director (or to the WMU director, if there is no Mission Friends director) for leading in planning, conducting, and evaluating the work of a Mission Friends organization. She will:

1. Serve on the Mission Friends council (or on the WMU council, if there is no Mission Friends council)

2. Participate in WMU annual planning and lead teachers in annual and regular planning

3. Work with teachers to develop a specific list of duties for each teacher

4. Plan ways to enlist prospects and contact absentees

5. Visit in the homes of members

6. At organization meetings, lead small-group activities and the large-group activity, if there is one

7. Report progress of organization work to Mission Friends director (or to WMU director, if there is no Mission Friends director)

8. Work with Mission Friends council (or WMU council) to secure literature and supplies and to secure and maintain furnishings and equipment

9. If there is no Mission Friends director, work with persons in other church pro-

Churchwide Missions Projects
Coordination of WMU-Brotherhood Joint Action

Essential Actions	WMU/Brotherhood Age-level Organizations	WMU/Brotherhood Councils or WMU and Brotherhood Directors as Representatives of Councils	Church Council
1. Suggest churchwide projects (on an annual basis)	Suggest projects for year	Suggest projects and assignment of overall initiative for each project during the year	
2. Approve projects and assignment of overall initiative for each			Approve projects to be conducted and assignment of initiative for each project. Add additional projects and make other suggestions if desired
3. Suggest work to be done in conducting a project and the assignment of responsibility (to be completed nearer time when project is to be conducted)		Suggest work to be done and assignment of responsibility to WMU and/or Brotherhood	
4. Approve work to be done and assignment of responsibility			Approve work to be done and assignment of responsibility
5. Make work assignments		Assign work to be done to officers, council, and age-level organizations	(Some assignments may be made to church council members such as Sunday School director, Church Training director)
6. Make detailed plans (with review as necessary)	Make detailed plans for work as assigned	Make detailed plans for work as assigned	
7. Conduct activity	Conduct activity	Conduct activity	
8. Evaluate work	Evaluate work completed by age-level organization	Evaluate work completed by the organization	Evaluate total project

Figure 25

194

grams to coordinate the church's work with preschoolers.

Mission Friends Teacher

The Mission Friends teacher is responsible to the Mission Friends leader for helping to lead the organization. By agreement with the leader she may assume some or all of these duties (if there is more than one teacher, divide the duties). She will:

1. Participate in WMU annual and regular planning

2. Assume responsibility for contacting some prospects

3. Assume responsibility for visiting in the homes of some of the members and absentees

4. Plan and lead in some of the small-group activities at organization meetings

5. Assume responsibility for particular missions projects appropriate to the age group

6. Keep records of work

7. Assume other duties as assigned

8. Serve on the Mission Friends council, if teachers are to be included on the council.

Notes

1. This is an assumption that frequently exists only as an ideal. Church leaders are prone to become positioned as either job- or person-oriented. This author views the ideal as workable and practical in churches in which evaluation and adjustment are normal parts of educational administration.

2. Information in this section is drawn from Reginald M. McDonough, *A Church on Mission* (Nashville: Convention Press, 1980).

3. For more specific information and guidance related to a program or organization, check materials listed in the bibliography, or consult your denominational office, bookstore, or publisher for recommended resources.

4. This material is reprinted from Bernard M. Spooner, "How to Enlist and Encourage Workers," *How to Improve Bible Teaching and Learning in Sunday School,* comps. Ernest R. Adams and Mavis Allen, pp. 85-89. © Copyright 1976 Convention Press. All rights reserved. Used by permission.

5. This material is reprinted from *Developing Your Church Training Program,* comps. Philip B. Harris and Lloyd T. Householder, pp. 24-33. © Copyright 1977 Convention Press. All rights reserved. Used by permission.

6. This material is reprinted from Henry F. Campbell, Jr., "Planning for Effective Training," Ibid., pp. 47-49.

7. All material in this section is from *Building an Effective Music Ministry,* comp. William J. Reynolds; © Copyright 1980 Convention Press; all rights reserved; used by permission; or from *Music Ministry Plan Book;* © Copyright 1980 Convention Press; all rights reserved; used by permission.

8. All material in this section is from Wendell Belew, *The Purpose and Plan of Baptist Brotherhood* © Copyright 1979 Brotherhood Commission. Used by permission.

9. All material in this section is from Carolyn Weatherford and Bobbie Sorrill, *Woman's Missionary Union Work in a Church,* rev. ed. (Birmingham: Woman's Missionary Union, n.d.).

7
Administering Educational Support Services
Charles A. Tidwell

Administration is enabling persons to become the persons they are capable of becoming and to do what they are capable of doing, by God's grace. There are certain support services which are vital to the optimum process of helping persons to become and to do what they are capable of becoming and doing. Among these support services in a church are the media center or library, the curriculum materials and supplies, records and reports, budgeting and purchasing, equipment and facilities, and office support. Administering these support services includes having the right things in the right places at the right time in the right quantities, ready for appropriate use. That is what this chapter is about.

Media Center/Library

The media center/library of a church should be designed to involve media in the life of the members and in the work of the church's programs. The task of the media services is to "educate persons in the use of media and provide media and media services to support the church in the achievement of its mission."[1]

Organization and Leaders

How does a church proceed to provide adequate media services? Begin with the enlistment of some carefully selected people who will train and work diligently at the task. For full details related to the media center/library, begin with a careful study of a manual such as *How to Administer and Promote a Church Media Center,* compiled by Jacqulyn Anderson. This good book, which can be studied individually or in groups, can get you properly started on the way to having an effective media center/library. Many of the suggestions which follow are from this source.

Decide how many workers you will need to provide the services you want. There should be a minimum of three persons in even the

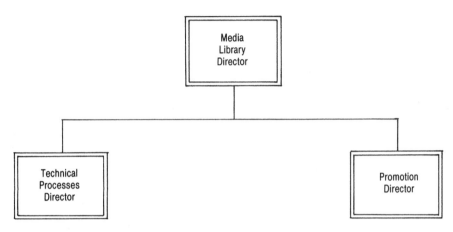

Figure 1

very small, beginning media center. A guideline in determining the number of staff members is to have a minimum of three persons, plus one additional staff member for every 250 resident church members. For example, a church with five hundred resident members would need at least five persons on the media center staff.

In a church with only three on the media center staff, there should be a media center director, a technical processes director, and a promotion director, as shown in Figure 1.

The success of the media center operation and ministry is often determined by the person elected to serve as director. This director becomes for many the embodiment of the media center. His major functions are to put other people to work, coordinate their activities, and represent the media center to other leaders and to the congregation. The director is responsible to the congregation. In churches where there is a paid director, he may be responsible to the minister of education, or to another designated person. The primary responsibilities of the media center director are as follows:

1. Supervise and make assignments to staff members.
2. Recruit new staff members, following church policy.
3. Plan and conduct a training program for the staff.
4. Plan for and preside over staff meetings.
5. Represent the media center officially in all areas of church life:
   a. Meet with the church council.
   b. Enlist media center staff members through the church nominating committee.
   c. Prepare and submit media center budget request to church stewardship committee.
   d. Make regular reports to the church.
   e. Interpret the media center ministry to church membership.
   f. Work with the church building committee in improving or enlarging media center space and furnishings.
6. Be responsible for the selection of all material.
7. Coordinate the weeding of all media.
8. Coordinate the rental of audiovisual materials.
9. Administer media center finances according to church policy:
   a. Purchase media center materials, equipment, and supplies.
   b. Handle all other finances according to policy.
10. Coordinate preparation and distribution of mediagraphies.[2]

The technical processes director has an important job in the media center. Processing media includes all operations necessary for preparing media for circulation. The technical processes director needs to become skilled in the technical areas and diligent in their completion. Often the work load is heavy, and the technical processes director needs to expedite his work as efficiently as possible.

The technical processes director will be responsible for these activities:

1. Prepare new materials for circulation:
   a. Classify and catalog all materials
   b. Type
      (1) Accession records
      (2) Pockets and cards (books)
      (3) Booking cards (audiovisuals)
      (4) Book plates
      (5) Gift recognitions for other media
      (6) Catalog cards
      (7) Labels
   c. Routine steps
      (1) Open books properly
      (2) Check for defects
      (3) Clean soiled books and audiovisuals
      (4) Stamp (books, periodicals, vertical file items, manuals)

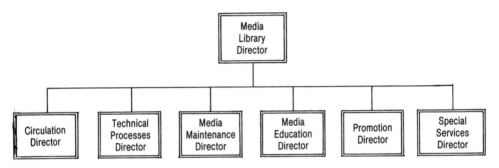

Figure 2

     (5) Paste
     (6) Affix book jackets
     (7) Premend paperback books
   d. File
     (1) Catalog cards
     (2) Shelf cards (books)
     (3) Booking cards (audiovisuals)
 2. Process and file vertical file items.
 3. Process and store miscellaneous media.
 4. Keep inventory of supplies.[3]

A media center/library with a staff of seven workers might be organized according to the chart in Figure 2. With twenty-one or more persons on staff, the media center/library organization chart might look like the one in Figure 3.[4] Notice on this largest chart that some are directors; some are specialists; and some are librarians. Suggested job responsibilities for all of these positions are found in Jacqulyn Anderson's book, mentioned earlier in this chapter.

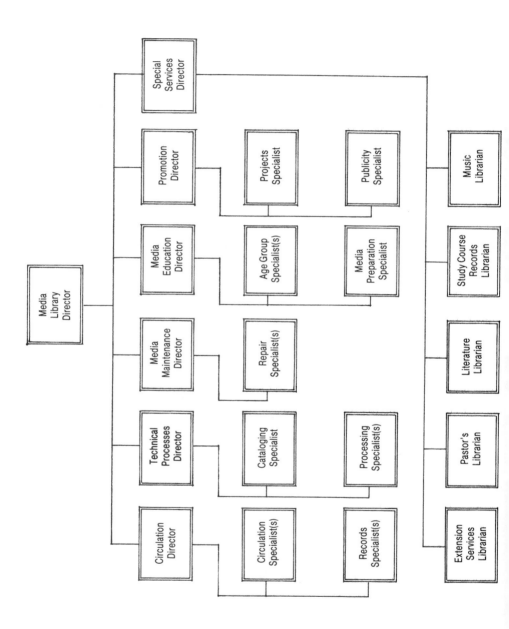

Figure 3

Media center staffers should be Christians and members of the church in which they are serving. They need time available to complete the assignments they accept. They must be willing to train, and to do their work properly. They must be responsible, dependable, patient, tactful, discreet, and willing to change for the better. They are unique in having the opportunity of working with all age groups and all organizations in the church. This work provides a challenge in its potential to change and develop persons in the church in every aspect of their lives.

The media center/library staff must work together. When the directors on the staff meet, they form the media center/library council. They need to meet regularly to plan routine and special activities related to the media center/library. At least one monthly meeting is recommended for the council to analyze the work and to make plans for improving or expanding services. The entire staff (in instances in which there are more than directors on the staff) should meet at least quarterly. The media center director should plan these meetings and preside over them. The following outline from the Anderson book may serve as a guide in determining staff meeting activities:

1. Have a brief devotional period.
2. Make reports on work accomplished and special assignments.
3. Evaluate work and special projects:
   a. Discuss progress toward goals.
   b. Discuss problems and shortcomings, if any.
   c. Discuss ways activities could be improved in the future.
4. Consider special needs involving such areas as space, furniture, budget, or policies.
5. Plan promotional activites, new services, and special projects.
6. Review new media or demonstrate the operation of new equipment.
7. Teach a lesson in this series or a chapter in another media center training resource.[5]

In order for the media center/library to be most effective, *The Church Media Center Record and Plan Book* should be used throughout the year. It gives suggestions for planning, plus important dates to help in planning. Circulation and financial records from the previous year can help to focus on areas where planning is needed.

A significant feature of this book also is the inclusion each year of the Church Media Center Achievement Guide. The guide may be used by churches of all sizes in evaluating their past and present services and in planning for the future.

The guide is organized into nine specific areas of achievement: program foundations, program, relationships, organization, leaders and users, physical resources, finances, planning and evaluation, and records and reports. Within each of these areas there are actions or achievements to be completed by the media center staff.

Guidelines

An effective media center/library needs guidelines for its operation. It needs to have rules, hours of service, and records and reports to help assure that the best service is rendered.

Rules or procedures for the media center/library should be drawn up by the media center staff and presented to the church in business meeting for approval. When approved, these rules become the action of the church rather than that of a few people on the staff. Rules are needed in areas like the schedule for the media center use, who may use the center, the length of loans, the number of items to be borrowed, fines for overdue materials, responsibility for lost or damaged materials, and authorization for circulation.

Media center/library hours should be determined by the staff and approved by the church in business meeting. The hours must reflect the needs and desires of the church family and not just the convenience of the media center staff. Most centers operate in connection with the major activities of the church by being open at least thirty minutes prior to each activity and for a short time after services and certain meetings. Sunday morning, Sunday evening, Wednesday afternoon or evening, other weekdays, and during special emphases are times when the media center might be needed to serve the church. It is vital that announced hours for the center be maintained. It hurts the ministry tremendously for the center not to be open at times when it is scheduled to be open.

Certain records should be kept and used to show the progress and ministry of the media center. Circulation records give the best picture of the actual use of the media center. *The Church Media Center Record and Plan Book* provides space for these records for the entire year.

At least limited financial records should be kept, such as fines, special gifts, and budgeted amounts. The media center director should verify expenditures related to the center. The church treasurer or financial secretary should keep the director informed concerning the balance in the media center account.

Other records may be kept, such as the hours the center is open during a given period, special events and gifts, the number of new users, and other indicators of the center's ministry. The chart in Figure 4 illustrates how these records might be presented to the church.

Circulation of media involves checking out and checking in, counting and recording the circulation. Procedures differ according to the type of media being circulated. All persons who work at the circulation desk need to know the procedures for circulating each type of media. Media center staff should make users feel that they consider it a privilege to serve the users, and not a chore.

Certain supplies should be acquired before the center begins circulation. Among the essential supplies are a media center ownership stamp, a stamp pad, a charging box or tray, blank guides for the charging system, a band dater, overdue reminder cards, scheduling sheets, and membership cards.

Many other facets need to be managed well in order to have adequate service via the media center/library. Procedures for circulating audiovisuals, both for use within and without the church building, need to be established and followed. Reservation procedures need to be developed, both for books and for audiovisuals. Overdue notices via card, telephone, or visit must be given. Regular work periods for accessioning new materials and for mending are essential. Adequate space and furnishings are needed. Gifts must be recorded and acknowledged, and recognized suitably. Good public relations must be maintained. Inventories are needed. The media center/library must be promoted. This support service is essential for the best success of a church's ministries.

Curriculum Materials

Curriculum materials are as vital to the life and growth of the members of a church's educational ministries as food is to the human body. Just as certainly as you are what you eat, it is true that your study materials determine your intellectual, and to some extent, your spiritual growth and development. It is of critical importance that the leaders of a church's educational organizations and other units choose the right curriculum materials.

Selecting Curriculum Materials

There should be a known procedure in a church for selecting and

Quarterly Media Library Report

Quarter ending _____, 19___

	Month of ____	TOTALS	Month of ____	TOTALS	Month of ____	TOTALS	Quarter TOTALS
HOURS							
Total hours open							
CIRCULATION							
Books circulated							
Filmstrips, slides, recordings, tapes, and cassette tapes circulated							
Other Audiovisual materials circulated							
Audiovisual equipment circulated							
Vertical file items circulated							
Periodicals circulated							
Total materials circulated							
MATERIALS							
Books added							
Books lost or withdrawn							
Total books							
Filmstrips, slides, recordings, tapes, and cassette tapes added							
Filmstrips, slides, recordings, tapes, and cassette tapes withdrawn							
Total filmstrips, slides, recordings, tapes, and cassette tapes							
Other visual materials added							
Other visual materials withdrawn							
Total other materials							
Audiovisual equipment added							
Total audiovisual equipment							
Total materials							
FINANCES							
Cost of supplies							
Cost of materials							
Total costs							
Special gifts							
Fines							
Budget receipts							
Total income							

Figure 4

204

Curriculum Selection Checklist

Use this checklist to compare lines of curriculum you might consider for use with a given age group. Secure samples of each line you wish to consider. Examine the materials carefully. Check each item on the list below. Indicate by _✓_ which line is best on each factor. Compare the basic pieces of each line: the pupil's material; the teacher's material. Choose and use the curriculum that best meets your needs.

Factor to Consider	Curriculum Lines		
	A	B	C
1. There is ample, appropriate use of the Bible.	___	___	___
2. The teachings are doctrinally sound.	___	___	___
3. Doctrinal emphases are balanced.	___	___	___
4. Coverage of the Bible is comprehensive.	___	___	___
5. The educational philosophy is valid.	___	___	___
6. Concepts presented are suited to the age group.	___	___	___
7. Content addresses life needs appropriately.	___	___	___
8. Teachings encourage appropriate responses.	___	___	___
9. Methodology is properly related to content.	___	___	___
10. Methods are suited to our workers' skills.	___	___	___
11. Training materials are available to develop worker's skills.	___	___	___
12. Learning activities are right for the age group.	___	___	___
13. The materials support the church program.	___	___	___
14. Materials advance purposes of this organization.	___	___	___
15. Quality teaching/learning aids are readily available.	___	___	___
16. Supplementary commentaries are available.	___	___	___
17. Art use is in good taste.	___	___	___
18. The layout is attractive to the user.	___	___	___
19. The binding is sufficiently durable.	___	___	___
20. The paper quality is adequate.	___	___	___
21. The print size is right.	___	___	___
22. The print is clear and easy to read.	___	___	___
23. Uses of color in materials is attractive.	___	___	___
24. Service for ordering, receiving, paying is good.	___	___	___
25. Consultation in use of materials is available.	___	___	___
26. Volume (number of pages) in each piece is adequate.	___	___	___
27. The cost in relation to the benefits is suitable.	___	___	___
28. The cost per comparable items is least.	___	___	___
29. _____	___	___	___
(Other factor we consider important)			
30. _____	___	___	___
(Other factor we consider important)			

Based upon this comparison, curriculum line _____ seems best for us. It is available at the following address:

_____

_____

_____

Figure 5

approving curriculum materials. A church has the responsibility and the right to determine what its members will study under the sponsorship of the church or in the name of the church.

A church might delegate the responsibility for selecting curriculum materials to the church council. It would be wise for the council to recommend the curriculum line or lines for the church to approve. Then in case of need to consider variations from the church-approved lines, the parties advocating a change could present their suggestions to the church council.

Such a procedure might assume that the leaders in a given organization represented on the church council had already approved the variation. Then the church council could determine whether to advise that the church approve or not approve the variation. In this manner the church could exercise control and guidance that are essential to the best interests of the church as a whole.

Use the Curriculum Selection Checklist, Figure 5, to help in the selection of the curriculum line most suited to the needs of the particular organization you have in mind.

The provision for literature should be made via the church budget. In anticipating costs, be sure to allow for current enrollment, new members, special outreach and ministry projects, and new items that might be produced during the year.

Ordering, Securing, and Distributing Curriculum Materials

Curriculum publishers usually provide order forms and information bulletins for their materials. For example, The Sunday School Board of the Southern Baptist Convention sends the "Church Literature Order Form," the "Undated Materials Order Form," and "The Mailbag" to churches each quarter.[6] The order forms provide a complete listing of all items available. New materials and special emphases are highlighted for ease in ordering. A news bulletin, "The Mailbag," includes: announcement of new items; features concerning existing literature; special order blanks; and instructions on ordering.

To get best results in ordering materials, consider these tips:

—Study information bulletins, catalogs, and order forms prior to ordering.

—Order early. This should be done at least six to seven weeks before you need the materials.

—Appoint one person to handle all your orders.

—Establish a permanent mailing address to which all materials will come.

—If a regular order form is provided, use it to speed processing.

—Be accurate and complete in filling out the order form.

—Order adequately but not excessively. For example, order one pupil's book for each pupil enrolled, each teacher, and some for new members. One teacher's book should be ordered for each elected regular and substitute teacher. Order only one resource kit for each class.

—Open and check packages upon arrival. Allow time for any "stray" packages to arrive. Report discrepancies immediately.

It would be helpful to have and to follow a *literature handling schedule,* such as the one in Figure 6. Modify it as needed to suit your church situation.

Media center/library personnel can be very helpful in the proper distribution of curriculum materials. Plan together with their staff to make sure the materials are placed where they will be used. This is especially true of materials which serve across organizational lines, such as materials for the family. Any material which is not used before obsolescence, especially the dated materials, is doubly expensive—it costs the initial price, plus the loss of the value from its use! Churches cannot afford such losses.

Records and Reports

It is important in the church's educational work that leaders and members keep informed regarding the progress of the various units in the organized effort. Each group, class, department, division, and entire organization should keep records of its activities, and report regularly to the next larger unit. All organizations (Sunday School, Church Training, Music Ministry, Woman's Missionary Union, Brotherhood, Pastoral Ministries, media center/library, recreation, and any others) should report regularly to the church. This latter report usually comes in the monthly or quarterly church business meeting, and a summary report at the church's annual business meeting.

Records

General organization leaders, as in Sunday School, should study their organization to determine what information they and others would need in order to keep informed and to give adequate guidance to the work of the organization. In most instances there is some history to consider regarding records. Certain items of information have been

Literature Handling Schedule

1. Plan with Church Leaders

    Study "Mailbag," *Church Materials Catalog,* and other materials pertaining to changes in literature and circulate to church leaders.

    Review with church and/or organization leaders the literature to be ordered.

2. Collect information from Teachers and Leaders

    Fill out all items on literature requisition form except "Quantity" and "Special Instructions."

    Distribute literature requisition forms. Give to organization directors or directly to each leader—leaders in Sunday School, Church Training, Music Ministry, Media Center, Recreation, and mission organizations, as well as the pastor and other church staff members. Call or see all leaders who have not returned the forms. All forms should be collected before beginning to tabulate the main order.

3. Prepare order

    (1) Transfer the requests onto the literature order form. Remember that a monthly or weekly publication is ordered only one time per quarter.

    (2) Multiply the number of each title ordered by the price, and enter the amount in the space provided.

    (3) Total the amount, using an adding machine if available. Check several times or have someone else check your multiplication and addition.

    (4) Subtract any allowable discount, if remittance is enclosed, and enter total. Add sales tax if applicable.

    (5) File church's copy of order form.

    (6) Check address label attached to literature order form.

    (7) Enter customer account number on every order.

4. Mail the Order

    Request check from church treasurer. Enclose check and order in return envelope. Check return address. Mail order. To assure having your material on time, have your order completed and in the mail by the date suggested on the order form. For rush orders, indicate the required date. The materials services department will determine the method of shipment and bill the buyer for shipping charges.

5. Verify the Shipment

    Open packages immediately upon arrival and check against your copy of the order. Keep notes on discrepancies or damage, and notify the publisher. Allow time for "stray" packages to arrive.

    Store literature until time to begin distribution.

6. Distribute the Literature

Each Quarter

Write names of teachers and leaders on their materials to expedite distribution and the return of lost items. Insert mediography (list) of supporting Media Center materials.

Distribute leadership materials to teachers and leaders either directly or through organizational directors. Distribute member materials to classes and/or departments. Suggest to teachers and leaders that members write their names on their materials.

Each Month

Distribute the monthly reading pieces on the first Sunday of each month, and the monthly leadership pieces for the *coming* month on the third Sunday.

Each Sunday

Distribute the weekly reading pieces.

Other Times

Distribute materials for groups which do not meet on Sunday such as deacons, missionary organizations, and persons engaged in outreach projects.

Figure 6

Literature Requisition Form (Sample)

(This form will also be used to guide in distribution)

Return to
Literature Librarian
(Literature Orderer)

Name_____ Organization_____ by _____

(teacher, leader, director, or church officer)

date

Grade_____ Age Group_____ Room No._____

(class, dept., or office)

Quarter _____   _____   _____   _____

Oct.-Dec.   Jan.-March   April-June   July- Sept.

Item Number	Title	Current Quarter	This Quarter Last Year	Quantity Needed

SPECIAL INSTRUCTIONS (distribution of leadership materials, etc.)

_____   _____

_____   _____

_____   _____

Signed (Organizational Leader) Date

Figure 7

found helpful to leaders in prior times. Systems have already been established which have generated record-keeping materials others have found to be adequate.

A study of the denominational suppliers' catalogs would be a good way to discover what systems and supply items have already been devised. For example, each year's *Baptist Book Store Catalog* lists systems, revised systems, and alternate systems of records, forms, books, binders, folders, and other supply items you need not reinvent. These probably could meet the needs in your church.

Some have found it feasible to use computer systems to serve the records needs in a church. Individuals and companies are in business to assist churches with their uses of computer records not only in the educational records, but also in the financial records and the general church membership records. Many benefits are possible to churches wishing to use a computer service to assist in their records, and in their reports as well. A report to the church for the monthly business meeting, for instance, which would take a secretarial worker hours and hours to prepare for copying, can be printed out of a computer in a very few minutes, ready for duplication and distribution to church members.

Once leaders select an appropriate record system and secure the essential supplies for its operation, there should be scheduled periodic training sessions to assure proper use of the system. An annual training session for those who "do" the records can be a great help in getting accurate and complete information needed to make the system fulfill its purposes. For example, in Sunday School such training sessions could be useful for group leaders, class secretaries, department secretaries, division secretaries, the general secretary of Sunday School, and classification officers (those who receive guests, get information from them, and help them find the appropriate group according to the church's grouping and grading plan).

The important point about records is to find out what you need to know about what is occurring, so that action which might be indicated by the records can be taken in time to meet the need.

A secondary but important point about records is their historical value. Those who need to can look at the records over a period of years and see trends and needs which inform them in their leadership roles. In a study of small businesses which failed, a major cause of their failure was shown to be inadequate records. The leaders didn't know what they had in inventory, who owed them money, and other vital facts. They were not informed enough to give successful leadership to their businesses. The church's enterprises in education should be operated on the basis of good information. Good records are essential.

Reports

Each unit in an organization should report essential information to the leaders of the next larger unit of which it is a part. General leaders of a church organization need accurate and complete information about the effectiveness of the major units within the organization. Report forms which summarize the key items of information can serve this need well. Individuals in designated places of responsibility within each unit should supply the requested information via such summary forms.

It is important that the general organizations of the church periodically report to the church. In some churches the time to report is in a monthly church business meeting. Other churches call for such reports in a quarterly business meeting. An annual summary report should be submitted to the church, and often this comes in a church meeting designated as the annual business meeting.

Some churches are experiencing good results and increased interest in the public reports (such as those given in a church business meeting) which are given in terms of actions and activities accomplished instead of the traditional and usually dull list of figures. The figures for enrollment, attendance, and other statistical data are vital, but often not interesting when given apart from some account of events, actions, activities, and ministries accomplished.

Accurate and lively presentations, possibly media-assisted, of ministries performed for specific persons bring real interest for the members receiving the reports. Even the addition of the report of expenditures required for the ministries becomes more attractive when presented in terms of ministries to persons. This concept fits the idea of "ministry-action budgeting" which is described later in this chapter.

The church's publications should carry certain features by way of report. A weekly church paper, an organization's weekly report summary at the midweek meetings, and highlights given orally in meetings of the congregation can be very useful as part of the process of reporting. Many churches use "register boards" to place key items of report before the church members. Some churches use boards in their sanctuary for the Sunday educational reports, while others place the boards prominently in a foyer, a hallway, or some other conspicuous place. Reporting is very important to an informed membership.

Budgeting

It is important to work in an orderly fashion to provide adequate financial resources to support the church's education ministries. One significant part of an orderly support system is the budgeting process. In view of the fact that there are materials widely available which support the more traditional line-item budgeting process, while there is not as much available in print about ministry-action budgeting (a form of program budgeting), the latter will be the major focus of this chapter's presentation about budgeting.

This writer acknowledges deep appreciation to Robert F. Polk, Secretary, Church Stewardship Department, Baptist General Convention of Texas, and to his able associates, for extensive use of materials from their uncopyrighted publications, "The Church and Its Ministry of Stewardship," and "Ministry-Action Budgeting."

In ministry-action budgeting, the budget takes the shape of programs (actions and services) and is commonly arranged according to the importance, urgency, or priority of each program. This system leads the church to think of the budget as a budget-of-programs or a package of ministry-actions to be carried out by the church in its response to the leadership of the Holy Spirit.

The following steps are to be followed in ministry-action budgeting:

1. *Prepare Ministry Proposals*—The key instrument in ministry-action budgeting is the case-proposal made by every program or ministry of the church. The preparation of this case-proposal (usually one page, as seen in Figure 8) is the beginning step in budgeting and should include:
   a. a description of the purpose of the program and an indication as to how this supports the church's basic purpose;
   b. an identification of the needs that are to be met by this action and the benefits that are to come to the church;
   c. a list of things to be done next year (reachable goals);
   d. the cost in detail, not in lump sums;
   e. the long-range implication of the program (where this program will lead the church in three years, five years, etc., what it will be costing in three years, five years; what it will

A Ministry Action Proposal

For_____   Subject_____

1. A description of proposed plan and how it relates to the church's basic purpose.
_____
_____
_____

2. Why this ministry is needed. _____
_____
_____

3. The costs to the church (in detail)._____
_____
_____

4. What this will mean to the church in opportunities and cost in 2, 3, 5 years.
_____
_____
_____

5. Alternative. _____
_____
_____
_____

6. Alternative. _____
_____
_____
_____

For every plan proposed there are alternatives. They are very important to the budget committee because they give variables for making judgments between one ministry and another.

Figure 8

be expected to accomplish in the future);

f. an evaluation of possible alternates.

2. *Evaluate Program Proposals*—The second step in budgeting is to evaluate the priority of each program. Merit or priority should be assigned in terms of the church purpose and goals by asking these questions:

   a. To what degree does this program make a contribution to the purpose of the church?

   b. What help will it be in assisting the church to reach its major objectives (goals)?

   c. Is this program needed any longer, or is there an alternate or better way to do this task?

   d. If the church should project this program, where will it lead the church in future years, and what will be its cost?

   e. Is there a "program" waiting to be included that is better, but excluded because of this program?

3. *Prepare the Budget*—Putting the programs together into a budget is the next step. It is good to let the format of the budget clearly reflect that it is a budget-of-programs, showing what is to be done and what it is going to cost.

4. *Present the Budget to the Church*—When the church is asked to discuss and finally vote, it is extremely important that the program be presented as well as the amount of money involved. The act of approving a budget is also then an act of approving the programs of work.

5. *Promote the Budget*—Members should be asked to give to the support of this budget-of-programs. Again, this step in budgeting is distinguished by the accent on the program. It is not a case of raising money to meet or subscribe the budget; it is a case of support for the programs of work. Budget shortages are then considered program shortages or failures, and budget overages are seen as opportunities to do more in the programs of work.

6. *Report on the Budget*—The monthly report should be a program progress report. It should reflect:

   a. money given and how it was used in support of programs;

   b. progress in the program goals (for example, a monthly report could be a combined money report and program report);

   c. creative and varied techniques that help people understand and grow in interest.

There is a temptation to take the shortcut in budgeting. There are much easier ways to get a budget together than the proposal just offered. However, the test is not, "How little work did it take?" but "How valuable is it to the future of the church?" It is important to understand that while ministry-action budgeting claims the prime virtue of making the church more aware of its purpose, the approach does not give up the needed controls of good financial procedures.

The "Flow Chart" in Figure 9 portrays this process of ministry-action budgeting. A minimum of ten weeks is required to adequately develop, prepare, and present a ministry budget:

Weeks before adoption	Step #	
10	1	Analyze ministries available to church
		Elect a budget committee
8	2	Show filmstrip, "Ministry Action Budgeting."[7]
		Prepare ministry-action proposal
5		Proposal hearing by budget committee
4	3	Evaluate proposals and set priorities
3	4	Prepare budget for distribution
1	5	Present and discuss ministry budget
	6	Ministry Adoption Day

For an excellent model of the more traditional budgeting plan and financial system, see the *Church Finance Record System Manual,* by Marvin Crowe and Merrill Moore (Nashville: Broadman Press, 1959).

Purchasing

A good leader might be a more effective leader by having available for use the right materials, supplies, and other essential items, in the right quality and quantity, at the right time. It is the task of those who purchase for the church to meet these needs, and at the right price. In many churches it has been found that one person should be identified as the purchasing agent for the church and all purchases handled by that agent. As in the procedure sample below, this person is often a member of the church staff.

Sample Purchasing Procedures

A church should design its own statement of purchasing procedures. This sample statement illustrates major concerns which should

Flow Chart

Steps that make Ministry-Action Budgeting a Simple Committee Procedure.

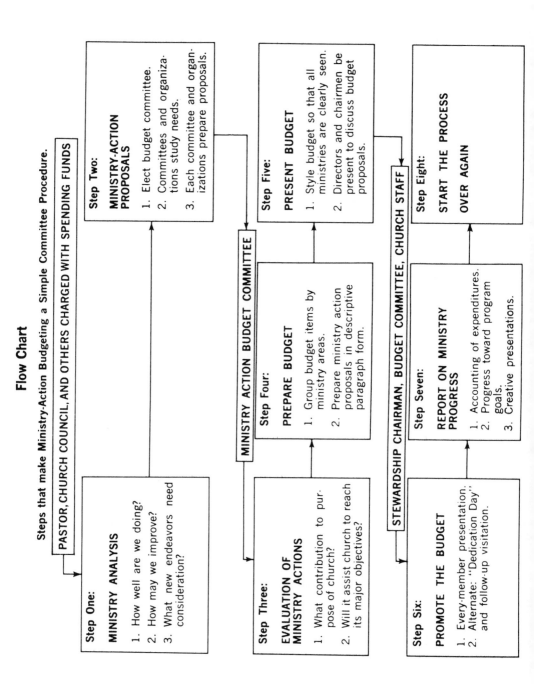

PASTOR, CHURCH COUNCIL, AND OTHERS CHARGED WITH SPENDING FUNDS

Step One:

MINISTRY ANALYSIS

1. How well are we doing?
2. How may we improve?
3. What new endeavors need consideration?

Step Two:

MINISTRY-ACTION PROPOSALS

1. Elect budget committee.
2. Committees and organizations study needs.
3. Each committee and organizations prepare proposals.

MINISTRY ACTION BUDGET COMMITTEE

Step Three:

EVALUATION OF MINISTRY ACTIONS

1. What contribution to purpose of church?
2. Will it assist church to reach its major objectives?

Step Four:

PREPARE BUDGET

1. Group budget items by ministry areas.
2. Prepare ministry action proposals in descriptive paragraph form.

Step Five:

PRESENT BUDGET

1. Style budget so that all ministries are clearly seen.
2. Directors and chairmen be present to discuss budget proposals.

STEWARDSHIP CHAIRMAN, BUDGET COMMITTEE, CHURCH STAFF

Step Six:

PROMOTE THE BUDGET

1. Every-member presentation.
2. Alternate: "Dedication Day" and follow-up visitation.

Step Seven:

REPORT ON MINISTRY PROGRESS

1. Accounting of expenditures.
2. Progress toward program goals.
3. Creative presentations.

Step Eight:

START THE PROCESS

OVER AGAIN

Figure 9

216

be clarified in such a statement. For a much more detailed treatment of this subject, see *Church Purchasing Procedures,* by Julian Feldman (Englewood Cliffs, New Jersey: Prentice-Hall, Inc., 1964).

1. The minister of education will serve as purchasing agent for the church.
2. All purchases amounting to $100.00 or more must be purchased with the submission of at least three bids. The lowest bid need not necessarily be accepted. Purchase is to be made to allow for service, need, and availability.
3. All purchases, where possible, will be acquired by centralized purchasing:
   a. Paper products will be purchased in quantities which will allow for maximum discounts.
   b. Maintenance supplies will be purchased on a yearly bid basis. Delivery will be, where possible, distributed throughout the year.
   c. All supplies and equipment for the kitchen will be handled by the church hostess. Funds for these purchases will be from that budget.
4. All purchases will be made in the following manner:
   a. A purchase request will be filled out and deposited with the education secretary.
   b. The minister of education will authorize a purchase order to be completed, if the request is approved, and mailed.
   c. If the purchase is to be made on a bid basis, a quotation request will be mailed to obtain estimated cost.
   d. When material arrives at church, it is checked against the purchase order to see that correct shipment has been made.
   e. No purchase exceeding $20.00 may be made in cash.
   f. All invoices will be paid by check. The invoice number will be included on each check, and a copy of the purchase order will be attached to each invoice.
   g. No purchase will be made until a purchase request has been approved.
      (1) For petty cash items (less than $20), a purchase request must be approved even though the individual person himself is to make the purchase.
      (2) The petty cash fund will be handled by the education secretary. No funds are to be released unless a purchase order has been approved.

5. Planning for purchases:
  a. Each organization will submit an estimate of planned expenses for each new year to the stewardship committee. Purchases for these organizations will be made out of these accounts. Amounts exceeding the budgeted figure must be approved by the stewardship committee or the church.
  b. If possible, large amounts of materials will not be ordered for frequently used supplies, but repeat orders will be placed.

Purchase order forms may be designed to suit the specific church needs. They may also be bought already printed, via office supply outlets.

A church needs to have well understood policies for the total financial operation of this vital support area. The sample policies statement which follows could serve as a guide for a church to develop its own policies statement.

1. It is understood that membership in this church involves financial obligation to support the church and its causes with regular, proportionate gifts. Each new member shall, therefore, be immediately approached by a representative of the church for a commitment to the church's unified budget; and at least annually, plans shall be put into operation for securing a worthy subscription from each member of the church.

2. The fiscal year of the church shall run concurrently with the church year, which begins on October 1 and ends on September 30.

3. All funds, for any and all purposes, shall pass through the hands of the church treasurer and be properly recorded on the books of the church.

4. The treasurer shall render to the church at each regular business meeting an itemized report of the receipts and disbursements for the preceding month. The treasurer's report shall be audited annually by an auditing committee or a certified public accountant.

5. A financial secretary shall receive the empty collection envelopes after the money has been removed and counted by the proper persons selected by the church to serve in turn. From these the secretary shall give donors individual credit. The secretary shall also be responsible for preparing and mailing quarterly or semiannually records of contributions to all contributing members.

6. The trustees shall affix their signatures to legal documents involv-

ing the sale, mortgaging, or purchase or rental of property or other legal documents where the signatures of trustees are required.

7. The church shall select and elect a seven-member properties committee to assist the church in matters related to properties administration.
8. The stewardship committee, in consultation with the church council, shall prepare and submit to the church for approval an inclusive budget, indicating by items the amount needed and sought for all local and worldwide expenses.
9. The minister of education shall serve as purchasing agent for the church. All purchases must be approved and the standard purchase form filled out in advance of any purchase.
10. The church shall bond those who handle funds.
11. The Broadman Finance Record System shall be the accounting system utilized in the financial operations of the church.

Managing Resources

Much of what has been said earlier in this chapter has implications for managing such resources as supplies, equipment, and facilities. However, it seems in order to add some definitive suggestions here.

Supplies are needed to support the educational ministries in the manner which they deserve. Technically, supplies include primarily the more expendable items such as record forms, crayons, paper, and the semidurable items such as flipcharts, choir robes, and recordings. Leaders of the various groups might need assistance to facilitate the planning for adequate supplies.

The purchasing agent for the church could help leaders by making available to them the sources of information (catalogs, brochures, order forms) about supplies they might choose. Further assistance is essential in securing items selected. Good purchasing procedures should be followed.

Distribution plans should be established and followed. In large churches with expansive buildings, supply "substations" in various parts of the buildings could be useful. Good inventory procedures need to be developed, whether there is a central supply station or several.

In some instances, training and follow-through supervision regarding the use of supplies are needed. Further, the storing of certain supplies needs careful attention. Management of materials and supplies might well be an indicator of the seriousness of those who lead. Waste, improper use, and other evidences of carelessly managed supplies might indicate poor stewardship of a larger nature. To avoid such situations, leaders should give careful and specific attention to developing and implementing systematic ways of managing supplies. Keep in mind that a supply which is not available as needed might as well not be there at all.

Similarly, equipment must be provided and managed well. Equipment includes items for the church office, sanctuary, recreation services, media center/library, restrooms, plumbing, heating, cooling, lighting, tables and chairs, special teaching tools, sound, audiovisuals, kitchen/food services, and others.

Leaders must provide for appropriate planning of construction (in some instances), financing, and use and maintenance of equipment and furnishings. A word of caution should come here. Many churches experience a serious lack of equipment and furnishings, but many others actually have too much. Workers, curriculum materials, and space should take prior claim on the concerns of a church over equipment and furnishings. The goal should be to have all of these elements in balance, as needed to support the ministries of a church. Many wise educators feel that too much equipment and furnishings, as well as the wrong kinds (not suited to the age group and program needs), might be worse than having too little or none. Equipment and furnishings are more durable than supplies. Extreme care should be used in selecting and managing these important and usually expensive items.

The term *facilities* usually means the buildings used by the church. Churches normally have no category of investment or expense that represents a larger financial outlay. Sometimes the long-term expenditures for personnel, program, or missions causes exceed the investment in buildings. In any event, facilities management commands continuing attention to assure that the buildings serve well the purposes for which they were provided.

Consider these suggestions:

> Maximum use of church facilities is the ideal. To accomplish this ideal the church should (1) make a thorough inventory of its facilities and possible uses to which they may be put, (2) establish policies regarding the use of its facilities, (3) survey its surrounding community to determine which needs are not being filled by other community resources, (4) assign the properties and space committee the responsibility of administering

policies on the use of church facilities and delegate to the church council the coordination of the various ministries, and (5) secure helps for specialized ministries from denominational offices and agencies.[8]

Policies regarding the use of the facilities should be developed to help assure that the facilities are available and are in order as needed for the church's ministries. Policies should include the church's positions on such things as whether and under what conditions outside groups may use the facilities; procedures for scheduling the use of facilities; rules for care of properties and facilities, including the responsibility for any damages incurred; financial charges, if any; and provision for restoring the facilities for use by subsequent groups.

Housekeeping and other concerns for upkeep of the facilities call for attention. One of the best procedures you might follow is to secure copies of the *Church Custodian's Manual,* by Idus V. Owensby (Nashville: Broadman Press, 1974), and follow its suggestions. Train those who are responsible for caring for the church facilities by means of this book.

Office Services

One of the most important support service areas related to facilitating the church's educational ministries is the church office. The church office is essentially an information center. It is more than the place where paper work is handled. It is the center for providing meaningful data that conveys usable knowledge. Such an assignment as this requires good management skills.

Providing meaningful information that conveys usable knowledge calls for developing (creating) information. This is not to suggest that you should make up false information! It is to suggest that the office workers take initiative in finding out what information might be needed. The workers in the office assist in collecting information. The information gathered in the various organizations should find its way to the church office for whatever future use might be made of it.

The church office should process information—that is, put it into meaningful, usable form. This facilitates supplying the information when the time comes to make the data available.

Retaining information is vital. Certain kinds of data need to be kept, ready for those who need it. It is important that the retention system be designed in such a way as to make retrieval efficient. Having data is of limited value if it cannot be found as needed.

Distributing information is a significant aspect of office services. A church should develop regular channels for distributing information that could be useful in the programs. In addition to a weekly church paper, there might be organization data sheets, memos of a regular nature, bulletin boards, Sunday bulletins, announcement sheets for key leaders in organizations, and other outlets for distributing information.

Many factors need consideration if the church office is to serve effectively. Among the most important is the factor of the physical arrangement of the office area. Significant criteria for arrangement in an office should include job responsibilities of the workers, number of workers in the office, routing of the work, equipment, convenience and comfort, aesthetics, and future expansion. In all of these, the church's financial ability to provide a suitable office must be taken into account.

The amount of space provided for office workers is important. Current specifications should be secured from competent consultants. A church committee, architects, and manufacturers of furnishings and equipment are good sources of information about provisions for the office.

Those who work in the church office become the church's front line of communication with other church members and with the nonmembers who contact the church. It is vital that their relationships with all persons be conducted at a high quality level. It is important, too, that leaders and members make only reasonable demands of the church office workers.

Notes

1. *Church Base Design 1979 Update,* an unpublished document of the Inter-Agency Council of the Southern Baptist Convention (Nashville: The Sunday School Board of the Southern Baptist Convention), p. 102.

2. *How to Administer and Promote a Church Media Center,* comp. Jacqulyn Anderson (Nashville: Broadman Press, 1978), p. 14.

3. Ibid., p. 15.

4. Figures 1, 2, and 3 from Ibid., pp. 18-19.

5. Ibid., p. 24.

6. To receive these, one may write the Materials Services Department, The Baptist Sunday School Board, 127 Ninth Avenue North, Nashville, Tennessee, 37234.

7. This filmstrip may be obtained from the Church Stewardship Department, Baptist General Convention of Texas, 102 Baptist Building, Dallas, Texas 75201.

8. Joseph R. Estes, "How to Make Maximum Use of Church Facilities," *Church Administration* (February 1973), p. 6.

8

Administering Specialized Educational Activities
Jerry M. Stubblefield

Introduction

All church educational activities do not necessarily fit under one of the existing educational organizations of the church. When specialized educational activities can be supported and administered by an existing organization, they should be. However, special organization is needed when objectives and goals for an area of ministry cannot be fulfilled by an existing organization.

Specialized educational concerns include youth activities, activities for senior adults, for single adults, family life, Vacation Bible School, kindergarten, Christian schools, child care ministries, and day camps. These activities usually meet on days other than Sunday and require more than the one hour to one and one-half hours normally given to the program organizations.

Activities may be conducted daily, weekly, monthly, quarterly, or annually. How frequently the group meets is determined by the nature of the programs and the needs and numbers of persons in your church to participate in the activity. Some function at special times of the year, for example, Vacation Bible School and day camps.

For any program to be effective, someone must be responsible. Even though a church may have a staff member charged with this responsibility, volunteer leaders in the church often can provide leadership and the administrative functions vital to an effective program. What is described below is applicable for any size church where there is a need for a particular specialized educational activity. For any program to be effective, four ingredients are necessary: (1) the need for such a ministry; (2) a dedicated volunteer who believes that this ministry needs to be done; (3) a pastor and church leaders who are supportive; and (4) the church's decision that "this is our ministry."

This chapter seeks to answer these questions: How do you determine what specialized educational activities or organizations are needed? How do you decide whether an activity should be short-term or an ongoing program? How do you develop short-term and ongoing programs? What are suggested objectives and goals for specialized educational activities? What organizational pattern is needed? Specialized educational activities will be grouped according to appropriate age divisions—preschoolers (birth through 5), children (ages 6 to 11), youth (ages 12 to 17), and adults. Some activities include all ages; these will be listed under the primary target groups. The chapter concludes with *Suggested Resources*.

To Have or Not to Have

Does your church need to begin a specific ministry? Consider two warnings before initiating new activities. An activity need not be started just because a neighboring or influential church is doing it. The other group may be doing it very effectively and may be willing to do it for *all* the community. Because of their involvement, your church may become sensitized to a need that you should be meeting. If so, do not try to duplicate what they are doing; make it *your own program* to meet the unique needs of your congregation and community. Communicate with the other church. Learn from their mistakes and their successes.

Second, be careful about starting programs you read about. Such a ministry usually is presented in idealistic terms, implying, "Do it the way we do, and success is guaranteed." The difficulty is that success usually is not instantaneous nor without its problems. Remember, *that* church began a specialized ministry because it met a need it had. Programs cannot be transferred from one location to another without some modification.

Discover what other churches are doing in specialized educational activities and read about as many as possible. Recognize that programs in your church have become a reality because you had a need, the program was designed to meet local needs, and it was done in your way. Enough cautions—how do you decide whether to begin a specialized educational activity?

First, you must determine that there is a need for a particular program. Ask questions such as:
- What needs are not being met by the church both for its members and also those in the community? (I do not believe that a church exists only to meet members' needs. Ministry and/or specialized activities should not be manipulative tools for outreach. These

activities should be done or not done on one criterion—whether they meet genuine, human needs.)

- How many persons are potential participants in this activity?
- What other churches and/or community organizations have programs/activities for this target group?
- What kind of facilities and/or equipment would be needed?
- Who has the best facilities and/or equipment? The church? The community?
  (The church could sponsor and lead activities at community sites as well as at the church.)
- What kind of organizational structure would be necessary?
- How many volunteers are needed to staff it?
- What specialized skills must volunteers possess?
- What financial resources will this activity require? (This question should be the last question asked.) Figure 1 provides a work sheet.

Once these questions are answered a church must ask: "Are we able to do this activity? Do we have the necessary resources—facilities, volunteers, finances, etc.?"

How do you gather such information? Begin by interviewing community organizations to see if a need exists. Visit organizations that have special interest in persons in need. Needs can be discovered by a minister who is sensitive to persons. Personal needs may be known to the minister through pastoral counseling and visitation. Programs cannot be started because a community organization confirms that there is a need. More data is necessary before you begin a new program.

What specific persons could benefit from this activity? Names, addresses—people—are necessary to insure success. Publicize specialized ministries through newspapers, radio, television, posters, handbills, and other ways. People must know that a program exists before it can fulfill their needs.

How to Decide Between Short-Term or Ongoing Programs

What kind of program should it be—short-term or ongoing? What determines whether it is a short-term or ongoing program? A short-term program would be one designed to meet a specific need through a one-time event or a series of activities held over a brief period of time. It would have a rather narrow objective, or similar objectives. It

Special Ministry Plan Sheet

What needs are not being met by the church both for its members and also those in the community?

How many persons are potential participants in the activity?

What other churches and/or community organizations have programs/activities for this target group?

What kind of facilities and/or equipment would be needed?

Who has the best facilities and/or equipment? the church? the community?

What kind of organizational structure would be necessary?

How many volunteers are needed to staff it?

What specialized skills must volunteers possess?

What financial resources will this activity require?

Figure 1
226

could be an annual emphasis, or it could be done only once.

Religious organizations have a tendency to repeat activities indiscriminately year after year. Church leaders frequently announce, "This is the first annual ...." Some events may need to be held only once. Each activity should be critically evaluated. Answers should be sought for the following questions:

- What was the objective or purpose?
- Was the objective achieved? How? If not, why?
- For whom was the event planned? Who was the target audience?
- Who participated in the activity? Who came?
- Does the need still exist?
- What other needs were revealed during the session(s)?
- Should this activity be done again? Why?
- What additional benefits would be forthcoming if done again?
- Is there another event that should be done?
- Did the response justify the cost?

Short-term programs that meet periodically should be scheduled as other activities. Short-term events should be seen as a vital part of the church's total program. These programs should be well-planned and supported by the church.

Ongoing programs are those that have multiple objectives that cannot be accomplished in a brief period of time. Needs to be met are diversified and cannot be fulfilled in one or two sessions. Ongoing programs necessitate a variety of approaches both in the time structure and the methodology to be employed. Each activity or event should be critically analyzed, using the questions listed above. Obviously, ongoing programs require more planning, administrative organization, and finances than most short-term projects.

Specialized Educational Activities

Preschoolers

Weekday activities conducted for preschool children have been called Church Weekday Early Education. For such a program to be more than "baby-sitting," it must be seen as an extension of the church's educational ministry. Before mentioning specific activities, a brief description of the values of weekday early education is in order.

- Weekday education is a function of the church, like Sunday School. It is financially supported by the church. Church members pay for this ministry.

- It is ministry in action. Christian teachers show Christ as they teach and care for the needs of the children.
- Weekday education includes Christian teaching which is not found in other public and private programs. It is a holistic approach to education.
- It seeks to relate to the child not only in the classroom but in the home as well. The home is seen as an integral part of the learning process.
- It is family-oriented. Follow-up visits can be made to witness to the families who need to know Jesus Christ or to minister to whatever needs the family may have.
- It achieves maximum use of the church buildings. The church becomes an activity hub. People begin to see the church as more than a place for Sunday activities.[1]

The values of such a program should be kept in mind. One should be aware of certain myths or misunderstandings as well. There are five myths that I want to counter.

- *Weekday education activities automatically bring unsaved and unenlisted parents into the church.* Evangelistic outreach comes about only by the deliberate effort to reach persons who are without Jesus Christ. Church leaders must be sensitive to the needs of parents and family members of children enrolled in the weekday education program. Family information must be secured and used in an appropriate way. The primary objective of a weekday education program should be to provide authentic educational activities for preschoolers.
- *It will guarantee religious education.* Weekday education seeks to minister to the total child. The child is approached in his wholeness. Religious instruction will be a part of his total educational experience. The teaching of religious values and concepts must be done in a natural manner as a factor in the child's learning processes.
- *Weekday education provides additional income for the church.* Unless fees are set exceptionally high, the church can expect to subsidize the weekday education activities. Fees normally cover personnel and supplies cost. Weekday programs require additional lights, heat, air conditioning, janitorial services, and more frequent painting due to heavy use. A weekday education program must be seen as a ministry to be performed, not a source of additional revenue.

- *Every church should have a weekday education program.* Such programs should be begun only after the need has been established in your community, not because you believe it should be done. Not every church has the facilities, personnel, or financial resources to have an effective program. Unless your church can have a first-class program, it should not have one. The program does not need to be extravagant, but it should be equal or superior to that offered in the community.
- *All church members approve of the program.* A good public relations program should be directed to the community-at-large and also to the church. Keep church members informed of what is going on. Volunteer leaders frequently believe that what they are doing is the most important. Sharing of rooms and supplies can cause friction. Help each part of the church's program see that all are engaged in a ministry that is significant to the advancement of the church and the gospel.[2]

Before beginning church weekday early education activities, answers should be formulated to the following questions:

- What administrative structure needs to be developed? (All such activities should be under *one* church-elected committee. This helps eliminate friction and rivalry between activities.)
- What kind of staffing will be required? Volunteer? Paid?
- How will this program be financed? Fees? Church support? A combination?
- Does this program require state licensing?
- What are the space needs for this activity?
- Will this require additional equipment? If so, how is it to be financed?
- What are the objectives and goals of this program?
- What is the philosophy by which this activity is to function?[3]

Mother's Day Out

This program usually operates one day each week, enabling mothers to relax, shop, visit friends, or tend to other matters. Modest fees might be charged to defray some of the operational expenses. The child engages in educationally-sound activities on his developmental level. Children can be supervised and taught by church volunteers or paid persons. This is to be an educational activity, not simply baby-sitting. Usually, one worker is needed for each six to eight children attending. The objective is to provide educational activities for the child while the mother has time away from her child.

Day Care

This is an all-day, five-days-a-week program involving teaching, rest, and at least one meal plus snacks. This ministry helps working parents provide adequately for their children while they work. It is open to children ages birth through five. Fees are charged, and the program is under professional supervision. State licensing is usually required for day-care activities. One teacher would be responsible for ten students. Separate rooms should be provided for each teacher and her children. Requirements for day-care programs necessitate more equipment than that usually provided for the church's regular educational activities.

Nursery School

This program meets for one-half day, with the children coming two, three, or five days per week. It is designed for children ages three and four. Each teacher works with ten children. The emphasis is on teaching and educational activities, with socialization being stressed. Some churches include two-year-olds on a one-day-a-week basis. The sessions are usually two hours in length. Costs are offset by fees. The program is under the direction of professional teachers. Churches that have ministers of music and recreation/activities could use these ministers to strengthen their programs. The nursery school schedule follows closely that of the public schools in the community.

Kindergarten

This is a program for five-year-olds which normally meets for one-half day, with a major emphasis on teaching. Some churches include four-year-olds in their kindergarten program. Much of that which describes the nursery school applies to the kindergarten. A teacher may teach fifteen children, due to their maturation and the activities in which they are engaged. Halbert states that kindergarten "places emphasis on intellectual, social, physical, and emotional growth within the scope of Christian education."[4]

Children

Specialized educational activities for children occur primarily in the summer when they are out of school: day camping; resident camping; and Vacation Bible School. Weekday education has functioned as an after-school activity operating concurrently with the school year.

Day camp—Day camp is a program in which children are daily transported to a nature setting. These may operate five or more consecutive days, or they may be one-day experiences repeated over several weeks in the summer. Primarily, this program is for children ages six through eleven, or grades one through six. Some churches have one-day camp experience for fours and fives, with a shortened schedule. Larry Haslam has stated the objectives of day camping as: "(1) To reach children (and their families) for Christ; (2) To help children develop new friendships, good life habits, a love for nature, and an understanding of God's plan for all of life—then, the camper may be led to see God's plan for his own life."[5]

Staff should include a director, a Bible study leader, camp craft leader, cook, nature study leader, a lifeguard if swimming is available, and unit leaders and counselors. Older youth can be enlisted to work in day camp. Careful attention must be given to site selection, transportation coordination, and the safety of the day campers. Each staffer should be trained prior to beginning activities with the children.

Funding for the day camp must be considered. Various ways of handling it are the church budget, camping fees, or a combination of the two. Registration in advance helps you know how many persons to plan for, the necessary staff, and your transportation needs.

Day camp can be the vehicle to minister to special groups of children who cannot participate in ordinary day camps. Such groups include the handicapped, the mentally retarded, and the deaf. Persons possessing professional skills will be needed as leaders.

Resident Camping—Resident or church camping takes the camper away from home for several days and nights. It is "camping which utilizes the resources of the natural environment for Christian education, fellowship, evangelism, ministry, and personal growth experiences."[6]

Camping experiences usually begin in the early morning or early afternoon. Recreational activities help the camper become acclimated to camp life. Administration of the camp is under the leadership of the camp director. He is assisted by the camp pastor, camp missionary (camping is an excellent time to teach missions), camp counselors (one for every eight campers), nurse, activity directors, cook, and other kitchen personnel. Depending upon the nature and objectives of the camping situation, persons possessing special skills may be needed.

Camping objectives are to communicate the gospel of Jesus Christ to the unsaved and to assist persons in the process of Christian growth leading to Christian maturity. Evangelism takes place through the clear presentation of the good news of Jesus Christ.

Camping is an extension of the church's educational activities. It is more concentrated and, like other educational activities, also allows for development of personal relationships.

The camp pastor should participate in various activities, thus gaining additional information on the campers' spiritual experience. Non-church children should become a part of the church's prospect file and become objects of the church's outreach program. Care should be exercised to see that each decision is genuine and not the product of emotionalism or peer approval.

Responsibilities of the camp director include answering the following questions:

- Where will the camp be held?
- What program emphases should there be?
- Who should be camp pastor, missionary, etc.?
- What is the total camp budget? How much of this cost will be paid by the church? By each camper?
- What shall be the criteria for selecting counselors? Age? Special skills? Training needed?
- What will be the daily schedule?
- Determine the schedule for planning, preparing, and executing the camping experience.
- For whom is the camp designed? Members? Nonmembers?

Camping should be seen as a part of the church's total educational program for children. Activities should be planned for children appropriate to their developmental stage. The age span needs to be restricted so that your objectives are attainable. Usually, resident camp experience begins with children age nine, or those who have completed the third grade. An adequate number of counselors should be provided. Older youth make excellent counselors. They must understand that the camp is for the children, not for the counselors. Too many adults and youth tend to overpower the children and add greatly to the cost.

Vacation Bible School—"Vacation Bible School is an age-graded, Bible-centered activity conducted during vacation time."[7] Until recently, Vacation Bible School has been considered a preschool, children, and youth activity. It now provides for adults as well. Children comprise the largest age group enrolled in it. It is a significant part of the church's Bible teaching program. The prepared curriculum is sometimes for ten sessions lasting three hours each. Most churches meet for five sessions, or a total of fifteen hours.

Purposes of Vacation Bible School include:

- Supplementing and supporting other church educational programs;
- Providing consecutive and concentrated educational activities;
- Focusing on Bible study;
- Contributing to the church's outreach and evangelism programs;
- Strengthening and helping the church in the exercise of its functions;
- Providing mission features and encouraging mission support;
- Encouraging Christian witnessing;
- Utilizing music—providing a better understanding of hymnody;
- Emphasizing the Christian living of Bible truths.[8]

Vacation Bible School is a vital part of the church's educational program. Its leadership should be church-elected. Its budget should be provided by the church. Offerings taken during the school should be given to a mission project or the mission program of your denomination, not used to defray expenses.

A successful Vacation Bible School is dependent upon: (1) early election of the faculty; (2) faculty training sessions; (3) both general and departmental faculty meetings; (4) adequate information and publicity both within the church and the community; (5) provision of curriculum materials and other learning aids; and (6) a planned follow-up of nonchurch members and their families.

The chief administrative officer is the director. He/she is assisted by other persons in the total operation of Vacation Bible School. A refreshment chairperson and a secretary are vital. Good refreshments are appreciated by both young and old. Your faculty will be grateful for a faculty room which has refreshments and a place to relax briefly. This is a small way for the church to acknowledge the good work being done. The secretary needs to keep good records. These records will help you know the enrollees. Your planned follow-up will be more effective if your registration cards contain accurate information. Keep your records as simple as possible.

Each department (age group) has a director who functions as a lead teacher. Workers should be enlisted in the same teacher/student ratio as the Bible teaching program. It is essential that each department have a minimum of two adult workers.

A schedule needs to be drawn up for the entire Vacation Bible

School and for each individual department. Each activity must be listed showing the amount of time allotted to it. Failure to abide by the schedule creates confusion and frustration. All faculty members should know the time of the joint worship service, playground time, and when and where their group is to have refreshments.

Pastor and other church staff persons should participate in the various activities as much as possible. Be supportive even when you are not in a leadership role. All faculty persons should receive evangelistic training so they can deal individually with children in the normal process of the day's activities. Commitment services ought to be kept simple, not highly emotional. The child should be encouraged to respond to Jesus Christ, but not pressured.

Nonmembers should be visited and invited to participate in the activities of the church. Unsaved persons need to hear the gospel and to know how to become a Christian. The fact that a person attends Vacation Bible School is no assurance that he will attend either Sunday School or a worship service. Good information secured through the registration process may reveal other family members who are prospects. If they are to be effective, follow-up visits should be made as soon as possible.

Christian Day Schools—In recent years Christian day schools have greatly increased in number. This is a return to a major historic function of the church. Christian churches in the United States basically supported the public schools as they emerged in this country, for they reflected the attitudes of the dominant Christian society. This has changed in the last few years.

What factors should churches consider in establishing and operating Christian day schools? What should be the objectives of such schools?

- Each child should be afforded the best education possible. *Quality* of education should not be sacrificed. Education in the Christian day school should be *superior* to public education. Teachers should possess academic credentials in addition to their spiritual qualities.
- The Christian day school exists to aid each child to discover and develop his God-given gifts.
- The mission of the Christian day school is the development of the future leadership of the community, the state, the business and professional groups, and the church.
- Children need to learn that there is a Christian option to be considered in every field of learning and in the living of life. J. Ralph McIntyre declares, "Christian options are best taught in the class-

rooms where the issues of biological life, mathematical searching, literature probing, business procedures development, physical education involvements, and all other subjects equate the Christian life with real life."[9]

- The Christian day school's mission is to honor Jesus Christ through the lives of the students and to minister in the name of Christ.[10]

Administration of a Christian day school can be complicated. In addition to a principal, office staff, and faculty, the church will need to elect a committee charged with the responsibility of operating the school, much like public school trustees. This committee would determine policies, elect faculty and administrators, set tuition fees, and give general oversight to the school activities.

The school must be licensed by the state board of education and meet all state requirements. Other important considerations include transportation, lunch program, and provision of textbooks. The committee should meet regularly and have the authority to make decisions. One member of the church staff should work in liaison with the committee. Sometimes, a church designates an associate minister to be the principal. If so, this should be his major responsibility, to insure that the Christian day school functions effectively and adequately.

Youth

Youth ministry has become popular in many churches. Some churches have professional youth ministers; others rely upon lay volunteers. Youth are ministered to through the regular educational activities of the church. Various definitions of youth ministry have been proposed. One is, "Youth ministry is all of that which takes place for and with youth in and through the local church."[11]

Youth ministry is a comprehensive term which includes all efforts a church might make because of a concern for youth. Bob R. Taylor affirms, "Youth ministry is a church's effort to minister to the total needs of the members of its family between the ages of twelve and seventeen. It is more than fun and games. Youth ministry is deep, healing, redemptive, and affirming."[12]

Youth ministry must be viewed as an integral part of the basic church programs meeting the needs of youth. In 1963 the following objectives for youth work (ministry) were proposed:

1. To help youth to make a commitment to Jesus Christ as Lord and Savior.

2. To help youth to be sensitive to the guidance and the power of the Holy Spirit.

3. To guide youth in meaningful church membership and in Christian discipleship.

4. To help youth to experience worship.

5. To help youth to learn to increase their knowledge and understanding of Bible truths.

6. To help youth to learn to apply Christian principles in every area and relationship of life.

7. To guide youth in the stewardship of their money, time, talents, and skill.

8. To guide youth to participate in Christian ministries and world missions.

9. To help youth to recognize and respond to the will of God in all decisions.

10. To help youth grow in understanding and acceptance of self.

11. To guide youth to witness to their experiences with Jesus Christ and to direct others to him.

12. To guide youth in their use of leisure time.[13]

Youth ministry is a team endeavor. It involves the pastor and staff of the church, parents of the youth, youth workers in the youth-related program organizations and services, and the youth.

A youth ministry should provide opportunities for youth to minister, as well as be ministered to. Mission and ministry options should be open for the youth locally and on mission trips. Many activities are possibilities for youth ministry. Church resources and location greatly influence and determine youth activities.

Administratively, the youth program should function under the leadership of a youth council. Each church must determine its representative base and the specific functions of the youth council. Representatives should be selected from church members, adult youth leaders, youth from the various program organizations, age-group representatives, and the youth minister/youth coordinator. Youth activities need to be planned in accordance with church objectives and church policies.

Adults

Specialized educational activities for adults will be examined in the areas of single adults, senior adults, and family ministry.

Single Adults—Many single adults are involved in the church's educational program. Attention will be focused on developing a weekday ministry with and to single adults.

Singles now constitute one-third of the American adult population. They are found in many varieties—never-married, divorced, deserted, separated, single parents, or widowed.

Before beginning a single adult ministry, three questions need to be answered:

- Who are the singles? How many singles are presently members or attending your church? How many singles are in your community?
- What are the needs of singles which your church can meet?
- What types of activities, programs, and organizations will be required to meet these needs?

Some of the needs of single adults include self-worth, companionship, acceptance, financial assistance, help with children, sexuality, the desire to know the will of God, and loneliness. If these and other needs are to be met, it will require a plan, a program. Single adult activities can be implemented and evaluated by a single adult council. The council is composed of the single adult minister (or other staff member), the lay coordinator, and representatives from each of the church program organizations which minister to single adults. Elected representatives are members of the various unit organizations and must be a member of that local church.

The single adult council has responsibility for coordinating the total single adult organizational and weekday activities, planning and administering the weekday program for single adults, reporting directly to the church or through the church council, determining single adult activities before planning events, and evaluating the single adult activities.[14]

Senior Adults—The number of senior adults is rapidly increasing. Senior adult clubs and other activities have been organized to meet the needs of these persons. Objectives of senior adult ministries include:

- Providing materials and activities which will enhance spiritual enrichment.
- Offering learning opportunities for continuing growth toward self-actualization.
- Providing attractive socialization activities to combat loneliness and to give a sense of belonging.
- Meeting physical and safety needs as possible and appropriate.
- Providing barrier-free facilities conducive for use by senior adults.
- Determining available community resources to help meet needs and interests of older persons and to assist older members in obtaining that help as required.[15]

A senior adult ministry can provide:

- A weekly or monthly program to help give a fuller purpose to the total church program for senior adults.
- A way for the church to show love and concern for senior adults in an environment which leads them to feel they are wanted in the worship and life of the church.
- A way for senior adults to use their natural and learned abilities by providing opportunities of service through the total church program, assuring them of uninterrupted Christian service.
- A way to combat loneliness through Christian fellowship, new interests, and a sense of belonging.
- An opportunity for senior adults to actively contribute to society by enlarging their areas of responsibility through the program of the church.

The senior adult council provides the administrative structure for an effective senior adult ministry. The group should have a coordinator and representatives from each church organization which has senior adult participants. The council discovers the needs of senior adults, plans and implements senior adult activities, coordinates the calendar of activities, reports to the church or the church council, and evaluates the senior adult program.

The senior adult weekday ministry is usually called a senior adult club. Officers needed include a president, program chairman, enlistment chairman, and a secretary. Additional committees may be added as the activities and needs expand.

It would be good if some funds for the senior adult program could be provided by the church. Senior adults have fixed incomes but want to feel that they are paying their own way. Senior adult activity funds could be budgeted, similar to those the church furnishes for youth activities.

Family Ministry—With the increased fragmentation of the family, the church has been forced to consider the needs of the family. Family ministry involves all ages. Adults hold the key to wholeness for younger family members. Objectives for a family ministry program in a local church include:

- Helping family members learn to communicate with one another and to understand and solve family problems.
- Aiding couples to enrich their relationship.
- Assisting those who are divorced to find acceptance in the church and to grow in their personal lives.
- Sustaining single parents as they try to understand and cope with

problems they encounter in rearing children without mates.

- Facilitating all single and senior adults to grow in self-understanding and to assume responsibility for making their lives worthwhile.
- Providing opportunities for single adults and for senior adults to form wholesome friendships and to enrich their lives.
- Encouraging families in times of crisis.[16]
- Teaching family members the biblical bases of sexuality, marriage, and family life.
- Preparing young persons for their future roles in marriage and family life.
- Training individuals to develop competence in interpersonal relations.
- Providing opportunities for families to develop competence in Christian family living.[17]

No church program organization has responsibility for family ministry. The church council could assume this responsibility, since this group is charged with planning for the total needs of the church. No program of family ministry should be initiated before the needs of the congregation are known. Identified needs should be listed in priority order. Instead of assuming that all the family ministry needs can be met during a special week, a year's plan of action needs to be projected. Multiple-year plans need to be developed. These proposals should be presented to the church for adoption.

Notes

1. William H. Halbert, Jr., *The Ministry of Church Weekday Early Education* (Nashville: Convention Press, 1977), pp. 9-11.

2. Ibid., pp. 12-14.

3. Halbert's book provides information relating to these questions. Additional information is available in William H. Halbert, Jr., *Church Weekday Early Education Director's Guide* (Nashville: Convention Press, 1972) and Robert A. Couch, *Church Weekday Early Education Administrative Guide* (Nashville: Convention Press, 1980).

4. Halbert, *Church Weekday Early Education Director's Guide*, p. 4.

5. Larry Haslam, *Day Camp Director's Guide* (Nashville: Convention Press, 1972), p. 1.

6. John LaNoue, *A Guide to Church Camping* (Nashville: Convention Press, 1976), p. 6.

7. *Administering a Vacation Bible School*, comp. A. V. Washburn (Nashville: Convention Press, 1970), p. 3.

8. Ibid., p. 11.

9. J. Ralph McIntyre, "The Mission and Ministry of a Christian Day School," *Christian Day School Administrative Guide* (Nashville: Convention Press, 1978), p. 10.

10. Ibid., pp. 7-11.

11. John L. Carroll and Keith L. Ignatius, *Youth Ministry: Sunday, Monday, and Every Day* (Valley Forge: Judson Press, 1972), p. 11.

12. *The Youth Ministry Planbook,* comp. Bob R. Taylor (Nashville: Convention Press, 1977), p. 6.

13. *Coordinating Youth Work in a Church* (Nashville: The Sunday School Board of the Southern Baptist Convention, 1963). See also Ibid., p. 10.

14. Ann Alexander Smith, *How to Start a Single Adult Ministry* (Nashville: The Sunday School Board of the Southern Baptist Convention, 1980), pp. 23-24.

15. Horace L. Kerr, *How to Minister to Senior Adults in Your Church* (Nashville: Broadman Press, 1980), p. 55.

16. Joseph W. Hinkle and Melva J. Cook, *How to Minister to Families in Your Church* (Nashville: Broadman Press, 1978), p. 28.

17. *Family Ministry in Today's Church,* ed. B. A. Clendenning (Nashville: Convention Press, 1971), p. 45.

Suggested Resources

Preschoolers

Couch, Robert A., *Church Weekday Early Education Administrative Guide.* Nashville: Convention Press, 1980.

Halbert, William A., Jr., *Church Weekday Early Education Director's Guide.* Nashville: Convention Press, 1972.

————. *The Ministry of Church Weekday Early Education.* Nashville: Convention Press, 1977.

Children

Christian Day School Administrative Guide. Nashville: Convention Press, 1978.

Haslam, Larry. *Day Camping Director's Guide.* Nashville: Convention Press, 1972.

LaNoue, John. *A Guide to Church Camping.* Nashville: Convention Press, 1976.

————. *A Notebook for the Christian Camp Counselor.* Nashville: Convention Press, 1978.

Washburn, A. V., comp. *Administering a Vacation Bible School.* Nashville: Convention Press, 1970.

Youth

Carroll, John L., and Keith L. Ignatius. *Youth Ministry: Sunday, Monday, and Every Day.* Valley Forge: Judson Press, 1972.

Richards, Lawrence O. *Youth Ministry—Its Renewal in the Local Church.* Grand Rapids: Zondervan Publishing House, 1972.

Taylor, Bob R., comp. *The Youth Ministry Planbook.* Nashville: Convention Press, 1977.

Adults

Single Adults

Brown, Raymond K. *Reach Out to Singles.* Philadelphia: Westminster Press, 1979.

Christoff, Nicholas B. *Saturday Night, Sunday Morning: Singles and the Church.*

Smith, Ann Alexander. *How to Start a Single Adult Ministry.* Nashville: The Sunday School Board of the Southern Baptist Convention, 1980.

Wood, Britton. *Single Adults Want to Be the Church, Too.* Nashville: Broadman Press, 1977.

Senior Adults

Gray, Robert M., and David O. Moberg. *The Church and the Older Person,* rev. ed. Grand Rapids: William B. Eerdmans, 1977.

Kerr, Horace L. *How to Minister to Senior Adults in Your Church.* Nashville: Broadman Press, 1980.

Family Ministry

Clendenning, B. A., Jr., Ed. *Family Ministry in Today's Church.* Nashville: Convention Press, 1971.

Hinkle, Joseph W., and Melva J. Cook. *How to Minister to Families in Your Church.* Nashville: Broadman Press, 1978.

Mace, David and Vera. *Marriage Enrichment in the Church.* Nashville: Broadman Press, 1976.

9

Training Teachers and Leaders

Charles A. Tidwell

Church leaders of Christian education must provide for the training of teachers and leaders. Several reasons support the truth of this statement. First, the general leaders cannot possibly do all the teaching and leading themselves. The task is simply too much for these few to do without the help of many others. Furthermore, it would neither be wise nor right for these few to do all the work of teaching and leading, even if it were possible. Doing so would deprive others of the joys of productive and meaningful service and of the personal growth that accompanies service.

Achieving the goals of Christian education calls for teaching and leading masses of people. But people are not best led in masses. They are best led in smaller, more manageable groups. The best teaching and leading in Christian education is done by teachers and leaders who are encouraged to know personally those who are being taught. This goal implies the use of large numbers of workers. A church's efforts in education will remain superficial at best if only a few teachers and leaders engage in the enterprise. A few cannot effectively work with masses of people.

Training teachers and leaders is itself a highly significant educational accomplishment for a church. Think about it! Having a sufficient number of teachers and leaders trained for their tasks represents an achievement accomplished by relatively few churches. And who else is to train the teachers and leaders if the church does not? A church must train its teachers and leaders.

Can a church expect to train its members and to educate them in large numbers if it cannot train the ones who will teach and lead them? The quantitative and the qualitative success of a church in educating those who are its responsibility is directly related to the quantity and quality of those whom the church enlists for teaching and leading.

There is a continuing, critical lack of qualified and trained teachers and leaders for churches. The work of the church in fulfilling its mission awaits the availability of such persons. From the operational perspective, this need for "laborers" seems to be the greatest need of the church. There is much work for the church to do. There is a world in need. A sufficient number of committed and trained teachers and leaders could turn "the world upside down" (Acts 17:6, KJV) for Christ in this generation. As a church sets its hopes on teaching and leading a growing number of persons in Christian education, it must also set its hopes on training teachers and leaders in growing numbers. Otherwise, there is little hope of succeeding in the larger task.

In this chapter we will present the task of training teachers and leaders through a variety of ways suited to preservice and inservice training needs. We shall consider training from the standpoints of who should be trained and who should do the training; what should make up the training experiences; when (both in terms of preservice and inservice needs, and with sample schedules) the training should take place; and how to approach and do the work of training teachers and leaders.

Who Shall Train and Be Trained?

Identifying all who should train and be trained in a church would involve naming the leaders and members of all church program and ministry groups. Consider the categories that follow. You might have others to add to these. List those in your church, and think of providing training for their leaders.

There are those who lead in the pastoral ministries of a church. Usually these ministries are led by the pastor, most of whose training is accomplished prior to and away from the training offered by a church. A pastor surely learns much as he leads the church, but his principal training usually occurs elsewhere. Growing numbers of churches, however, are providing sabbatical leaves, financial support, and other encouragements for their pastors to extend their training for ministry.

A church would do well to consider its opportunities in this regard, both in reference to the pastor and to others who serve on the church staff. This is very important to a church for the effective performance of all the church's ministries. One of these is providing training for the leaders in the church and its organizations, a function for which the pastor and the staff have the major responsibility. The future effectiveness of a church may depend on the sensitivity and effectiveness of the pastor and staff in providing training for church leaders. Those who lead in pastoral ministries will be no more effective than their training allows. They should be taught and trained so that they can lead in teaching and training others.

Church members who are selected to assist and to lead in pastoral ministries, such as deacons, need training. There is vital work to be done by these members. They support and assist the pastor and others in leading the congregation to perform its ministries to members and to others. They are active in leading the church's ministry of proclaiming the gospel to believers and to unbelievers. They work directly with the members in a planned program of caring, as an extension and a multiplication of the pastoral ministries of the church. All of these important ministries call for trained leaders. A church should plan for and provide training for these leaders.

Those who lead in the church's Bible teaching program need training. Some leaders work to administer the Bible teaching program. They lead in planning, implementing, and evaluating the program. They need training. Many churches' major outreach is through the Bible teaching program organization (Sunday School and related Bible teaching groups). It is essential that the people who work in outreach be trained, if they are to reach people who will take part in the Bible teaching and learning activities. A church must reach people before it can teach them anything.

The teachers must be trained. Not only must they teach the biblical material, but teachers also must be examples of the spiritual and moral qualities taught in the materials. Too, the role of a Bible teacher in a church suggests that the teacher should lead in the class's ministry of caring for its members. This includes the teacher's personal involvement with individual members in times of need. All of this awesome job calls for training.

Training plans for a church's Bible teachers should receive high priority in a church's educational ministry. Ponder this question: If a church cannot train those who teach, why should a church think it can train its members? It is impossible to "skip" the training of teachers and still hope to be effective in teaching others. Many teachers must be trained, not just a few select ones. Remember, if you want to multiply teaching and learning, multiply the teachers—they are the ones who are apt to learn the most!

Other leaders might be responsible for training new church members. This includes new church members who are new Christians and those who come into the membership from other churches. These new members need instruction in a wide range of subjects. They need nurture. They need to understand the meaning of discipleship. They need to know how to continue their growth in Christ. They need to know their church, and how it goes about its work. They need to know how they relate to the church's ongoing ministries. Those who lead new members have special training needs.

Some members lead in the ongoing training of church members (after the new church member period). These leaders in learning work in areas like Christian doctrine, Christian ethics, denominational doctrine, church polity, and organization. They also need to know how to train in special ministries, such as witnessing and discipling. Such leaders require a very high level of personal preparation in order to do their best possible work. A church should invest appropriately in training these leaders.

There are teachers and leaders in the mission education and action programs of a church. They teach the missionary message of the Bible. They teach the great history of missions and missionaries. They teach of contemporary missions, and of current needs for missionaries. They lead in mission activities, and in support of missions through prayer and through financial resources. They need training. An essential way for a church to multiply missionaries is to teach missions effectively. Good training of teachers and leaders in this significant field is imperative.

Leaders of a church's family ministries need specialized training. This critical concern should call forth a concerted effort to meet the needs. Part of this effort would be to provide leaders with adequate training.

Some churches have ministries to people in special needs categories. Examples are social ministries, ministries to exceptional children, jail ministries, hospital ministries, special student groups, and others. All of these kinds of ministries require training for those who would minister effectively.

A continually expanding ministry area is that of recreation. Some churches have need for leaders such as lifeguards, referees, aerobics specialists, and leaders of social recreation. These leaders need training.

Media center/library personnel in churches need training. The ministries of these workers can enhance the work of many other ministries, and they should have adequately trained people.

There are people who specialize in the various age-group ministries, usually coordinated through the more formal program organizations such as Sunday School. These are people who work with preschool nursery or other preschool children; those who work with elementary children; those who work with youth through high school age; those who work with young adults, in or out of college; those who work with college students and/or career young adults; those who work with median adults; and those who work with senior adults. In several of these age groups are workers who work with single adults—the ones who have never married, the ones previously married, and widows and widowers. Adequate training can make the difference in their success or their failure.

Many churches have a variety of ministries that include weekday ministries like child care and kindergarten. These ministries require qualified, trained workers. In some parts of the nation there are certification standards that demand minimal training. A church should at least meet these requirements.

There are officers of the congregation who need training, such as the moderator (presiding officer), the trustees (legal officers), the clerk (clerical officer), and the treasurer (financial officer). Their tasks are very specialized, and their training should reflect their special needs. In an incorporated church, similar training would be needed for the officers of the corporation, such as the president, vice-president, and secretary-treasurer. All of these people act on behalf of the church membership as a body, and they need to be trained for their responsibilities.

An area of extensive training needs is that of the church committees. Chairmen and members need training regarding the work of their committee and how the committee goes about doing its work in relation to other committees, persons, groups, and the congregation. It is not uncommon for a church of moderate size to have as many as twenty "regular" committees, and some "special" (temporary) committees. Some churches have considerably more committees than that. These committees render various specialized services, and they need training for their tasks.

Music leaders, including accompanists, need training suited to their responsibilities. While many of these leaders received their music training outside the church they serve, they have additional needs for training opportunities which might be provided by the church. Often their need is to better understand the human growth and development needs and the administrative needs of the groups with whom they minister.

Those who work in the nonmusical educational organizations often need to learn about music appropriate to the group they lead. In many churches, the division of labor between the educators who are not musicians and those who are has left too wide a gap, so that little or no appropriate music is used in the educational programs, and limited educational concepts are used in the music programs. Good, continuing training could, in great measure, solve this problem.

Music is too powerful a teaching approach to be relegated to professional musicians only, and educational know-how among musicians could enhance considerably the music ministries in many churches. Musicians and educators, and any who are qualified in both areas, must work out the training needs and help with the training itself.

Perhaps there are still others in your church who need training—like ushers, parking lot traffic directors, broadcast technicians, and others. Think what a magnificent achievement it would be in the educational ministry of any church to have all the teachers and leaders training, intermittently, frequently, regularly. This is a church educational program in itself!

Who should do the training? The continuing initiative for training teachers and leaders must come from general church leaders, like the pastor and staff and the elected leaders of church organizations. While these leaders cannot possibly do all the needed training themselves, they must lead in planning for and in providing adequate training opportunities.

Often it is essential for those whose scope of responsibility encompasses the entire church to serve as the catalyst to those whose responsibility is restricted to a single unit of church ministry. The pastor, for instance, is concerned with and responsible for helping to meet the total church needs, but he cannot be expected to be the trainer for those who lead in meeting all these needs. What he can do, and must do, is to ask the leaders of the respective ministries in the church what their training needs are and how they are planning to meet these needs for those in their organizations. He can make suggestions regarding training approaches they might consider. He can refer them to training resources. He can point them to people and other resources where they might find help. He can encourage leaders and members to be receptive to training opportunities. By his example as a continuing learner/trainee, he can inspire others to train.

The same could be said of other church staff leaders. Such an approach by the general church leaders is essential if a church is to do an adequate job of training church leaders and teachers. This positive attitude can be contagious, but the absence of such an attitude virtually rules out the probability that a church will adequately meet its training needs.

The Church Training organization might offer general leadership training that cuts across program organization lines. This would include training for any type of leadership role commonly held by church members; training potential leaders in basic leadership knowledge, understanding, and skills; and training which enables a person to develop as a leader beyond the responsibilities of a given job.

In consultation with leaders of other church groups, Church Training leaders should plan to make available the desired and needed training for their teachers and leaders. In some church organizations which cannot offer their own specific training there might be need for the Church Training organization to assist. For example, some administrative services groups (such as committees) might work with the Church Training leaders to train chairmen and members of committees. On the other hand, the Bible teaching organization of Sunday School might handle its own specialized training with minimal assistance from Church Training.

The leader of a given organization, or any subgroup of an organization, must be responsive to the training needs of those who serve in that unit. A major contribution of a leader is to develop the people in the organization who share the leadership tasks. General leaders of an organization must develop departmental leaders, who in turn must develop the leaders of groups in the departments for which they are responsible.

At times this responsibility of developing leaders requires help beyond the resources of the organization whose leaders need training. This is an occasion when the general Church Training organization might assist.

At other times the leaders of given organizations can provide the necessary training from the resources of their own organizations. Part of the leaders' responsibility is to see that the training needs are met in the organizations for which they are responsible.

Not all the responsibility for training should be borne by the pastor and staff, the Church Training organization, or the leaders of other organizations or organizational units. The individual Christian who receives the full impact of the call to discipleship—which encompasses learning to live Christ's way in relation to the Father, to self, and to others, and sharing with the Lord in the redemptive enterprise—must take some responsibility for becoming an effective disciple. Such a sense of responsibility includes being receptive to opportunities for training which are offered at others' initiative. It also includes recognizing one's own needs for training, and requesting help to get it. Further still, it includes taking initiative to self-train, especially in the absence of available group opportunities or one's inability to participate in such group training due to work schedules or other obstacles which hinder participation with others.

In short, there is over the long-term virtually no excuse for not training. An individual Christian who wants training can get it in these times, even if he must arrange it for himself alone.

The author once knew a humble, devoted senior adult member who deeply desired training. She could not attend many of the scheduled training opportunities. She operated a day-care program in her home for long hours throughout the day, at times providing care single-handedly for twenty-five or more children ranging in age from a few months to twelve years. She did not drive a car, lived alone, and did not venture out at night to training events.

She was introduced to the idea of completing training courses by home study. In one year she submitted written answers to the personal learning activity questions in the thirty-five books she studied! When asked how she could work as she did and still have the energy to undertake such a vast personal training program she replied, "I often have trouble sleeping at night, so I just use that time to read and study." Surely one who wants to grow through training can do something for himself, whether the "system" meets his needs for training or not.

Beyond the local church opportunities for training there are vast opportunities available. Groups of churches many times offer jointly-sponsored training classes. These often provide very highly skilled and qualified persons as leaders to train teachers and leaders from a group of churches or an entire association. The regional, statewide, and national training events (such as those provided at training conventions, conference centers, and other settings), present an impressive array of training opportunities. Church leaders do well to encourage participation in these for all.

Who should train and who should be trained? An answer might be found in this question: Who should *not?*

What Training Should Include

The content and the experiences a church should provide for training its teachers and leaders are as comprehensive and as complex as the scope of the life and work of the church itself. The suggestions which follow will be illustrative, but, admittedly, not exhaustive, of the possibilities. Later in the chapter there are some suggestions for providing training for specific positions of leadership.

Teachers and leaders need training like that needed by all members of the church. Even before they become teachers or leaders, they need training in Christian discipleship. This involves the Christian's lifelong commitment to the person, teaching, and spirit of Jesus Christ. It involves progressive learning, growth in Christlikeness, application of biblical truth in life, responsibility for sharing the Christian faith, and responsible church membership.[1]

Teachers and leaders need training to be able to live and serve as effective members of the body of Christ. They need certain understandings and relationships skills to enable them to be effective Christian disciples. This training in the Christian way and in the life and work of the church must be seen as spanning the entire life cycle, not as some plateau reached in some terminal sense. Teachers and leaders need to continue to grow in skills of worshiping, witnessing, learning, and ministering.

Teachers and leaders need training that will enable them to develop a valid system of biblical beliefs about God and his relationship to man. This training in Christian theology and Baptist doctrine should include a study of God, man, sin, salvation, the church, the Bible, and other important themes of study which would enable the individuals to organize their beliefs into a personal theology which they could express and apply in daily life.

Teachers and leaders need training to help them grow in Christian character and the ability to express and apply it in every relationship of daily living. Teachers and leaders must surely manifest by their personal lives the knowledge of Christian ethics, the practice of which might well be the most vital teaching or leading they could hope to accomplish. Someone has said that more is caught than is taught in the field of spiritual and moral education. What is to be caught from or taught by the Christian teacher or leader must first be in his possession. Better still, it must possess him.

Teachers and leaders need training that helps them discover and appropriate the meaning and the values of Christian history and the history of their denomination. Biblical history is the foundational area of such training. Subsequent history of the life and problems of the church in relation to society's sectors and to the internal problems of the church itself should greatly enhance the wisdom and the usefulness of teachers and leaders.

Teachers and leaders need training to equip them with know-how regarding the operation of their church—church polity. They need to know how best to organize and work together in such a way that the practice matches the theory to which their faith subscribes and reflects the best stewardship of time, talents, money, and other resources in fulfilling the church's mission.

Teachers and leaders who have not yet or not recently been enlisted to serve in specific places of leadership need training which provides basic knowledge and understanding of Christian leadership and helps develop basic skills in this crucial area. Introductory studies in church leadership should help the trainees develop understanding of leadership roles, both formal and informal, in which they are likely to be most effective. This potential leader training can help make the difference in the success or failure of a prospective leader.

Once recruited, a teacher or leader might need some basic job training related specifically to his new position. Such training comes best just prior to or just after the recognition of need, usually around the time of his initial assignment to a specific job. The training content could consist of studies of age-group characteristics and teaching/learning methods; or how to work with special groups in the church. Those in administrative positions might need training in planning, directing, and evaluating an organization, including relating their unit of organization appropriately to the total effort of the church and to its other units.

When to Train

Train when you want to win! Other factors being reasonably equal in any contest, training makes the difference between those who win and those who lose. Training reflects commitment and desire to accomplish. Some can talk of their commitment and their desire, but the ones who are willing to show their faith by disciplined preparation and training are most likely to succeed in getting a job done. One of the basic "laws" of teaching and learning suggests that one's readiness for learning is at its highest just prior to the time one needs to know.

Preservice Training

Preservice training is training timed to equip those who are just about to go on duty. They might not have been recruited as yet, but

Schedule of Sessions and Assignments
Plan 2: Fast Track—8 Weeks
Course Sequence B

Week	Time	Date	Sessions	Assignments
			Unit I—Learning About Teaching and Learning	
1	Sun. AM		1—Overview of the Course	xxx
	Sun. PM		2—How Learning Occurs	Ford, 138-139
	Wed. PM		3—Teaching Preschoolers and Children—Survey	Allen, ___ ___
2	Sun. AM		4—Observation in Preschool or Children's Department	Caldwell
				xxx
	Sun. PM		5—The Teaching-Learning Process	Ford, 140-141
	Wed. PM		6—Teaching Youth and Adults—Survey	Allen, ___ ___ Caldwell
3	Sun. AM		7—Observation in Youth or Adult Department	xxx
			UNIT II—Introduction to the Bible	
	Sun. PM		8—What Kind of Book Is the Bible?	Johnson, 1-16
	Wed. PM		9—How God Is Related to the Bible Places and People of the O.T.— Part I	17-30, 31-42.
4	Sun. AM		10—Places and People—Part II; How the O. T. Came to Be	45-53, 54-69.
	Sun. PM		11—Places and People of the New Testament—Part I	70-84
	Wed. P.M.		12—Places and People—Part II	85-98
5	Sun. AM		13—How the New Testament Came to Be	99-113
	Sun. PM		14—How the Bible Came to Us; the Bible Speaks Today	114-129, 130-147
			UNIT III—Basic Sunday School Work	
	Wed. PM		15—Reaching People for Bible Study: Outreach	xxx
6	Sun. AM		16—The Weekly Worker's Meeting: Key to Bible Learning Improvement	xxx
	Sun. PM		17—Questions and Answers About Working in Sunday School; Preparation for Student Teaching	xxx
			UNIT IV—Student Teaching	
	Wed. PM		18—Preparing to Teach in Chosen Age Group	Prepare Lesson S.S. Lesson
7	Sun. AM		19—Teach as Assigned	
	Sun. PM		20—Evaluate Student Teaching Experience	xxx
	Wed. PM		21—Prepare to Teach in Chosen Age Group	Prepare Lesson S.S. Lesson
8	Sun. AM		22—Teach as Assigned	
	Sun. PM		23—Graduation of Student Teaching Experience	xxx
			UNIT V—Course Conclusion	
	Wed. PM		24—The Worker's Life and Spiritual Growth; Course Evaluation	xxx

Figure 1

252

they are interested enough in the prospect of teaching or leading that they are willing to train. Perhaps someone has noticed their readiness and has recommended them to receive training to become a worker.

Teachers and leaders of adult and youth groups in regular church organizations should continually be alert to such persons, and should take delight in helping them move along in their growth and development, and into service. One of the marks of effective teachers or leaders is that as a result of their leadership some other teachers or leaders develop to the point of being ready for service. Periodically ask your present leaders to recommend to you those in their group who might be growing toward leadership readiness.

In many churches the largest single organization for education is the Sunday School. It usually has more groups—divisions, departments, classes—than any other organization. It has more teachers and leaders. It probably has a larger number of positions vacant, in need of teachers and leaders, than any other organization at a given time. More plans have been designed for preservice training for Sunday School workers than for other organizations.

The preservice Sunday School training manual in use in many churches of the Southern Baptist Convention was prepared by this writer: *Training Potential Sunday School Workers* (Nashville: Convention Press, 1976). This manual describes three options for scheduling preservice training for Sunday School workers. "Plan 1" is a semester-length plan which calls for two sessions per week for sixteen weeks, with meetings on Sunday mornings and either Sunday nights or Wednesday nights.

"Plan 2" is an eight week "Fast Track" plan with two alternate sequences from which to choose—"Sequence A" and "Sequence B." In "Sequence A," Sunday morning and evening sessions go together for the study of methods, teaching, learning, basic Sunday School work, and student teaching. Wednesday evening sessions are used for biblical study and the course conclusion. In "Sequence B," which is shown in the schedule in Figure 1,[2] each unit is scheduled straight through Sunday morning, Sunday evening, and Wednesday evening until its completion, followed by another unit similarly scheduled. The idea is to offer several courses each year. By doing so, after completing several cycles of the course some churches actually have a waiting list of trained workers. Some have been able to staff dual Sunday Schools or maintain a branch Sunday School after several years of such training. A course overview of "Sequence B" is shown in Figure 2; and a

Course Overview
PLAN 2: Fast Track— 8 Weeks
Sequence B

8 Weeks	1	2	3	4	5	6	7	8
	Unit I—Learning About Teaching and Learning			Unit II—Introduction to the Bible		Unit III Basic Sunday School Work	Unit IV Student Teaching	Unit V Course Conclusion
Sessions	1 2 3 4 5 6 7			8 9 10 11 12 13 14		15 16 17	18 19 20 21 22	23 24

Home Study	Doctrinal Book—The Baptist Faith and Message	"Teaching" book for age group of student's choice

Note: An alternate plan for the home study (individual study) line might be one of these:

(1) Allow seven sessions for the completion of each, leaving no such study during the student teaching unit; or,

(2) Offer one or both of these after the course as part of the leadership training portion of the regular Church Training program; or,

(3) Schedule them for a "lab" or "study blitz" some additional time during the course.

Figure 2

DESCRIPTION OF THE COURSE FOR
TRAINING POTENTIAL SUNDAY SCHOOL WORKERS

We are training for a PURPOSE. Actually, there are several parts to our PURPOSE. We want to *provide trained teachers for present places of service* in our Sunday School. We want to *upgrade our efforts in reaching more people* for Bible study, for Christ, and for church membership. We want to *provide more workers for future expansion* of our Sunday School. We want to *complement other training opportunities* offered by our church. We want to help *remove feelings of inadequacy* which might hinder potential workers from accepting leadership responsibilities. We want to *raise the level of Bible learning and living* for all who attend our Sunday School. We want to *reduce the rate of worker turnover* among Sunday School workers. These are major factors in our PURPOSE.

We have several GOALS. During the next ____ weeks we plan to prepare ____ workers to begin effectively to serve in Sunday School. Of these, we plan to have at least ____ workers prepared to serve in each age division: Preschool, Children, Youth, and Adult. We plan to graduate ____ percent of those enrolled, indicating satisfactory completion of all requirements of the course. • • • • •

HOW shall we do this? We will meet together for the next ____ weeks, ____ times per week, on _____ and _____ to study these units: Learning about Teaching and Learning, and Basic Sunday School Work. We will have a brief introduction to the Bible. We will do student teaching. We will study the worker's life and spiritual growth. We will evaluate our experiences. We will study on our own *The Baptist Faith and Message*, and the "Understanding" book for an age group of our choice. We will conclude with a graduation/recognition service for all who complete the requirements for graduation. We will receive a certificate indicating that we are graduates of the course. We likely will have occasion to consider a specific place of service in our Sunday School, which we then will be better prepared to fill. However, we are free to return to our former class if we so desire.

All of this is made possible in our church because we are committed to the idea that we should offer the Lord our very best effort as we serve him through helping others.

Figure 3

description of the course, designed to be given to prospective students in an organizing session, is in Figure 3. Sample policies for the course are in Figure 4. The manual gives complete details for how to organize and conduct a course for potential Sunday School workers, including directions for each session for those leading in the course.

For other groups, such as church committees, there might be preservice training in brief clinics. These could be one-night meetings, with all committee members meeting together for general training, followed by the first regular meeting of the committees. The conference outline in Figure 5 illustrates what might be presented during the general session of a committee workshop.

In the meetings of individual committees that might follow the general session, responsibilities and other matters of particular interest to each committee could be reviewed and clarified. The committee could then be organized. A more extensive experience for committee training is found in the Equipping Center module *How to Train Church Committees,* produced by The Baptist Sunday School Board, Church Training Department, in conjunction with the Church Administration Department. The Church Training organization could plan and conduct this course in the church.

There are numerous other ways to accomplish preservice training. Some of these ways are the same as those for inservice training for those already at work as a teacher or leader.

Inservice Training

Inservice training is the place where one really learns to teach and to lead. Preservice training can help one make a better beginning as a teacher or leader, but it cannot fully equip one for service. One must learn while doing, and continue to learn and to do.

The pamphlet *Using the Sunday School Leadership Diploma to Train Workers* by Joseph M. Haynes, suggests many of the possible ways and times to accomplish training. Consider these suggestions adapted from the pamphlet:

Times to Accomplish Training

1. Friday night and Saturday morning workshops
2. All-day workshops
3. Consecutive night sessions or a week of study
4. Weekend training sessions, using Saturday morning and afternoon

Policies for the
Potential Sunday School
Workers'
Training Course

The following are policies developed to help make our training course as productive as possible in preparing persons to begin to serve effectively as Sunday School workers.

1. Members attend regularly all sessions. In case of unavoidable absence, members notify director as soon as possible.

2. Class begins promptly at the time scheduled. Members are present at least five minutes before the scheduled time to begin, at which time the roll is checked. Three "tardies" equal one absence on the member's record. (Workers must learn to arrive early in order to be "on time" as leaders.)

3. Members complete all textbooks and other work as required. Make-up work is completed as directed for any sessions missed, and is due at the next session attended.

4. Members do not substitute-teach during the course. They do student teaching as part of the training, but are not called upon to substitute or to teach at any other time. This is intended to protect the student from interruptions during the course.

5. Members who complete the course requirements might be offered a place of service in Sunday School by persons authorized by the church nominating committee. No member is expected to accept a position against his/her wishes. Members may return to their own class following the course if they wish.

6. Requirements for graduation are as follows:
   (1) Attend 75 percent of the total sessions, including student teaching. One who misses more than half the sessions in student teaching may not graduate (see statement about make-up work below).
   (2) Complete all textbooks required.
   (3) Make up all work as directed by the last session, or by the extended time set in consultation with the course director (not longer than two weeks after the end of the course). If time beyond this is needed, the student may complete the work and graduate with the *next* class.

Figure 4

HOW A COMMITTEE GETS HOLD
OF ITS JOB

For the Entire Committee
1. Have a job to do.
2. Have only the persons needed as members of a committee.
3. Know your job.
4. Know the limits of your committee's responsibility.
5. Meet when you must.
6. Look for ways your job *can* be done.
7. Set par for the course.
8. Report to the parent body.
9. Evaluate your work.

For the Chairman

1. Communicate.
2. Lead members to know their job.
3. Plan the agenda for meetings.
4. Begin meetings on time.
5. Understand the problem-solving approach.
6. Lead members to share in decision making.
7. Assign responsibility, and follow through.
8. Briefly summarize the committee's progress in the meeting.
9. Stop the meeting.
10. Supervise the committee secretary's work.
11. Report for the committee.

For the Members

1. Learn what the committee's job is.
2. Be on time for meetings.
3. Discuss freely, and expect others to.
4. Bring solutions, not problems.
5. Accept assignments, and follow through.
6. Report to the chairman on assignments.

Figure 5

    5. Training retreat
    6. Associational Training School
    7. Sunday night training time
       a. Ongoing Church Training groups
       b. Interest groups for Sunday School workers not attending a
          Church Training group
       c. Equipping Center concept
    8. Individual study, using "personal learning activities"
    9. Combination of reading book and joining others for writeup
       sessions
   10. Courses offered one night or day a week until completed
   11. Duplicate sessions offered one day and night until completed
   12. State and/or regional training endeavors
   13. Leadership conferences at Glorieta and Ridgecrest
   14. Sunday morning for potential workers
   15. One night for three weeks with covered-dish supper in homes
   16. One-night training blitz from about 6:00 to 11:30
   17. Two nights (Monday and Tuesday) each week for two weeks
   18. Wednesday afternoon or evening
   19. Weekly workers' meeting time
   20. Mimeographed questions for individual study
   21. Job descriptions, directed reading/listening programs, directed observation/evaluation

Teachers and leaders must train continually. A church should have a training plan which includes a schedule that projects well ahead the opportunities which will be available. Again considering the Sunday School work force, a sample calendar for continuous training is illustrated in Figure 6.[3]

How to Train

Some ideas for how to train teachers and leaders have appeared throughout this chapter already. Many other ideas could be useful.

Using the training program guidelines which follow could be an excellent way for a church to plan to train almost all its teachers and leaders.[4] Consider these guidelines as they might relate to your church.

1. Use the Church Study Course system as the basic resource for training workers. This system consists of a variety of short-term credit courses for adults and youth, as well as noncredit foundational units for children and preschoolers. There are more than four hundred

Sunday School Training Calendar

October-November
- Training for outreach leaders
- Potential worker training class, meeting usually on Sunday morning, Sunday evening and/or Wednesday evening for eight to sixteen weeks, using *Training Potential Sunday School Workers* (diploma requirements included)
- Sunday School evangelism workshop: Training in evangelistic visitation and in improving skills to make faith-sharing visits to members and prospects, using *Witness to Win.* Or schedule at a time when Adult and Youth lesson course materials support workshop purpose (diploma requirement-elective)

December-January
- Preenrollment for participation in January Bible Study Week
- January Bible Study Week
- Ten-week Sunday evening session on *An Introduction to the Bible* (diploma requirement)
- Individual study for *An Introduction to the Bible* for workers unable to attend sessions

February-March
- Associational Training School (diploma requirement)

April-May
- Baptist Doctrine Study (diploma requirement-elective)
- Understand-your-member write-up session: An all-age training effort for all church organizations, using *Understanding Adults, Understanding Youth, Understanding Children,* and *Understanding Preschoolers,* with mimeographed questions distributed ahead of time (diploma requirement)

June-July-August
- Sunday School Leadership Conferences at Glorieta and Ridgecrest Baptist Conference Centers and state assembly training (diploma requirements)
- Age-group workshop: *Teaching Adults in Sunday School, Teaching Youth in Sunday School, Teaching Children in Sunday School, Teaching Preschoolers* (diploma requirement)
- Individual study of teaching books for workers unable to attend workshop, using *Personal Learning Kit* for each book

August-September
- Training recognition banquet to recognize workers' achievements in training, giving special recognition to those earning a Leadership Diploma
- Preparation Week (diploma requirement)
- Preenrollment for Bible Survey Series, beginning in October.

Figure 6

courses in twenty-three subject areas. Some of the courses are also presented in Spanish. Here are the subject areas:

The Church
Evangelism and Witnessing
Christian Growth and Service
Bible Studies
Baptist Doctrine
Christian Ethics
Christian History
Stewardship
Missions
Church Music
The Christian Family
Basic Church Leadership
Age-Division and Special-Group Characteristics
Sunday School Leadership
Church Training Leadership
Woman's Missionary Union Leadership
Brotherhood Leadership
Church Music Leadership
Pastor and Staff Ministry
Deacon Ministry
Church Administrative Services
Church Media (Library)
Church Recreation Leadership

2. Determine the training needs of workers. Talk with workers individually and in groups. Check the long-range plans of the church. Consult the leader groups of each church organization (like the Sunday School council, the Church Training council, music council, Woman's Missionary Union council, Brotherhood council, Committee on Committees). Anticipate organizational expansions which will require additional workers.

3. Enlist potential leaders who are willing to train. In the enlistment interview, the prospective worker's attitude and commitment to training should be evident.

4. Adopt a church policy on training. This policy could establish some minimal acceptable goals for training for those who are to serve as elected workers. For example, each person in a place of leadership could be expected to complete at least one training course each year and to work toward a diploma appropriate to his area of responsibility.

5. Interpret the requirements for the various leadership diplomas

and for diplomas in other categories that might fit leaders' needs. The *Church Study Course Catalog,* updated annually, lists the requirements, and gives ample information for use of this plan. The same information is also in the annually updated *Church Materials Catalog.*

6. Prepare a calendar of training opportunities, such as the sample shown in Figure 6. Use this calendar for planning with individuals and with groups to develop plans for training throughout the year.

7. Include training expenses in the church budget. Consider costs of outside personnel, materials needed, and expense assistance for persons attending training events at conference centers, assemblies, associational, regional, and other opportunities.

8. Maintain a record of training for each teacher and leader. A person could be elected for this important assignment, or a clerk in the church office might have this job. The pamphlet *Using the Sunday School Leadership Diploma to Train Workers* gives detailed guidance for record keeping, which could be adapted to serve the entire records needs for all training of teachers and leaders of the church.

9. Present diplomas to workers as soon as they are received. Recognize these workers personally, and in church publications.

10. Conduct a recognition banquet. Some find that September is a very good time for this event, since it immediately precedes the new church year in many churches. Recognize those who have completed diplomas during the year. Call attention to others who have previously earned or made progress toward diplomas. Have a good time of fellowship at the table and some inspiring encouragement to move forward in training.

There is much more about training that could be helpful to know and to use in training teachers and leaders. For instance, some workers might desire training on the college or seminary level. There are almost four hundred Seminary Extension Centers located over the country, with more than ten thousand persons engaged in continuing education under the guidance of the Seminary Extension Department. Many are also enrolled in the Home Study Institute for correspondence study, offered by the Seminary Extension Department.

Churches must train teachers and leaders. Give this emphasis a place of high priority in your church, and observe the vast difference over a reasonable period of time. You can reach more people for Christ through adequate training, and reach them in a better way!

Notes

1. For further discussion of this and other general training needs of teachers and leaders, see *A Church on Mission,* comp. Reginald McDonough (Nashville: Convention Press, 1980).

2. Figures 1—4 come from Charles A. Tidwell, *Training Potential Sunday School Workers* (Nashville: Convention Press, 1976).

3. Joseph M. Haynes, *Using the Sunday School Leadership Diploma to Train Workers* (Nashville: The Sunday School Board of the Southern Baptist Convention, n.d.).

4. Adapted from Ibid.

10

Guiding Outreach and Enlistment

Bruce P. Powers

Outreach and enlistment are major activities for evangelical churches. Along with their educational endeavors, these churches stress reaching and involving new persons in their activities, with the hope of making and maturing Christian disciples.

Why Combine Education and Outreach?

Efforts to involve more people in an organization must be viewed from two perspectives: individual growth and corporate growth. The *individual* perspective of growth is focused on providing educational experiences which will enable individuals to discover their existence as children of God, and grow to their full potential as part of a loving, supportive community of faith. This type of growth might be selfish and self-centered, however, unless complemented with a commitment to *corporate* growth.

Corporate growth relates to the spiritual growth of a group or congregation; to the development of a maturing, caring, cohesive body; to the process of discovering, developing, and using spiritual gifts; to the reaching of the multitudes for Jesus Christ.

There are those who dichotomize individual and corporate growth, usually at the point of meeting personal needs *versus* reaching the masses. This is unfortunate because neither can be fully accomplished without the other. Each supports the other and makes the other more effective.

The Great Commission (Matt. 28:19-20) focuses on four great action words that bring individual and corporate growth together: *go, make* (disciples), *baptize,* and *teach.* It is this *mandate* that calls leaders to seek growth not only for each person but also for the entire body of which they are a part.

Guiding Outreach

Ongoing visitation that is a natural outpouring of inward conviction and concern is central to reaching people. For many persons, such contacts are a natural part of life-style witnessing, whether telling others about the good things happening, visiting a sick person, or inviting someone to visit a Sunday School class. Others, however, find it helpful to have some structure to assist them in outreach, and most congregations find a support system increases the quantity and the quality of visitation.

A Time

Set aside regular times for churchwide (or department, class, etc.) visitation. This might be weekly, biweekly, or monthly, morning and/or evening. The key is to make it *regular,* and to provide all the encouragement and support necessary for the congregation to *believe* this is a priority. Promote the time, schedule no competing activities, and, if needed, provide child care for those visiting.

A Place

Determine a regular meeting place to serve as an administrative and rallying point. Often this will be the church building, but it could be any place that is convenient to visitation points and where parking and meeting facilities are available.

A Visitation File

Maintain a file of prospects and other persons who might be responsive to a visit. Classify persons in three categories—nonmembers, inactive members, and sick/shut-in members—and give equal attention to each group. Before each visitation time, priorities for visits should be set so that visitors will know exactly whom to visit, why, and where.

To develop a system for a visitation file, arrange for

- Information gathering—Set up channels to receive names and contact data for persons in each of the three visitation categories. Designate a person (and place) to whom outreach leaders, department directors, teachers, and other interested church members will send names. Provide cards in pew racks so that worshipers can indicate if they need a visit or give the name of someone who does (see Figure 1). Make contact, through church members if possible, with realtors, newcomers clubs, and utility companies to arrange for sharing of newcomers lists. At least once a week, transfer all names and contact information to prospect file cards. (See Figure 2.)
- Setting up the file—Arrange cards in three categories, nonmem-

Combination Visitor and Pastor's Card

Please fill in   DATE _____

YOUR NAME _____

ADDRESS _____ PHONE _____

CITY _____ STATE _____ ZIP_____

BUSINESS _____

YOUR HOME CHURCH _____

WOULD YOU LIKE A VISIT FROM THE PASTOR? _____

PLEASE CHECK AGE GROUP

☐ Under 12   ☐ 18-29   ☐ 45-over
☐ 12-17   ☐ 30-44

(Front)

pastor's card

BROADMAN
B P
SUPPLIES

NAME _____

ADDRESS _____

PHONE _____

THIS PERSON   ☐ IS SICK   ☐ IS NEW RESIDENT
☐ DESIRES PASTORAL CALL   ☐ WANTS OFFERING ENVELOPES
☐ PROSPECTIVE MEMBER   ☐ HAS CHANGED ADDRESS TO

_____
(Name of person giving information)
PLEASE USE THIS CARD FREELY.
Code 4333-06, WV7, Broadman Supplies, Nashville, Tenn., Printed in U.S.A.

_____
Place in offering plate.

(Back)

Figure 1

PROSPECT FILE CARD								

PROSPECT FILE CARD
Form 5

Date	Prospect's name

Street address	City	State	Zip Code	Home phone no.

Mailing address (if different)		Date of birth	School grade

Church member?	Church to which prospect belongs	City

☐ Yes   ☐ No

Additional information

Assigned to:	Department	Class/group/choir/etc.	Date

Visited by	Date	Results

Code 4380-05, Broadman Supplies, Nashville, Tenn., Printed in U.S.A.

Figure 2

bers, inactive members, and sick or shut-in members. In a small church, all cards might be kept together. If many cards are involved, code them by marking a different color in the corner of each to distinguish the categories. In large churches, or in urban areas, it might be helpful to maintain a separate set of files according to area of town, community, or zip code.

- Using the file—Cards should be filed in each category by priority, with the most important coming first. Cards should be removed and visits made according to priority. Once contacts are made, appropriate information should be recorded and the cards placed in a Return Box.
- Maintaining the file—Review comments recorded on visitation cards. Reclassify the card if appropriate; channel it to a class outreach leader or other responsible person; recycle for another visit; or place in an inactive file.

A Leader

Effective visitation requires a committed leader who will promote and coordinate activities. This person would review the visitation file; arrange and distribute assignments; support, encourage, and participate in visitation; and assist in collecting, evaluating, and reporting results. A church staff member or a highly motivated layperson could provide this leadership. If visitors gather at several meeting places, a coordinator for each location would need to be enlisted by the leader to assist with leadership responsibilities.

Guiding Enlistment

Closely related to outreach is enlistment. Rather than having a general purpose, however, the aim of enlistment is to secure participation in specific organizations or activities. Although usually administered by leaders at the department/class/group level, persons with churchwide educational responsibilities often are called on to provide assistance.

To help you give guidance in enlistment, here are the basic principles involved in reaching and involving new people in educational organizations. Included in this chapter are a training session work sheet (Figure 3) and an enlistment plansheet (Figure 4) which could be used in training workers.

Why Do People Respond?

People are need-oriented. That is, they tend to respond to needs they feel or can be caused to feel. The greater the need one feels, the stronger the desire to satisfy that need. For example, if a person has a longing for a more active social life, the tendency is to try to satisfy this need. If a person feels a need for training in how to witness, he will attempt to meet this need.

People usually respond to invitations that, in their opinion, promise some satisfaction or benefit. For example, if you were to invite someone to join your group, he would wonder, "Why?" The appeal must answer this question if the expectation is to reach and involve the person in that group.

How Are People Reached?

The prospect has in his mind the question "Why should I?" To reach him, two things must be done: (1) Determine and/or help him recognize a need that he has; and (2) offer a *benefit* that, in the prospect's opinion, will meet his need. The prospect has needs; a group must offer benefits. When needs are *matched* with appropriate benefits, the potential is greatly increased for reaching and involving prospects.

What Is Enlistment? What Is Publicity?

Most people are familiar with the word *enlistment,* but if you had to describe what it means, what would you say?

We must also be concerned about *publicity.* What does this word mean? How are enlistment and publicity related?

Basically, enlistment is reaching and involving someone in an activity. It may involve informal contacts, personal visits, telephone calls, or a personal note. *But the contact is usually person to person.*

Publicity, on the other hand, is designed to provide information, to create awareness or an image, or to develop a desire on the part of the person receiving the message. Publicity may involve posters, newspaper announcements, skits, signboards, and mass mailings. Usually the contact is impersonal in that an impersonal *message* is intended to reach people.

Once enlistment and publicity are distinguished, one can tell that they have similar purposes—that is to reach people. Yet, strangely, they do *not* accomplish similar results.

Publicity, as it provides information or creates an image, simply increases the potential for response. It does not "sell" anything unless the person receiving the message feels or can be caused to feel a need related to the "product" offered by the publicity. If the publicity offers a benefit that will meet a need felt by the receiver of the message, then the potential for positive response is present.

Now here is the problem. *Most of what is done in enlistment endeavors is actually publicity.* Consider the manner in which most churches try to reach new members: posters, bulletin announcements, announcements from the pulpit and in Sunday School departments, skits, newsletters, and various other types of mailings. All are publicity, and publicity never enlists anyone unless a person feels a need which can be met by the "product" offered.

Enlistment, however, can build on a potential for response and, because of the personal contact, focus on the needs and concerns of the prospect, showing him the benefits that would meet his needs.

Enlisting Members in Educational Organizations

A. Distinguish between publicity and enlistment.
   What is publicity?_____

   _____

   What is enlistment?_____

   _____

   Notes:

B. Evaluate your group's publicity.
   1. What image is your group conveying to the church through its publicity?_____

   _____

   2. What are some ways your group has made people aware of study opportunities available to them?_____

   _____

   3. What types of publicity are used most often?_____

   _____

   Is there good variety?_____ Yes _____ No
   4. Where are some places that would be good to locate publicity?_____

   _____

   5. What other channels for publicity are available to your group?_____

   _____

C. Evaluate your group's enlistment.
   1. Who is responsible for enlistment in your group?_____

   _____

   2. What methods of enlistment are used most often? How are these related to the topics studied?_____

   _____

   3. How effective has your enlistment been?_____

   _____

   4. What are some suggestions you would make to your group?_____

   _____

D. Application
   The work sheet on the following page is based on the information given above. Select a coming unit of study and work through it as if you were planning activities for enlistment and publicity.

Figure 3

269

Training Group Publicity and Enlistment Work Sheet

Enlistment Leader—*Prepare work sheet for each unit studied* in continuing and short-term training groups.
(Prepare in duplicate. Give one copy to your Director of Enlistment or your Church Training Director.)

UNIT FOR STUDY _____ Date of Study _____ Enlistment Leader _____

Who	Where	What	by Whom
1 DECIDE ON "TARGET GROUPS" List in this column some special groups of people or individuals who need this unit, or are interested in it, and might be enlisted.	**2** PUBLICITY & ENLISTMENT LOCATIONS Write in this column the best place to find and influence these groups. (S.S. depts, homes, meetings, bulletins, services)	**3** WHAT SPECIFIC METHODS AND PLANS will you use to publicize the unit? (posters, skits, announcements in S.S. depts, letters, visits, bulletin, articles, telephone calls, etc.)	**4** ASSIGN RESPONSIBILITY for each of the enlistment plans to some person. Write names in this column.
TARGET GROUP (1)	WHERE	WHAT	BY WHOM
TARGET GROUP (2)	WHERE	WHAT	BY WHOM
TARGET GROUP (3)	WHERE	WHAT	BY WHOM
TARGET GROUP (4)	WHERE	WHAT	BY WHOM
SPECIFIC INDIVIDUALS this unit might reach.	WHERE	WHAT	BY WHOM

5 Joy in Fellowship

(Plan at least one social activity per quarter.)

What kind of fellowship or social activity could we plan which would both aid our present membership and possibly assist in enlisting other persons? (visitation night climaxing with a social or fellowship: social or picnic to which we bring guests; banquet, party, etc.)

Activity _____

Date _____ Person in Charge _____

Figure 4

Enlistment is always person-to-person and is capable of relating benefits and needs.

Planned or Unplanned Activities

Enlistment and publicity activities are usually of two kinds: those that are planned and those that develop out of the normal activity of the group and its members. Planned activities, such as posters and announcements, personal visits, and socials, are coordinated by the enlistment leader in a group.

Unplanned enlistment is the natural outgrowth of a well-functioning group. Members just naturally tell others what they are doing, and people can see desirable things happening in the group members' lives. Casual contacts are made when a friend says, "Come join our group."

Planning for and Conducting Enlistment

The key to reaching people effectively is to match a prospect's needs with the needs a particular unit of study or a particular group will meet. For example, a person who feels the need for a study on witnessing can most easily be reached when the group is studying witnessing.

Here is how to plan for effective enlistment and publicity:

1. Determine the needs a particular unit of study will meet.
2. Answer these questions:
   a. Who has these or similar needs (may be individuals or groups of people)?
   b. Where can these people be reached?
   c. What methods will be most effective in reaching these people? (Keep in mind a balance between publicity and enlistment activities.)
   d. Who will be responsible for each of these publicity and enlistment actions?

The important thing in this plan is to be specific and to involve the group in making enlistment and publicity plans. (A sample plansheet developed by Charles M. Lowery is illustrated. This could be used in planning sessions.) The enlistment leader should lead the group in this planning at least two weeks prior to the unit of study. An intensive enlistment effort based on a unit of study that will meet specific needs should be made at least once a quarter.

11

Christian Education and the Small Church

Daniel Aleshire

Several years ago, I was participating in a study to identify what issues and concerns volunteer agencies deal with as they seek to implement new programs. One of the routine questions asked was: "Do you think it is easier for large or small organizations to innovate new programs?" Persons in large organizations always answered that it was easier for a small organization to innovate. Persons in small organizations always responded that it was easier for large groups to implement new programs.

Large congregations, with all their complexity, often look wistfully at smaller congregations. Smaller congregations often think that all their problems would be solved if they were larger. Size does influence how a congregation goes about its tasks. There are positive characteristics that come from being large and from being small. However, there are also negative characteristics that are produced by congregational size, large or small. This chapter seeks to identify the special issues that are part of being a small church. There are both positive and negative concerns, and we will explore both.

Most Protestant churches in the United States are "small" congregations. For example, approximately 60 percent of the thirty-four thousand Southern Baptist congregations have memberships under three hundred. The United Methodist Church, the second largest Protestant denomination in the country, has an even larger percentage of churches with memberships under three hundred. A similar picture emerges for Presbyterian and Disciples of Christ congregations. Although an increasing percentage of the persons affiliated with a denomination are in larger churches, the average church in most denominations is still relatively small.

What is "small"? The definition of the small church is, of course, arbitrary. In some areas of the country, a Southern Baptist church with 300 members and an average Sunday attendance of 140 would be considered "large." However, many writers tend toward defining the small church as the church with fewer than two to three hundred members. Churches this size usually have one part-time or full-time minister. There is seldom a second staff person to aid the ministries of the church. Building facilities are usually limited. Small churches have a number of other distinctive characteristics that deserve consideration.

The Nature of the Small Church

Most churches are small, by the arbitrary definition that we have chosen, and a significant number of church members in this country receive all the Christian education they will receive in the small church setting. If these people are to receive the gifts of good Christian education, they will receive them because the nature of the small church has been taken seriously, and an appropriate educational program had been implemented. A consideration of the effective program rightly begins with several questions about the nature of the small church. Why are churches small? What are the advantages of the small church? What are the disadvantages of the small church? What might these various characteristics mean for the task of Christian education in small congregations?

Why Are Churches Small?

It would be easy, though improper, to assume that all churches are small for the same reasons. Paul Madsen identified a variety of reasons why a particular congregation may be small.[1] Consider first some of the positive elements that may make a congregation small.

Some congregations are small because they reach out to a limited target population. The influx of immigrants to the United States requires the establishment of churches that are either bilingual or non-English speaking. In many communities, the number of persons who are Korean, or Vietnamese, or Laotian-speaking may be only two to three hundred. Even if a special mission church reaches the entire population, it would still be a small congregation. Southern Baptists have been especially successful at establishing non-English speaking congregations. But in so doing, they have established many congregations which will not grow into large, multiple-staff ministries.

Other churches are located in sparsely populated areas. The church can reach out, win, and enlist a number of people. But if the total population within driving distance of the congregation is very limited, there is little chance that the church can grow very large. Some churches have been isolated by an interstate highway or some other major barrier that effectively cuts them off from a population area they might otherwise serve.

Still other congregations are small because they have a very intense concept of what it means to be the church, and demand that members abide by significant disciplines. This makes a particular congregation unattractive to some prospective members. For example, some congregations require that all members submit to the discipline of tithing, or that a certain number of hours be invested in ministry. These disciplines can be seen as consistent with the values of the gospel, but may have the effect of limiting the size of the congregation.

Many congregations remain small for less positive reasons. Some congregations are small because they have a limited vision of what it means to be the church. They are comprised of a few families who treat their church more like a family club than the people of God on mission. Their church is not large, even though it could grow by reaching more people.

A lack of any sense of evangelism keeps other congregations unnecessarily small. They may be happy to welcome any who come and anxious to receive them. However, they refuse to go into the community to enlist persons for Bible study, fellowship, or worship.

There are many churches that remain small because of serious internal problems. Division and strife are in the church. Every time the church begins to grow, some kind of power struggle emerges which saps the church's strength and the members' desire to reach out. There are many churches whose history is one of strong people who used the church for their own personal needs, or whose vision of the gospel was so distorted that they did wrong, thinking it right. The actual Christian education in some of these churches teaches that the church divides against itself and is a place where people struggle, fight, win, and lose.

The task of Christian education can be a very discouraging one in churches that are small for these negative reasons. Few programs can introduce the gospel's fresh wholeness and love in the middle of an environment that is destructive and punitive.

The reason for a church's small size will greatly impact the quality of Christian education that church will provide.

If the church is small because of its very intentional program of discipleship, or because it has adequately included all of the limited number in a particular region or group, it can be an ideal environment for Christian education. Much of this chapter is written for the church that does not have some congregational failure that explains its smallness. Healthy, small congregations have many strengths to bring to the tasks of Christian education.

Advantages of the Small Church

The small church is probably more sensitive to the disadvantages of being small than to the advantages. However, an effective program of Christian education grows out of the positive features of being small.

First, small size in no way restrains a congregation's ability to be all that the church was meant to be. The purposes of the church include worship, fellowship, evangelism, mission, and education. None of these purposes is dependent on size. Each is possible in the very small congregation.

Some of these purposes, in fact, may be more easily accomplished in small congregations than in larger ones. For example, fellowship is a task that gives large churches a great deal of difficulty. Large churches are frequently comprised of hundreds of people who do not know each other well, and who find it difficult to fellowship with each other. But fellowship comes easily and naturally to many small churches. People know each other. They are usually aware of each other's traumas and burdens and can easily provide the ministry of support and care. In many large churches, persons can be carrying very heavy burdens and no one ever knows. As the purposes of the church are defined, the small church is not disadvantaged. It can achieve all of them.

Another advantage of the small church is the quality of learning that can be accomplished. Christian education requires a certain kind of learning. It is not just the learning of facts and ideas, although those are important. It requires the learning of feelings and the learning of how to live life consistently with faith. This kind of learning requires involvement in doing the tasks of the church—not just hearing about them.

In many small congregations, youth are required to be leaders because of limited personnel. In large congregations, youth tend to be the recipients of program ministry. Faith can grow in both settings, but I think it takes on new dimensions when youth are leaders. The number of officers and helpers in the church programs in the small church represents a much higher percentage of the membership than it does in the larger congregation. There is more of a chance here than in large church settings that people in the small church will learn because they are serving and helping others learn.

The small church can make changes with less bureaucratic involvement than is possible in larger congregations. This characteristic represents a third advantage. While the smaller church may be limited in financial and building resources, it has decided advantages in the process of decision making and implementing those decisions.

Disadvantages in the Small Church

Of course, all is not rosy in the small church. It labors very hard in the face of the consumerism that has become a part of American church choosing. Many people are not looking for a place to invest their lives but for an environment with the best facilities, the most active youth program, and the best selection of ministries available. This attitude puts the small church at a disadvantage in seeking to reach out and attract persons in the community.

However, attitudes that people in the community have about a church may not be as much of a disadvantage as the attitudes that members of the small church may have themselves. There are a variety of debilitating attitudes that sometimes exist in small church environments.

Persons in the small church may be inclined to think that because they are small they are bad. The current emphasis on church growth may cause some churches to feel like failures if they are not large. The growth emphasis is positive and needed—it is in the mission of the church to reach out and to grow. However, no community can have all large churches. That idea not only denies a desirable preference for Christians who want to work and witness through smaller congregations, it is also numerically impossible. A community of twenty-five thousand just cannot have too many five thousand member churches! So church members should not feel guilty because their church is not large. Frequently, the guilt feelings become inhibiting attitudes which keep the church from making the most of its potential.

Another disadvantage in the small church is that it may feel it must do everything that denominational agencies and boards recommend. Those agencies are charged with the responsibility of relating to all the churches, and that includes providing ideas for very large and complex congregations as well as small ones. Many denominational leaders come to their positions from large congregations, and their experience in large congregations becomes an unintentional, though permeating, referent for them. The ideas and programs that flow from the agencies may appear excessive, if not oppressive, to smaller congregations. They are perceived as expectations and discourage the small congregation because it cannot do them all.

Sometimes small congregations put themselves at a disadvantage because they don't take their size seriously. They try to run all the programs and provide all the ministries that a congregation three times their size might provide. The result is that members are overworked and feel discouraged. Small churches need to recognize the limitations their size places on them. They should then perform those ministries of which they are most capable and which are most needed in a particular community.

Of course, small churches do face the limitation of resources and persons. These can be serious disadvantages. A small inner city church may need far more financial resources than it has to do the benevolent ministry that an urban, blighted area requires. There may be the legitimate need for recreation facilities in a rural area where there are none, or for a minister who can devote a great deal of time to youth or migrant workers who may spend much of the year in a church's community. But size frequently prohibits such ministries.

Finally, the small church may find itself at a disadvantage because of the reasons that keep it small. I have already suggested that a church may be small for some negative reasons such as divisiveness, or lack of vision or concern. The same dynamic that makes the church small can make any kind of ministry very difficult. It may not be the church's smallness that sabotages the ministry. Instead, the reason for the church's smallness may create the disadvantage.

Small congregations, just like large ones, must understand the mission of the church, identify the ministries they can effectively provide, and work diligently to provide those ministries. The small congregation should work with the conviction that its mission is to do the purpose of the church and accomplish the tasks which God has given to the church. It may discover, as it emphasizes these things, that growth may come. The small church need not always be small. Rather it may determine to use the advantages of being small while it is small, and emphasize the advantages of larger congregations as it grows.

Doing Christian Education in the Small Church

The reasons a church may be small, as well as the advantages and the disadvantages of being small, all influence the task of Christian education. This section discusses Christian education in terms of the realities of the small church, the organization and planning appropriate for a small church, the educational leadership needed in the small church, and the growth opportunities that emerge through the small church's program of Christian education.

Accepting Educational Realities in the Small Church

The small congregation cannot operate all the programs that larger churches can. It should not even impose the same expectations on itself that larger churches do. Rather, it should seriously examine the content of a good program of Christian education and determine how it can make that kind of education available within the limits of its resources. Such an examination begins by reviewing the objectives of Christian education (see chapter 2).

The primary objectives are to help persons become believers, mature as believers, and learn how to live as believers. This frequently translates into educational opportunities that include: Bible study; the study of doctrine, ethics, church polity, church history; missions; music; and opportunities to participate in mission and service activities. Larger churches can sustain programs with specially trained leadership in many of these content areas. But the smaller church may not be able to maintain separate programs. However, it can incorporate these learning areas into the programs that it can maintain.

If, for example, a rural church is a "half-time" church with preaching service every other Sunday, it may choose to meet for two hours during "nonpreaching" Sundays to study missions, ethics, doctrine, and church history after it has had Bible study during Sunday School. Reality may say that the church cannot support the detail of a variety of separate programs. But reality also says that a small congregation can systematically include the areas of study in Christian education.

Another reality which the small church faces is the lack of leaders. The scarcity of persons in the small church frequently means that the church must use anyone who will serve. For example, youth may need to help with the preschool and elementary children, or play the piano for worship. However, this is the limitation of the small church, and that limitation must be accepted with grace.

This limitation, however, can also be a strength. People grow in their own faith through accepting responsibility. Because they are working in the education and worship life of the church, youth may be receiving the most meaningful experience possible—even though they are not enjoying the benefits of special youth ministries. It may be that the best formation program of Christian faith is the doing of that faith. The small church provides many with that opportunity.

Small churches must confront their own attitudes about being small. Smallness is, in many ways, an advantage in learning environments. But if the only attitude is guilt and anger about size, none of those benefits are likely to have a chance to emerge. Some churches seem to feel that smallness is a condition which they must rid themselves of as soon as possible. Churches with this kind of attitude will be troubled by their smallness and will not use it effectively. A healthy concept of the benefits of smallness will make a congregation more inclined to set out on ministry and be attractive to many persons. The small church can teach the gospel, can help people live the gospel, and can reach out to its community. It needs to develop attitudes that reflect that positive reality!

Organization and Planning in the Small Church

Some small churches decide that because they are small and everybody knows everybody there really is no need for planning or structure. It is true, of course, that they do not have the same need for organization as may exist in larger churches. But even very small churches need to plan and organize their work.

Planning is a way of assuring the best use of limited resources. It is a process that can include evaluation, as well as impose the discipline of periodically examining the community, determining what ministry needs exist, and discovering ways of meeting those needs. Planning is an effort by which the church can reflect its stewardship and commitment to the gospel. If a small church does not have the resources to maintain all church programs, then planning becomes an important means of assuring that each of the areas that should be taught in a program of Christian education will be taught. Planning provides a systematic way of exploring means of reaching those goals.

The organization in the small church should be flexible and realistic. Basic class units can be formed for preschool children, elementary children, youth, and adults. If a church is able to sustain more units, the large age-span groupings can be subdivided and several classes formed within a department structure.

Developmental characteristics in children do mean that older preschoolers function better when they are separated from the younger preschoolers. However, families with a two-year-old and a five-year-old get along, and so can a Christian education class with two- and five-year-old children. It is more difficult, but it is not impossible. There is not one correct organizational pattern for the small church. However, developing class structure around basic age groups is one that has demonstrated its effectiveness.

The organization should include more than class or department groupings. It should also have a director, someone to maintain up-to-date records, and someone who will facilitate the tasks of outreach and enlistment. The organizational system is not the goal of a program of Christian education. It is a necessary ingredient for implementing those goals. Basic leaders and basic age groupings—those are the organizational necessities.

Leadership for Christian Education in the Small Church

Leadership for Christian education in the small church centers in the pastor. If the education program is not important to the pastor, the church will likely evoke little significant investment in it. The pastor is the key.

Pastors facilitate the program in three ways. First, they seek to motivate people to become involved and interested in the issues of Christian education. Second, they provide the expertise necessary for the program organization, direction, and planning. Frequently, pastors may be the only individuals in the small church who have had any opportunity for training in Christian education. And, even though they may not feel theirs has been adequate training, it is likely more training than anyone else has had.

A third way pastors facilitate the program is through the active training of lay leadership. Training is a very important ingredient in the program of Christian education. It is especially important in the small church. The large age spans in classes, for example, make teaching more difficult. Coping with this difficulty requires training. While pastors may not have the skills necessary to do all the training, they can encourage volunteer workers to attend training conferences that are held frequently in local associational gatherings.

The small church, even more than the large church, depends on the faithful work of volunteers. The small church needs to be careful not to overwork some willing individuals to the point of exhaustion. It must realize that the volunteers are the key to the accomplishment of its ministry. Volunteer workers should be openly appreciated by the congregation and encouraged. They should be recognized in meaningful ways. The small church, where everybody knows everybody, sometimes may not be inclined to give to individuals the amount of recognition which they are due. But this should not be the case. Leadership for Christian education begins with the pastor, and should be passed on by motivation, training, and affirmation to volunteers.

Education as the Growth Agent

One of the important ways that the program of Christian education can serve the church is that it can become the church's primary outreach agent. James Fitch suggests that "The genius of Sunday School is that it organizes all church members into outreach groups."[2] He goes on to suggest that the effectiveness of the Sunday School program as a growth agent emerges from training Sunday School members to the possibilities and responsibilities of outreach, helping teachers teach inspiring lessons, and motivating class members to bring prospects with them to church.

Growth does not just happen. It happens because people determine to grow, are willing to enlist and to incorporate new persons into the fellowship, plan for growth, and have the kind of organization that quickly accommodates growth.

Conclusion

The small church brings many advantages to the tasks of Christian education. Some of the things that come easily in the small church must be artificially manufactured in large churches. The small church must not lose sight of its true strengths. Neither should it be unwilling to be something other than a small church. Many small congregations have the responsibility to reach out in their communities to people who have not heard the gospel. Failure to reach out is a failure to accept the responsibility of being the people of God who function as the body of Christ.

There are disadvantages, as anyone who ministers or serves in the small church knows. But the disadvantages are not fatal. The small church is still boldly the church. It still can accomplish the education that can help people become believers, mature as believers, and live like believers.

Notes

1. Paul Madsen, *The Small Church: Valid, Vital, Victorious* (Valley Forge: Judson Press, 1975), pp. 19-30.

2. James Fitch, "Growth Through an Effective Sunday School," *Helping a Small Church Grow,* ed. Bruce Grubbs (Nashville: Convention Press, 1980), p. 30.

12

How to Get Started

Daniel Aleshire

If this volume contributes to the reader's learning, it should produce a number of new ideas. These include ways to improve existing programs, new programs to start, and new ways of doing the things that have been done the same way for a long time. All of these ideas mean that the educator is now faced with the task of getting started—which is the task of processing innovations through the organization. This task requires serious consideration in its own right.

Many excellent programs remain unused not because they are faulty programs, but because there was a faulty way of getting started. Few people reading this book are going to be starting a program of Christian education from scratch. It is far more likely that a program of some kind exists, and that it is in need of revision. But whether revision or an entirely new program is called for, getting started must be taken seriously.

Getting started—at least as this chapter characterizes the task—involves careful attention to three considerations. The first is a reminder that most programs of Christian education depend on the faithful support of a committed and volunteer labor force. It is important to understand what it means to be sharing ministry with volunteers. Leadership begins with the establishment of certain attitudes and concepts, such as trust. These become quite crucial when dealing with volunteers and innovations.

A second consideration is the importance of adequate assessment and evaluation to determine which needs a program should meet and what kind of programs will meet those needs.

A third issue concerns the process of innovation itself. It is a process that is hard, and frequently ends in failure. To be successful, innovation requires careful attention to several important variables.

This chapter will consider these three issues as they relate to the task of getting started. Together they comprise a comprehensive approach to innovations in local congregations.

Building an Atmosphere That Facilitates Innovation

Getting started means that a leader takes seriously the nature of the people with whom he or she is working. They are volunteers, but they are also sinners who have experienced the grace of God in their lives. Both facets of their identity will influence the leader's relationship to them.

Reginald McDonough,[1] for example, points out that people may volunteer for both positive and negative reasons. They may volunteer because they want to serve God, help their church, or help other people. These are certainly positive motivations. But people may also volunteer because they need recognition, want to be "in charge," feel guilty, or feel coerced. These are not so positive! Different motivations mean that volunteers cannot all be treated alike. A good leader is sensitive to the different motivations which bring volunteers to service, and varies leadership style according to those differences.

All volunteers in the church are sinners who are being touched by God's grace. That means they may be untrusting at times. They may even be undependable at times. And while they may accept these failures in themselves, they may not accept them in others. Sin has not been completely conquered in them, and that will influence their attitudes and insights.

These characteristics mean that leaders need to cultivate several attitudes among the people they seek to lead. Leaders begin to cultivate these attitudes in others by developing some attitudes of their own.

Attitudes to Be Cultivated

First, the leader needs to begin where the people are. They may not be well-trained. Caring leadership means that leaders will seek to implement programs which take into account the ability of the volunteers. Getting started frequently means leader training. When leaders can't be trained, it may mean a program is revised or left unused. Beginning where the people are may mean that the leader respects the degree of attachment volunteers may have to existing programs. Even though a program may not meet many needs, it may be meeting some very pressing needs in the lives of some people. People should not have their attachments torn from them. Be sensitive to the pain that sometimes accompanies necessary change.

In addition to these attitudes which the leader should reflect, there is one important attitude which must emerge among the volunteers: trust. Trust is not something that can be manufactured. It must grow over time in the presence of several fertilizing agents.

One of these agents is honesty. As the minister relates honestly, keeps promises, and lives consistently with his or her beliefs, an atmosphere of trust begins to emerge. Another characteristic that helps trust develop is a leader's ability to hear persons. Sometimes, leaders are so busy convincing people of a new idea that they spend very little time hearing—seeking to understand the needs, hurts, burdens, and concerns of the people they are serving. Time and energy expended in careful listening is time spent developing a legitimate basis for trust. The more persons are assured that they will be heard, the more likely they are to place their trust in persons.

Still another characteristic that nurtures an atmosphere of trust is the leader's careful effort to keep commitments. Keeping commitments is one way of demonstrating that an individual can be trusted.

The leader also needs to be caring and should know how to communicate that care. When persons feel that the minister is genuinely concerned for their welfare, the opportunity for trust emerges.

Another agent of trust in a church leader is that he or she be a person who in all ways, and all times, seeks to live the gospel. Nothing will build trust more graciously than the leader's being sincerely, consistently, and patiently Christian.

Regardless of these efforts, reality reminds us that a leader cannot create trust or force persons into trusting relationships. That violates the very nature of trust. An atmosphere where trust might emerge can be created; the qualities that nurture trust can be shown; but no one can make some people trust others. In fact, there are some people who are incapable of trust. They don't trust anyone. Ministers must accept the fact that some people will not trust them, and good leaders should not feel as though they are failures if some persons find them untrustworthy.

Getting started begins, then, with understanding the nature of volunteer workers and establishing some attitudes both in the leader and in these volunteer workers. But the establishment of an understanding and trusting environment is only the first phase of getting started. It is also important that the leader learn how to evaluate needs and programs and become sensitive to the technical process of innovation.

Assessment and Evaluation

One of the temptations which can lead to failure for the designer of a program of Christian education is fascination with a good idea. Now, on the surface, that appears to be a very good thing. But, though it may sound bizarre, Christian education that serves the people of a local church and community can never be based on good ideas. Rather, it must be based on the needs of particular people in particular places with respect to overarching objectives. Needs emerge through the processes of assessment and evaluation.

The problem with good ideas is that they may not relate to the particular needs of people. Sometimes, innovations in Christian education emerge in the following way. Someone returns from a visit to a friend's church with great enthusiasm about one of its programs. The church program sounds like a good idea to the local minister, who calls the minister at the friend's church to determine the details. The details make it appear that the program could be initiated and a valid ministry could be provided. The program is launched, but soon it becomes obvious that the program is not going to provide the ministry for which it was intended. It was a good idea, but it didn't work.

Problems like this one can be lessened by an adequate assessment of needs and a proper evaluation of existing and proposed programs in light of those needs. The task of revising old programs and designing new ones must always emerge from a commitment to assessment and evaluation.

The Task of Assessment

Assessment is the means by which the needs of a particular church or community are identified, and the available resources for meeting those needs determined. An educational innovation should clearly meet some need. Something should get started because it *needs* to get started—because its inauguration will enhance the doing of the church's objectives.

There are many ways of determining needs. A minister may be able to identify some by his or her own careful evaluation of existing programs or procedures. Or several people can be interviewed to determine what they perceive needs to be. Or, in a more thorough method, individuals throughout the congregation can be surveyed, their responses tallied, and a comprehensive perception of needs identified.

The difference in these approaches is that each increases the base of judgment by including more people. The perception of some needs may require a very limited base. For example, the need to change the records that are kept on individuals enrolled in the education program may be identified from a relatively limited base. But the perception of other needs may require a much larger base. For example, the need for a new educational facility may require a broad-based perception.

There will almost always be more needs than any church can meet. So the congregation must engage in a constant effort to determine which needs are most central to its task and which could be met by other institutions in the community.

The multitude of needs means that the congregation's available resources must also be monitored. Some needs may have to go unmet until additional resources are available. Good ministry includes both the use of available resources and the nurturing of others. But while those resources are being nurtured, some needs may go without the church's response.

If, for example, everybody in the church who can teach is already teaching twice a week, the implementation of a program involving a third hour of teaching may harm the overall ministry of the church. The problems of resources, such as too few teachers, may identify other needs—like training new teachers before a new teaching program is inaugurated.

The assessment of needs is an important part of getting started. It is also closely linked with the task of evaluation.

The Task of Evaluation

Evaluation, according to one writer, is a "pronouncement concerning the effectiveness of some treatment or plan that has been tried or put into effect."[2] Getting started not only means that needs must be assessed, but also that existing programs and approaches should be evaluated. Evaluation is possible when certain conditions exist.

The first is that there must be some meaningful definition of what success or failure is. This definition provides the criterion by which a judgment can be made. For example, an evaluation of a Sunday School outreach program can be made only after some definition of success has been determined. Is a Sunday School program of outreach in need of replacement if the Sunday School is growing by 20 percent, or 15 percent, or 2 percent? At what point does one evaluate the program (pronounce the effectiveness) as a success or failure? One of the advantages of taking evaluation seriously is that it imposes the discipline of seriously identifying the standard of success or failure.

Caution must be introduced at this point. Sometimes persons evaluate a program by irrelevant criteria because these criteria are readily observed. Thus, while attendance growth might be both a good and readily-identified criterion for the effectiveness of a Sunday School outreach program, numeric growth may not be a good point for the evaluation of the total Sunday School program.

If the Sunday School is growing but is teaching in ways that do not help persons become believers, mature as believers, or behave as believers, then the effectiveness of that program must be seriously challenged. Budgets and attendance are frequently used criteria, not because they are necessarily the most appropriate but because they are highly visible. Adequate evaluation not only imposes the discipline of determining identifiable criteria, it also insists that the criteria be appropriate standards for judgment.

A second characteristic necessary for adequate evaluation is some satisfactory means of conducting the evaluation. There are different ways in which evaluation can occur. It might be appropriate, for example, to evaluate a program that has been started to help persons grow spiritually by having persons who participated in the program complete a questionnaire. They could use the instrument to express how the program has helped them in their own devotional life and growth in faith.

Rossie, Freeman, and Wright[3] suggest that the ongoing process of administering programs includes at least four different kinds of evaluation. One is the evaluation of the planning process by which programs and events are determined necessary. This kind of evaluation monitors the planning process to see if the objectives are clear, and determines if the programs or innovations being considered are clearly related to those objectives.

A second kind of evaluation is the monitoring of existing programs. This evaluation seeks to answer questions like: Is the program functioning according to plan? Is it being conducted in accordance with its intentions? This kind of evaluation is necessary so that the final assessment of the program can be completed with the confidence that the program functioned as intended. If the program should be evaluated as a failure, for example, the leader can be confident it failed because it was an inadequate program—and not a good program improperly conducted.

A third kind of evaluation asks: Has the program achieved its intended goals? A fourth kind of evaluation is realistic but very hard for churches to ask or answer: Is the program cost effective? Of course, no one can place a dollar value on a person accepting Christ, but a church has a limited amount of money. Money invested in some programs may win and nurture some persons, but that same money invested in other programs may win and nurture even more. Somehow, the congregation must take seriously the stewardship of spending money the best way possible.

Assessment and evaluation—these are important parts of getting started. They can be used in a way that aids a congregation in doing its job. Of course, they can be useless nuisances, too. But properly understood and adequately done, they can help Christian educators know what needs are unmet, what educational and program innovations are needed, what programs or ministries need revision, and which ministries are effectively fulfilling their intended purposes.

Getting Started: What to Do

The proposal of almost any innovation in procedure, program, or ministry will usually be greeted by several obstacles. Obstacles, in at least one way, are very good. They are a church's way of protecting itself from needless change. Change requires a great deal of energy, and any change that can be avoided probably should be.

But the right kind of change, in response to properly identified needs, is crucial for a congregation's continuing ability to serve in effective ways. It is never enough simply to know what should be done. It is equally important to know how to go about the task of innovating. What are the issues that naturally arise when a new ministry is being started? What are appropriate responses to those issues? What is the most appropriate way to introduce new, meaningful programs of ministry?

Variables That Influence Innovation

There are different ways of looking at change. One of the more fruitful, and one appropriate for churches, involves eight variables which Howard Davis has termed A VICTORY factors.[4] While Davis did not develop this model from work with churches, much of what he says has been shown by other research to be relevant to the innovation of new programs of ministry in local church settings.[5]

The first factor is *Ability:* Does the church have the resources or the capabilities to introduce the ministry? For example, let us suppose that the need for space and an evaluation of building and energy costs lead a congregation to decide to conduct two Sunday School programs rather than build additional space. The question immediately arises: Are there enough qualified teachers to staff two Sunday schools which meet at different times? Questions like this one concern the church's ability to implement a particular innovation.

One of the issues that must be clearly determined is the ability of the church to do the proposed ministry. If the ability is present, then that reality needs to be carefully documented and demonstrated. Many good and needed expressions of ministry never move beyond introduction to church business meetings because the ability of the congregation to carry out the innovation has not been carefully ascertained.

A second factor that stands between the invention of a new education ministry and its innovation in the church is the issue of *Values:* Does the new program reflect the values of the congregation, its sense of ministry, and its understanding of the gospel? It is at this point, too, that many good programs become unusable in some congregations. Sometimes, a program does not fit the values of the congregation.

Chapter 2 of this volume discusses the mission and tasks of the church. One emphasis there is that programs of Christian education must reflect those purposes and tasks. In other words, programs must correspond to the values of gospel ministry which define all of the church's task. If a program does not correspond to those values, then it should not be implemented. The right concern for values will lead the congregation to implement the most appropriate ministries.

There is, however, a way in which concern for values can have a negative impact on a congregation's educational ministry. If a church has a misguided sense of values (for example, "We don't want those people to attend here"; or, "We are not responsible for teaching anything about ethics"), then those misguided values can prevent the innovation of a program that is wholly in harmony with gospel values.

Information is another of the variables that must be dealt with in the process of getting started. The persons considering the program, and those seeking to implement it, must have information about the program. That information must make sense, show that the program can indeed accomplish the goals for which it is intended, and provide a profitable addition to the church's ministry. Like the variable of abilities, this variable requires leaders to prepare carefully, and to make information available.

Sometimes persons seek to innovate by keeping some information secret, or by keeping some people uninformed. Such a practice not only goes against the earnest of the Christian faith, it also sabotages the program's chance of being implemented. Persons both require and deserve an adequate information base in the process of making decisions about innovations.

A fourth concern is the *Circumstances* in which the new program emerges. Sometimes, the circumstances are "right" for the introduction of a new program. When the spirit of the congregation is united and optimistic, the circumstances are amenable to accepting the challenge and hope of a new program of outreach or ministry. But when the people are divided and torn, when they are at odds with each other, then the circumstances all but guarantee that the new ministry will fail. Some congregations seem to be able to make almost anything work. Other congregations seem to be able to make nothing work. The issue may not be the quality of the innovation, or even the ability of the congregation. Rather, it may be that the circumstances in some congregations, and the circumstances alone, determine the ultimate adoption or nonadoption of a needed program of ministry.

A closely related variable is *Timing.* An innovative ministry might be more acceptable at one time than it is at another. *Obligation,* the sixth variable that Davis discusses, seems to be of less importance to innovations in churches in the free church tradition than might be true of other organizations. There are few changes which a congregation can be obligated by an outside agency to make. Few changes can be foisted on congregations; however, there should be a sense of internal obligation. That is, the gospel may imply the need for a revised program of ministry, and the church should feel obligated by the gospel's demand to make the revision. Thus, while the congregation may not be susceptible to obligation from without, it must ever be open to internal obligations that emerge from the leadership of the Spirit and the teaching of Scripture.

Frequently, the response of many will be, "Why change at all?" If innovations are really appropriate, it must be because they meet needs that are related to the church's mandate. Thoughtful people will frequently require the internal obligation before they are ready to start a program.

Even if all these criteria are accounted for, there is still another variable that can keep an innovation from being implemented: *Resistances.* No matter how needed, no matter how good, no matter how much anchored in the demands of the gospel, most educational ministry innovations will be met by some resistances. People may honestly disagree; feel threatened; they may just not want to change. Whatever the reason, there will frequently be resistances. Thoughtful attempts at innovation require individuals to consider these possible areas of resistance and deal with them forthrightly. They will not go away.

Sometimes, ministers and church leaders must proceed with an innovation even though some resistance remains. There are few times when everyone will be in agreement about every detail. It is inappropriate to think that one must wait to get started until everyone is "on board" and in agreement. That time may never come. Resistances should be taken seriously, considered objectively, and reacted to sincerely and patiently.

There is one last variable to consider in the process of getting started in a new ministry or revising an existing one: the *Yield* that can be anticipated. This variable deals with the potential benefit that might be realized from the implementation of a new program of ministry. Since starting new programs requires so much energy, a church has a right and a responsibility to inquire as to the yield that a new ministry will provide. Just what good will it do, after all?

This variable is sometimes very difficult to assess. The yield from many needed ministries to the community and church family is hard to define objectively. This difficulty can lead churches into beginning only those programs that have a clearly identifiable yield. Sometimes it is easier to build a new building than it is to do anything else, because the yield of such a project—a new building—is so self-evident. The definition of yield is important, both in the process of evaluation as discussed previously, and in the church's consideration of a new program.

The process of getting started depends, in part, on the skill of a minister or educational leader in dealing with these eight variables that influence the adoption or nonadoption of new or revised ministries.

Steps Toward Implementation

Much of the literature on change, in one way or another, deals with the variables that have been listed in A VICTORY model. But knowing the variables is not enough. They need to be incorporated into some basic steps which should be followed when initiating a new ministry. The first step includes defining the nature of the problem which requires some new ministry. The second step is to identify the kind of ministry that will meet the stated problem. The third step involves the development of motivation in the people who will vote on the change and who will work to bring about its implementation. A fourth stage involves the trial use of the program, and its consequent adoption.

1. The purpose of assessment and evaluation, as explained earlier in this chapter, is to provide information about the relative success of existing programs and the need for new ones. If an ongoing process of evaluation is working, then the need for change or new programs will not come as a surprise. The congregation can become comfortable with the idea that, from time to time, readjustments in the program will be necessary for the church to meet its primary Christian education goals. The process of evaluation will lead to awareness by some. But the level of awareness must always be increased beyond that of the persons directly involved in the evaluation process.

2. The second step is to provide detailed information concerning the nature of a proposed program, how that program would work, why a particular program is the best way of meeting an agreed-upon need, and what the cost of a prospective program might be.

The natural consequence of the information stage is that persons will raise questions about the proposed innovation, and an evaluation of the proposed innovation will occur. Sometimes persons read the questions and evaluations raised at this time as resistance to the change. While that may occasionally be the case, that is probably a less than fair interpretation of the evaluation that follows introduction to the detail of a new program. Many times, the questions lead to helpful clarification and needed revisions in the proposed innovation.

One of the things that occurs during this stage is that more and more persons hear about the innovation and place their evaluation on it. Christian educator Bruce Powers notes the importance of broadening the base of support that should undergird the implementation of the innovation.[6] However, it is probably wise not to artificially increase the base beyond what is adequate, appropriate, or necessary. For example, if the innovation involves some aspect of missions education for boys and girls, it may not need a larger base of support than the men's and women's missionary organizations. While the implementation of innovations should never be done on the sly nor people left deliberately uninformed, it is not necessary to have everybody informed about everything, nor to make the innovation contingent on everyone's stated or implied consent.

3. Any initiation of a new ministry or a change in existing ministry

requires motivation. Knowing that something should be and that a particular innovation is a good thing to do is never adequate to accomplish the tasks of an innovation. Motivation for change is necessary. It is also necessary that motivation be in keeping with the gospel that calls the ministry into existence in the first place.

Powers discusses three approaches to change.[7] In some ways, these three approaches reflect three ways of motivating persons. The first is to induce change based on power. Pastors or church staff members may, for example, appeal to the power of their position to motivate the congregation to change. In this motivational model, it is the role of the leader to make and enforce decisions, and the role of the congregation to follow and implement those decisions. There are certainly many ministers who appeal to this form of motivation.

Another approach to change is based on expertise. Some expert expresses what is best, and that motivates the group to implement the recommended change. Some research on the nature of innovation in volunteer organizations suggests that many churches use the expertise approach to change—though volunteer organizations are less likely to use this approach than some others.[8]

A third kind of motivation is through discrepancy. If people become aware of a discrepancy between what is and what is desired, that awareness will provide a stimulus for solving that problem. The motivational assumption is that once concerned people are informed of realistic needs, they will be moved to meet those needs. This kind of motivation reflects images of the church as servant and people of God. It is a very positive form of motivation, although at times it may appear abstract.

4. The fourth step deals with the actual innovation process. Some research suggests that a group is more likely to innovate if it can do so on a trial basis first. Many educational innovations should be instituted on a trial basis. This allows less commitment from the congregation, is more likely to be acceptable, and makes it possible for more permanent changes to be based on actual experience.

If a change is good, the trial usage gives it a chance to prove itself. If the change is not as effective as anticipated, the trial adoption allows it to be either revised or eliminated without major investment from the church. Of course, some innovations—like a new building—cannot be implemented on a trial basis. But most educational program innovations can be tested in this way.

Once the trial period has passed, the innovation finally needs to be adopted. While trial periods are usually desirable, there also must be a point at which the congregation makes a commitment to continue a particular ministry. Some programs are plagued by persons who consider them up for reconsideration every business meeting. If people are expected to invest energy and hopes in a program that has proved successful on a trial basis, they need to have the security that the program will not be capriciously eliminated.

A Few Other Considerations

As these variables and steps are being negotiated, the minister must keep a few other things in mind. The first is that persons become open to innovation differently. Some people are nonadopters—it just isn't in them to be open to new ideas, to work toward their inauguration in the church, or to support those who are open to innovations. There are such people in almost every church. While they have a right both to be a part of the church and to their position, they cannot be allowed to keep the church from doing what needs to be done. Church leaders need to remember that there are people like that in every church and not be discouraged because these persons resist change.

There are other people who are the opposite. They are true innovators, and will make use of almost any new idea that they discover. It is sometimes easy for the church leader to gravitate to these people when innovations need to be made. They are open and amenable; they are supportive; but they are not like the rest of the congregation. The minister needs to remember that they are exceptional.

The majority of people in most congregations will be open to change if they have a chance to understand the issues, can clearly identify the benefits, and are given time to participate in the decision-making process. But even within this group, some will innovate more readily than others.[9]

Another important thing to keep in mind is that innovation saps a great deal of energy from a church. A church can only handle a certain amount of innovation without actual damage. Some congregations become so innovative that all their energy goes into their innovations. Some of the energy should remain available for care, fellowship, worship, and growth in faith. Sincere leaders need to discipline the amount of change that is permitted to flow into the congregation's life.

Getting started is an important process. It is also one of the hardest things a leader can do. Imagining new programs, making plans, identifying structures, and designing organizational patterns can become attractive ends in and of themselves. But the reason one engages in these tasks is to come to a point of engaging in meaningful ministry.

Notes

1. Reginald McDonough, *Working with Volunteer Leaders in the Church* (Nashville: Broadman Press, 1976), pp. 12-18.

2. W. Edwards Deming, "What Is Evaluation?" *Handbook of Evaluation Research,* eds. E. Streuning and M. Guttentag (Beverly Hills, California: Russell Sage Foundation, 1975), p. 53.

3. Peter Rossie, Howard Freeman, and Sonia Wright, *Evaluation: A Systematic Approach* (Beverly Hills, California: Sage Publications, 1979), p. 32 ff.

4. Howard Davis and Susan Salasin, "The Utilization of Evaluation," *Handbook of Evaluation Research,* p. 643 ff.

5. See, for example, *Effecting Utilization: Experimental Use of Consultants, Phase I Report* (Minneapolis, Minnesota: Search Institute, 1978).

6. Bruce P. Powers, *Christian Leadership* (Nashville: Broadman Press, 1979), p. 52.

7. Ibid., p. 38.

8. Part of this information is in *Effecting Utilization: Experimental Use of Consultants: Phase I Report.*

9. McDonough, p. 73 ff.

13

Resources for Educational Ministry

Jerry M. Stubblefield

How does one find appropriate resources for educational ministry? A danger for any minister is the temptation to use only those resources learned about during school days. Books, tapes, and periodicals are being produced at a very rapid rate. The minister should have an in-depth acquaintance with the various resources developed by his denomination. He needs to be aware of products distributed by other evangelical denominations and Christian publishers.

Book reviews are published in many religious publications. *Search,* a quarterly periodical published by The Sunday School Board of the Southern Baptist Convention; *The Southwestern Journal,* produced by Southwestern Baptist Theological Seminary; and *The Review and Expositor,* a journal issued by Southern Baptist Theological Seminary, regularly have book reviews. Denominational state papers also list resources both in reviews and advertisements.

Many seminaries and divinity schools duplicate lists of resources for key areas of educational ministry. If you need help in a particular discipline, a request to a professor or a school could provide you with an up-to-date list. Obviously, you do not need an entire course bibliography. You want to know the significant works that are currently being used. Denominational seminars and workshops can acquaint you with helpful, up-to-date materials.

The Minister's Inner Spiritual Life

It is easy for a minister to devote much of his time to a study of mechanics—preparation of sermons, devotions, administration, program-oriented materials. Every minister must devote major attention to the development of spiritual resources—his own inner spiritual life. Attention needs to be given to serious, systematic Bible study, reading of the major devotional classics, and the development of one's prayer and devotional life.

Annotated Bibliography

Baillie, John. *A Diary of Private Prayer.* New York: Charles Scribner's Sons, 1949.
  Prayers for mornings and evenings for a month. A page is provided for personal reflections.

_____. *A Diary of Readings.* New York: Charles Scribner's Sons, 1955.
  365 readings from the mainstream of devotional writing. Stimulates serious thought and contemplation.

Barclay, William. *A Guide to Daily Prayer.* New York: Harper and Row, 1962.
  Prayers for morning and evening are arranged with appropriate Bible readings for forty days.

Donne, John. *Devotions Upon Emergent Occasions.* Ann Arbor: The University of Michigan Press, 1959.
  A series of meditations written during a dangerous illness.

Hallesby, O. *Prayer.* Minneapolis: Augsbury Publishing House, 1931.
  A profoundly simple and practical book on the important subject of prayer. It is written for those who need and desire help in their prayer life.

Kelly, Thomas R. *A Testament of Devotion.* New York: Harper and Row, 1941.
  A series of devotional essays written about the inner life. Practical guidance is presented about how one may lead a religious life in the world.

Kempis, Thomas À *The Imitation of Christ.* London: Collins, 1957.
  A manual of devotion intended to help the Christian in communion with God and the pursuit of holiness.

Law, William. *A Serious Call to a Devout and Holy Life.* Philadelphia: Westminster Press, 1955.
  A devotional classic intended to prod indifferent Christians into making an honest effort to live up to what they profess to believe.

Macdonald, George. *Diary of an Old Soul.* Minneapolis: Augsbury Publishing House, 1965.
  A unique devotional book of prayers in verse form for reflective meditation; one for each day of the year.

Rinker, Rosalind. *Communicating Love Through Prayer.* Grand Rapids: Zondervan Publishing House, 1966.
  Shows how prayer can be more than words; how it can be personal communication with God, when our attitudes are changed.

Educational Resources

To effectively lead a church's educational program, the minister must be aware of the various resources provided by his own denomination as well as general religious education resources. Every denomination annually publishes a catalog of available leadership resources. These include books, cassettes, filmstrips, films, and supplies. Each minister or church should receive a copy.

To limit oneself to one's own denominational materials would be to limit one's vision and growth potential. A minister should be learning new ideas and methods from many available sources. The annotated bibliography which follows is arranged under general headings and is selected from a variety of sources.

Christian Education

Cully, Kendig B. *The Search for a Christian Education—Since 1940.* Philadelphia: Westminster Press, 1965.
   Makes readily available the rational ingredients for a coherent Christian education philosophy.

Edge, Findley B. *A Quest for Vitality in Religion.* Nashville: Broadman Press, 1963.
   Institutionalism threatens the vitality of Christian churches. Clarifies what the "people of God" are to be and to do in the modern world in light of scriptural teachings.

Groome, Thomas H. *Christian Religious Education.* San Francisco: Harper and Row, 1980.
   A broadly ecumenical, foundational text. Draws from the best in contemporary philosophies of education, social theory, biblical scholarship, and theology.

Miller, Randolph Crump. *The Clue to Christian Education.* New York: Charles Scribner's Sons, 1950.
   Places a central emphasis on the beliefs of the Christian tradition as a solid base for the religious development of children.

_____. *Education for Christian Living.* 2nd ed. Englewood Cliffs: Prentice-Hall, Inc., 1963.
   Christian theology is the cornerstone upon which Christian education must be built and by which the theories, objectives, and methods of Christian education are determined and evaluated.

Powers, Bruce P. *Christian Leadership.* Nashville: Broadman Press, 1979.
   Effective Christian leadership is not based on knowing principles or acting in particular ways but in adopting a life-style based on certain principles.

Richards, Lawrence O. *A Theology of Christian Education.* Grand Rapids: Zondervan Publishing House, 1975.
   Discusses the theological concepts that form the content and underlie the method of Christian education. Emphasis upon the "whole-person focus" and the involvement of the entire church community.

_____, and Clyde Hoeldtke. *A Theology of Church Leadership.* Grand Rapids: Zondervan Publishing House, 1980.

Activities of the church are not task- or project-oriented but people-oriented. Church members are ends, not means, and the dynamic processes of growth come through interaction.

Schreyer, George M. *Christian Education in Theological Focus*. Philadelphia: Christian Education Press, 1962.
Thoroughgoing presentation of what is involved when Christian education is undertaken in its proper "theological-supernatural" setting.

Sisemore, John T., Compiler. *Vital Principles in Religious Education*. Nashville: Broadman Press, 1966.
Identifies the basic principles on which to build practical and relevant education programs.

_____, ed. *The Ministry of Religious Education*. Nashville: Broadman Press, 1978.
Foundations, organizations, vocational leaders—the broad sweeps and specific details of who, what, and why in the church's work of teaching and training.

Taylor, Marvin J., ed. *Religious Education*. Nashville: Abingdon Press, 1960.
Planned as a systematic study of religious education. Though dated, it provides some essential background data concerning religious education.

_____. *An Introduction to Christian Education*. Nashville: Abingdon Press, 1966.
Serves as an introductory survey of all of Christian education.

_____. *Foundations for Christian Education in an Era of Change*. Nashville: Abingdon Press, 1976.
Supplement to *An Introduction to Christian Education,* it offers exciting probes into religious education perspectives of the past decade. Takes account of the past and dips into the future of religious education in America.

The Church's Teaching Ministry

Bowman, Locke E., Jr. *Teaching Today*. Philadelphia: Westminster Press, 1980.
Suggests how the church can utilize volunteer lay leaders to achieve a successful Christian education program.

Coleman, Lucien E., Jr. *How to Teach the Bible*. Nashville: Broadman Press, 1979.
A practical approach to how to teach the Bible.

Cooperative Curriculum Project. *The Church's Educational Ministry: A Curriculum Plan*. St. Louis: Bethany Press, 1966.
A design of the church's educational ministry, appropriate to the urgency of the church's mission. Describes the scope of the curriculum combined with the sources for teaching-learning opportunities.

Edge, Findley B. *Teaching for Results*. Nashville: Broadman Press, 1956.
Stresses the importance of definite teaching goals, ultimately leading to Christian action.

Ford, LeRoy. *Design for Teaching and Training.* Nashville: Broadman Press, 1978.
Designed for effective self-study yet applicable for the classroom. Good description of the teaching-learning process.

Glen, J. Stanley. *The Recovery of the Teaching Ministry.* Philadelphia: Westminster Press, 1960.
Appeals for a reassertion of the teaching ministry of the church. Urges the uniting of teaching and preaching.

Little, Sara. *The Role of the Bible in Contemporary Christian Education.* Richmond: John Knox, 1961.
Proposes a philosophy of Christian education which must be understood in the light of the rediscovery of the biblical message.

Richards, Lawrence O. *Creative Bible Teaching.* Chicago: Moody Press, 1970.
Comprehensive encyclopedia to the basis, approach, and methods of Bible teaching—Bible teaching that will communicate God's Word in a contemporary, relevant manner.

Smart, James D. *The Teaching Ministry of the Church.* Philadelphia: Westminster Press, 1959.
Provides a theological basis for Christian education. A detailed plan for implementing a new church school program which recovers the historic meaning and power of ministry for Christ.

Age-Group Resources

Children—Birth through Eleven
Cully, Iris V. *Christian Child Development.* New York: Harper and Row, 1979.
Applies teachings of educators and psychologists to the religious education of children, birth through twelve.

Davis, Cos H., Jr. *Children and the Christian Faith.* Nashville: Broadman Press, 1979.
Help for parents and church workers interested in the instruction of children during the conversion experience and in the Christian faith.

Elder, Carl A. *Values and Moral Development in Children.* Nashville: Broadman Press, 1976.
Understanding values and moral development in children is necessary if parents and teachers are to fulfill their equipping tasks.

Fulbright, Robert G. *New Dimensions in Teaching Children.* Nashville: Broadman Press, 1971.
Practical assistance for those using the team teaching approach to teach children.

Ginott, Haim. *Teacher and Child.* New York: Macmillan, 1972.
Offers tools and skills for dealing with daily situations and psychological problems faced by all teachers.

Gordon, Ira J., ed. *Early Childhood Education.* Chicago: The National Society for the Study of Education, 1972.

Attempts to stimulate interest in and contribute to meeting the educational needs of young children.

Hendricks, William L. *A Theology for Children*. Nashville: Broadman Press, 1980.
A clear picture of systematic theology; suggests ways to help children understand the major doctrines of the church.

Youth

Richards, Lawrence O. *Youth Ministry: Its Renewal in the Local Church*. Grand Rapids: Zondervan Publishing House, 1972.
A practical guide to working with youth in the local church. Designed for the youth minister, sponsor, or leader.

Sparkman, G. Temp, ed. *Knowing and Helping Youth*. Nashville: Broadman Press, 1977.
Insight into helping youth find a meaningful Christian experience through insight into youth development.

Strommen, Merton P. *Five Cries of Youth*. New York: Harper and Row, 1974.
Presents a meaningful portrait of church youth, rather than a piecemeal attempt to grapple with their symptomatic problems.

Adults

Bergevin, Paul, and John McKinley. *Adult Education for the Church*. St. Louis: The Bethany Press, 1970.
An educational plan for adults utilizing participative procedures and processes.

Knowles, Malcolm S. *The Modern Practice of Adult Education*. New York: Association Press, 1970.
Explores a comprehensive theory that will give coherence, consistency, and technological direction to adult education practice.

Zuck, Roy B., and Gene A. Getz. *Adult Education in the Church*. Chicago: Moody Press, 1970.
Deals with the how-to of adult Christian education. Focuses on the need for family life education.

Bibliography

Adams, Arthur M. *Effective Leadership for Today's Church.* Philadelphia: Westminster Press, 1978.

Adams, Ernest R., and James E. Fitch. *Reaching People Through the Sunday School.* Nashville: Convention Press, 1979.

Adams, Ernest R., and Mavis Allen. *How to Improve Bible Teaching and Learning in Sunday School.* Nashville: Convention Press, 1976.

Allen, Mavis, and Max Caldwell, compilers. *Helping Teachers Teach.* Nashville: Convention Press, 1976.

Anderton, Lee, compiler. *Church Property and Building Guidebook,* Nashville: Convention Press, 1973.

Beal, Will, compiler. *The Work of the Minister of Education.* Nashville: Convention Press, 1976.

Belew, Wendell. *The Purpose and Plan of Baptist Brotherhood.* Memphis: Brotherhood Commission, 1979.

Beveridge, W. E. *Managing the Church.* London: SCM Press, 1971.

Bower, Robert K. *Administering Christian Education.* Grand Rapids: William B. Eerdmans, 1964.

Byrne, H. W. *Improving Church Education.* Birmingham: Religious Education Press, 1979.

Colson, Howard P., and Raymond Rigdon. *Understanding Your Church's Curriculum.* Nashville: Broadman Press, 1969.

Conner, Ray. *A Guide to Church Recreation.* Nashville: Convention Press.

Couch, Robert A. *Church Weekday Early Education Administrative Guide.* Nashville: Convention Press, 1980.

Craig, Floyd. *Christian Communicator's Handbook.* rev. ed. Nashville: Broadman Press, 1977.

Crowe, Jimmy P. *Church Leader Training Handbook,* rev. ed. Nashville: Convention Press, 1974.

Davis, Howard and Susan Salasin. "The Utilization of Evaluation" *Handbook of Evaluation Research.* Eds. E. Streuning and M. Guttentag. Beverly Hills, California: Russell Sage, 1975.

Deming, W. Edwards. "What is Evaluation?" *Handbook of Evaluation Research.* Eds. E. Streuning and M. Guttentag. Beverly Hills, California: Russell Sage Foundation, 1975.

Drucker, Peter F. "Long Range Planning: Challenge to Management Science." *The Management Process.* Comp. Carroll. New York: Macmillan, 1973.

Edgemon, Roy T., compiler. *Equipping Disciples Through Church Training.* Nashville: Convention Press, 1981.

Effecting Utilization: Experimental Use of Consultants, Phase I Report. Minneapolis: Search Institute, 1978.

Fitch, James. "Growth Through an Effective Sunday School." *Helping a Small Church Grow.* Ed. Bruce Grubbs. Nashville: Convention Press, 1980.

Flegal, Bob. *Sunday School Director's Handbook.* Nashville: Convention Press, 1979.

Furnish, Dorothy Jean. DRE/DCE— *The History of a Profession.* Nashville: Christian Educators Fellowship, 1976.

Grubbs, Bruce. *Helping a Small Church Grow.* Nashville: Convention Press, 1980.

Halbert, William H. *The Ministry of Church Weekday Early Education.* Nashville: Convention Press, 1977.

Harris, Philip B., and Lloyd T. Householder, compilers. *Developing Your Church Training Program.* Nashville: Convention Press, 1977.

Hendrix, John, *et.al. Nexus.* Nashville: Convention Press, 1974.

Hicks, Herbert G., and C. Ray Gullett. *Organizations: Theory and Behavior.* N. Y.: McGraw-Hill, 1975.

Hinkle, Joseph W., and Melva Cook. *How to Minister to Families in Your Church.* Nashville: Broadman Press, 1978.

Hinson, E. Glenn. *The Integrity of the Church.* Nashville: Broadman Press, 1978.

Holley, Robert. *Diagnosing Leader Training Needs.* Nashville: Convention Press, 1974.

How to Train Church Committees. Equipping Center Module. Nashville: The Baptist Sunday School Board, 1980.

Howse, W. L. "Understanding Changing Concepts," in *Vital Principles in Religious Education.* Comp. John Sisemore. Nashville: Broadman Press, 1966.

Kerr, Horace. *How to Minister to Senior Adults in Your Church.* Nashville: Broadman Press, 1980.

Kotler, Philip. *Marketing for Non-Profit Organizations.* Englewood Cliffs: Prentice-Hall, Inc., 1975.

Leas, Speed, and Paul Kittlaus. *Church Fights: Managing Conflict in the Local Church.* Philadelphia: Westminster Press, 1973.

Lindgren, Alvin. *Foundations for Purposeful Church Administration.* Nashville: Abingdon, 1965.

McCall, Duke K., ed. *What Is the Church?* Nashville: Broadman Press, 1958.

McClellan, Albert, compiler. *A Basic Understanding of Southern Baptist Missions Coordination.* Nashville: Inter-Agency Council, SBC, 1972.

McDonough, Reginald M., compiler. *A Church on Mission.* Nashville: Convention Press, 1980.

McDonough, Reginald M. *Keys to Effective Motivation.* Nashville: Broadman Press, 1979.

McDonough, Reginald. *Working with Volunteer Leaders in the Church.* Nashville: Broadman Press, 1976.

McGregor, Douglas. *The Human Side of Enterprise.* New York: McGraw-Hill, 1960.

McSwain, Larry, and William Treadwell. *Conflict Ministry in the Church.* Nashville: Broadman Press, 1981.

Madsen, Paul. *The Small Church: Valid, Vital, Victorious.* Valley Forge: Judson Press, 1975.

Martin, Mickey. *Woman's Missionary Union Manual.* Birmingham: Women's Missionary Union, 1981.

Maslow, Abraham H. *Motivation and Personality.* New York: Harper and Row, 1970.

Miller, Randolph Crump. *The Clue to Christian Education.* New York: Charles Scribner's, 1950.

Miller, Randolph Crump. *Education for Christian Living.* Englewood Cliffs: Prentice-Hall, 1956.

Newman, A. D., and R. W. Rowbottom. *Organizational Analysis.* New York: Heinemann, 1968.

Niebuhr, H. Richard. *The Purpose of the Church and Its Ministry.* New York: Harper and Row, 1956.

Pascal, Blaise. *Pensées,* trans. H. F. Stewart. New York: The Modern Library, 1967.

Piland, Harry. *Basic Sunday School Work.* Nashville: Convention Press, 1980.

Powers, Bruce P. *Christian Leadership.* Nashville: Broadman, 1979.

Prince, George. *The Practice of Creativity.* New York: Harper and Row, 1970.

Reynolds, William J., compiler. *Building an Effective Music Ministry.* Nashville: Convention Press, 1980.

Rossie, Peter, Howard Freeman and Sonia Wright. *Evaluation: A Systematic Approach.* Beverly Hills, California: Sage Publications, 1972.

Shinn, Roger. "Education is a Mystery." *A Colloquy on Christian Education.* Ed. John Westerhoff. Philadelphia: Pilgrim Press, 1972.

Sisemore, John T., compiler. *The Ministry of Religious Education.* Nashville: Broadman Press, 1978.

Smart, James. *The Teaching Ministry of the Church.* Philadelphia: Westminster Press, 1954.

Sorrill, Bobbie. *WMU—A Church Missions Organization.* Birmingham: Woman's Missionary Union, 1981.

This, Leslie E. *A Guide to Effective Management.* London: Addison-Wesley Publishing Co., 1974.

Tidwell, Charles A. *Training Potential Sunday School Workers.* Nashville: Convention Press, 1976.

Tidwell, Charles A. *Working Together Through the Church Council.* Nashville: Convention Press, 1968.

Todd, Wayne E. *The Media Center Serving a Church.* Nashville: Convention Press, 1975.

Van Fleet, James K. *Power With People.* West Nyack: Park Publishing Co., Inc., 1970.

Weatherford, Carolyn, and Bobbie Sorrill. *Woman's Missionary Union Work in a Church,* rev. ed. Birmingham: Woman's Missionary Union, Southern Baptist Convention, n.d.

Westerhoff, John. *Will Our Children Have Faith?* New York: Seabury Press, 1976.

Wyckoff, D. Campbell. *How to Evaluate Your Christian Education Program.* Philadelphia: Westminster Press, 1962.

Young, William E. "The Minister of Education as an Evaluator." *The Minister of Education as Educator.* Comp. Will Beal. Nashville: Convention Press, 1979.